英语专业系列教材

STYLISTICS AND TRANSLATION

新编文体与翻译教程

主编 纪蓉琴 黄 敏
编者 黎志萍 金 莹

清华大学出版社
北 京

内 容 简 介

《新编文体与翻译教程》是一本实用英汉互译技巧教程,以语域理论为框架阐述翻译理论,着眼于翻译实践需要,旨在培养学生的文体意识,帮助学生建立基本的翻译策略观。全书分为四编,共15章,分别讨论实用文体、商贸文体、科技文体、文学文体四种代表性文体;每编下分章节讨论该文体代表性体裁的翻译策略,包括文体简介、课前实践、文体特点、翻译要领、常用词汇句型(文学文体部分除外)、译文赏评、课后练习等板块。

本教材适合本科英语相关专业的学生及翻译硕士使用,也可供翻译工作者及英语和翻译爱好者学习和进修使用。

版权所有,侵权必究。举报: 010-62782989,beiqinquan@tup.tsinghua.edu.cn。

图书在版编目(CIP)数据

新编文体与翻译教程 / 纪蓉琴,黄敏主编. —北京: 清华大学出版社,2018(2025.1重印)
(英语专业系列教材)
ISBN 978-7-302-50773-4

Ⅰ. ①新… Ⅱ. ①纪… ②黄… Ⅲ. ①英语-文体-翻译-研究 Ⅳ. ①H315.9

中国版本图书馆CIP数据核字(2018)第178270号

责任编辑:黄智佳
封面设计:子 一
责任校对:王凤芝
责任印制:杨 艳

出版发行:清华大学出版社
网　　址:https://www.tup.com.cn,https://www.wqxuetang.com
地　　址:北京清华大学学研大厦A座　　邮　编:100084
社 总 机:010-83470000　　邮　购:010-62786544
投稿与读者服务:010-62776969,c-service@tup.tsinghua.edu.cn
质量反馈:010-62772015,zhiliang@tup.tsinghua.edu.cn

印 装 者:涿州市般润文化传播有限公司
经　　销:全国新华书店
开　　本:185mm×260mm　　印　张:18.25　　字　数:357千字
版　　次:2018年8月第1版　　印　次:2025年1月第8次印刷
定　　价:75.00元

产品编号:076951-02

前　言

　　信息时代和市场经济的迅猛发展，导致了当今翻译活动信息量更大、涵盖面更广、题材体裁更丰富多样、理论研究更活跃。在日常生活中，人们经常接触到的不仅有文学翻译，还大量地接触到实用文、商贸文书、科技论文等的翻译。各类文体的区分越来越精细，不同文体类型有各自不同的文体特征和风格。有鉴于此，译文是否能正确传达原文的显性和隐性信息、再现原文的语体风格特征，如何对译文质量进行科学、客观的评价，是现阶段翻译工作者面临的新课题。

　　不同的文体具有不同的语言特点，在词汇、句式、修辞、结构等方面都表现出很大的差异。条约、法律、学术论文需要庄重的文体；戏剧需要口语化的表达；广告文体注重语言的感召力，句子比较简朴，讲求凝练，大量使用省略句，并着意修辞手法的应用；而文学文体由于涉及的题材、体裁很广，词汇丰富，语言生动形象，使得句法变化多端，风格多样。翻译论述文时，要正确处理一词多义；在文学文体中要做到传神达意、意韵皆存。英汉词汇和句法文体色彩丰富，英汉语音和修辞手段文体特征显著，英汉语篇语相运用活灵活现，它们共同构成了英汉语言丰富的表达色彩和深刻的寓意。如何准确地识别原文的文体风格，采用恰当的翻译策略，原汁原味地传递出原文的文体风格，是《新编文体与翻译教程》要解决的问题。

　　本教材在阐述和选择翻译理论专题时，主要以语域理论为框架，着眼于实践意义，在分析各类文体时也主要着眼于翻译实践的需要，并未系统介绍文体学的基本理论。从这个意义上说，它是一本实用性技巧教程。

　　本教材根据近年来对文体类别的研究，结合实际教学需求，分为四编，共15章，每编讨论一类具有代表性的文体，即实用文体、商贸文体、科技文体、文学文体。同时，为了尽量配合每种文体类别的特点，每单元都安排了文体特征识别、翻译策略要点的讲解，旨在培养学生获取初步的文体意识，建立基本的翻译策略观。

　　本教材注重文体意识的培养，强调译文是否正确得体，语体是否对应，格式是否符合目的语规范等。教学的最终目标是培养学生独立翻译每一种文体的能力。为实现这一目标，本教材围绕以下特点进行规划和编写：

一、编写目的

（1）**代表性**。本教材涵盖文学文体和非文学文体两大类。每大类选取常用的代表性文体，包括职场交际类文本——通知、致辞等；商贸文书文本——合同、标书等；学术交流——论文、摘要等；文学作品——小说、散文等。力求较全面地、有代表性地涉及各种常用英汉文体。

（2）**工具性**。本教材涵盖文学和非文学文体。非文学文体选取了实用文体、商贸文体、科技文体，较大范围地涵盖了功能性文体的样本和翻译策略，配以简洁的文体特征描述，提供主要的常用词汇和句型，兼具工具性作用，方便随时查用参考。文学文体涵盖主要的文学体裁，提供了文体特征判别和翻译策略样本，便于与非文学文体对照参考识别。

（3）**条理性**。在体例设计、选材和举例方面充分考虑了循序渐进的原则，"课前实践"是热身环节，目的是调动学生的兴趣和求知欲，再以文体特点分析、翻译要领讲解、译文赏评等环节培养学生的基本文体翻译意识，最后以课后练习强化所学内容。

（4）**操作性**。教材编排以一学期32学时左右课时为量，编排了四个大部分，共计15章（另加绪论一章），每周一章，便于教师安排课程内容和练习。

（5）**资源性**。本教材选取了大量不同文体特征的英汉对比样文，便于通过样本学习、识别、掌握不同文本的文体特点。每章后附有翻译练习题，既有利于教学弹性的需要，又方便学习者根据兴趣和需要进一步练习。

二、教材体例

本教材编写体例按照文体简介、课前实践、文体特点、翻译要领、常用词汇句型（文学文体部分除外）、译文赏评、课后练习依序而成。

（1）**文体简介**。每章开篇简要介绍本章文体概念及翻译时可采取的策略，以便让学习者建立初步的文体概念，了解该文本的文体类型和基本功能。

（2）**课前实践**。培养学习者初步的文体识别意识，体现实践性和实用性。每章材料两篇以上，选材涉及该文体的各个方面，基本按从易到难阶梯排列，英汉或汉英对比，可供不同类别、不同层次的教师和学习者自由选取。

（3）**文体特点**。了解每一种文体独有的词汇、句法、修辞、语音、语相等特点，学会识别文体特征的技能。每章基本安排3个文体特点讲解，力求条理清楚、简洁明了，例句精当，分析简明，便于学生操作和领会。

（4）翻译要领。每章配有3个左右的翻译要领讲解。选取与本章文体特点最契合的翻译策略、原则、方法或技巧等，力求短小精悍，深入浅出，以点代面，说理精短，例证翔实。

（5）常用词汇句型。词汇以每个文体类型所涉及的基本词汇为主，缩略词为辅，充分考虑到实用性和人文性，供学习者翻译时查阅和参考，也可增进学习者相应的学识与修养。归纳翻译该文体所常用的句型结构，体现翻译是模仿的理念，供翻译时模仿和套用。

（6）译文赏评。提供2~4篇例文，正面或反面的材料，先给出原文，再列出译文，运用前面所学该文体的文体特点和翻译要领，对译文进行赏评，指出译文的优劣之处，旨在为学习者准确得体翻译该文体提供理论指导和实践模板，引导其朝着正确的路径发展。

（7）课后练习。设置了英汉互译练习题，旨在帮助学习者加强和巩固本章所学的文体翻译要领。

文体与翻译是实用性较强的翻译理论及技巧课程，编者力图给出一套详尽具体的公式化操作原则，并希望能起到一定的指导作用。然而，由于语言的丰富性，即使同一语言，上下文不同，词义的褒贬也可能不同；文体不同，译风也往往不同。因此在翻译实践中，不能墨守成规、循规蹈矩。此外，在重实践的同时，也不能忽视翻译理论对翻译实践的科学指导作用及其对翻译实践成果的指导意义。有些翻译理论是直接和翻译实践相通的，翻译理论因而能在整体上或宏观上指导翻译实践活动。

本教材适合本科英语相关专业的学生及翻译硕士使用，也可供翻译工作者以及英语和翻译爱好者学习和进修使用。

本教材借鉴、引用了大量学者的翻译实践成果及理论观点，在此谨致诚挚的感谢。

本教材为江西科技师范大学教材出版基金资助项目。谨此表示感谢。

由于编者水平有限，错误及遗漏在所难免。欢迎广大专家、学者、教师和读者提出宝贵意见，以便修订和完善。

编者

2017年6月

目 录

绪论 1

第一编　实用文体与翻译 11

导论 12

第 1 章　致辞 16
1.1　课前实践 17
1.2　文体特点 20
1.3　翻译要领 21
1.4　常用词汇句型 22
1.5　译文赏评 24
1.6　课后练习 27

第 2 章　通知、海报 29
2.1　课前实践 29
2.2　文体特点 31
2.3　翻译要领 32
2.4　常用词汇句型 33
2.5　译文赏评 33
2.6　课后练习 36

第 3 章　简介 39
3.1　课前实践 40
3.2　文体特点 41
3.3　翻译要领 43
3.4　常用词汇句型 44
3.5　译文赏评 47

3.6　课后练习 51

第 4 章　公示语 53
4.1　课前实践 54
4.2　文体特点 56
4.3　翻译要领 58
4.4　常用词汇句型 61
4.5　译文赏评 63
4.6　课后练习 65

第 5 章　广告 66
5.1　课前实践 66
5.2　文体特点 69
5.3　翻译要领 70
5.4　常用词汇句型 71
5.5　译文赏评 72
5.6　课后练习 73

第二编　商贸文书文体与翻译 75

导论 76

第 6 章　合同 87
6.1　课前实践 88
6.2　文体特点 89
6.3　翻译要领 93
6.4　常用词汇句型 94

6.5　译文赏评 95
　　6.6　课后练习 101

第 7 章　产品说明书 102
　　7.1　课前实践 102
　　7.2　文体特点 106
　　7.3　翻译要领 110
　　7.4　常用词汇句型 111
　　7.5　译文赏评 112
　　7.6　课后练习 116

第 8 章　标　书 118
　　8.1　课前实践 119
　　8.2　文体特点 121
　　8.3　翻译要领 122
　　8.4　常用词汇句型 124
　　8.5　译文赏评 125
　　8.6　课后练习 129

第三编　专用科技文体与翻译 131

导论 132

第 9 章　摘　要 136
　　9.1　课前实践 136
　　9.2　文体特点 139
　　9.3　翻译要领 139
　　9.4　译文赏评 142
　　9.5　课后练习 145

第 10 章　科技论文 147
　　10.1　课前实践 148
　　10.2　文体特点 151

　　10.3　翻译要领 152
　　10.4　常用词汇句型 155
　　10.5　译文赏评 155
　　10.6　课后练习 161

第 11 章　报　告 163
　　11.1　课前实践 163
　　11.2　文体特点 166
　　11.3　翻译要领 167
　　11.4　常用词汇句型 170
　　11.5　译文赏评 171
　　11.6　课后练习 176

第四编　文学文体与翻译 181

导论 182

第 12 章　小　说 190
　　12.1　课前实践 191
　　12.2　文体特点 195
　　12.3　翻译要领 197
　　12.4　译文赏评 200
　　12.5　课后练习 207

第 13 章　戏　剧 210
　　13.1　课前实践 211
　　13.2　文体特点 217
　　13.3　翻译要领 218
　　13.4　译文赏评 223
　　13.5　课后练习 238

第 14 章　散　文 240
　　14.1　课前实践 241
　　14.2　文体特点 245

14.3 翻译要领 248	15.3 翻译要领 267
14.4 译文赏评 251	15.4 译文赏评 271
14.5 课后练习 259	15.5 课后练习 276

第 15 章　诗歌 262

15.1 课前实践 263

15.2 文体特点 265

参考文献 278

绪 论

语言代码呈现出一定的文体特征。翻译是两种语言代码的转换过程。从一定意义上来说，翻译过程也是文体转换的过程。任何文章都是社会生活的反映，社会生活丰富多彩，文章表现形式也就多种多样。任何情景因素的改变都会引起意义上的变化，并导致语言运用的变化。文体有广义和狭义之分：狭义的文体指文学文体；广义的文体指包括文学文体在内的各种语言变体。狭义的文体也可指文章的体裁，依据文章内容、结构和表现手法分类，如记叙文、议论文、说明文、应用文等。一种语体可能会呈现某种表现风格，如新闻体较庄重，科技体较平实，广告体简洁明快，文学体中包含个人风格。文学文体有小说、诗歌、散文等之分，科技文体也有科普作品、学术论文、科研报告等之别。翻译不能脱离文体，得体与否正是评判译品高下的尺度之一。

文体包含语体、体裁、风格，翻译的译文也涉及语体、体裁、译者风格三个层次。

1 文体与文体意识

1.1 文体的概念

文体（style）的本质含义是说话或作文表现出的规律性特征，这些特征在一定时期内相对稳定。汉语中的"文体"可指"文章的风格或结构、体裁""字体""文雅有节的体态"。文体在语言文学研究领域的相关概念包括"体裁"（又称"文类"，相当于英语 literary form、type of writing 或 genre）、"风格"（相当于英语 author's writing style，即作家特有的写作或叙事方式）、"语体"（相当于英语 language style），这些在汉语中都可统称为"文体"。相对而言，英语中则有 genre、style、register、dialect 等概念表示以上类别。

一般认为，文体是写作者或说话者独特的语言选择；或者是对规范或常规语言用法的偏离，即有标记的语言使用方式。

文体是指一定的话语秩序所形成的文本体式，它折射出作家、批评家独特的精神结构、体验方式、思维方式和其他社会历史、文化精神。从表层看，文体是作品的语言秩序和体式；从深层看，文体还负载着社会的文化精神和作家、批评家的人格内涵。

Leech & Short（1981：10）将文体 style 定义为"特定语境下，特定人物出于特定目的对语言的使用方式"。他们进一步说明：① 文体是语言的使用方式；② 文体属于言语而不是语言的范畴；③ 文体是由从语言总存中所做的各种选择组成；④ 对文体的定义是根据语言使用域 domain 来进行的，如特定作者在特定文类或特定文本中会做出何种选择。Crystal（1999：323）认为，文体是个体或群体在一定情境中对语言的独特使用。英语中的 style 一词并不仅指汉语中的"文体"，有时它还被用来指"语体、风格"等。

不同的语篇具有不同的文体特征，但语篇的文体特征不是一个空泛的概念，而是通过语音、语相、词汇、句子、修辞、语篇等层面的语言形式体现。

1.2 文体意识

文体意识是指由文体知识的感性认识发展而成的语感，它包括文体识别和分析意识、文体思维意向意识和文体选择运用意识。翻译中的文体意识是指译者面对具体的文本时，对其在语言表达上显示出来的文体特征的识别与理解、分析与判断、翻译选择与实现三个层次。

文体意识是古今中外各种翻译理论最为关注的现象之一，实践证明，一个没有文体意识的译者，不可能译出高质量的译文。

培养文体意识，我们首先要区分文体特征，选择文体的风格，才能实现文体翻译知识的扩展与意识的强化。

"文体虽各异，语言的总体则一"（王佐良、丁往道，1987：i）。不管实际语篇的文体类别如何变化，其基本体现方式与构成因素不变。所谓文体构成因素，是指任何语篇的基本组成部分都包含语音、语相、词汇、句子、修辞、语篇等因素，任何具体文本的文体特征识别与分析都可以从这几个方面入手。

① 语音。语音贯穿全部说话活动，并渗透到文字描述的各种形式。语音是语言的基础，也是研究文体的要素。英语中"The moment you speak, you are placed."的说法就充分表明某些语音特征还能区别说话人在地理区域、社会阶层、文化程度乃至职业、年龄和性别上的差异。其他诸如头韵、谐音、半谐音、双声叠韵、押韵、重音、节奏等也使语言体现出明显的文体特征。一般情况下，语音特征分析在诗歌欣赏中地位突出，但在非诗歌文体中也会有所体现。

② 词汇。词汇选择与文体特征密切相关。词汇选择因语言使用领域与场合的不同而大相径庭，如政府白皮书中多用庄重大词，而童话故事多用小词；学术论文词义明确，用词严谨，而抒情散文往往词义模糊，引人遐思。在同样的领域与场合，词汇选择也因作者风格的不同而相去甚远，故有"文如其人"之说。翻译中对词汇的分析选择可从词的本义、引申义、词义的演变、词义的褒贬、语气的轻重、修辞色彩等方面入手。

③ 句法。不同的文体，其句式也有不同之处。如长句让人觉得沉闷压抑，而短句则能创造明快有力的文体特色；新闻语言中丰富的信息往往以从句、插入语等形式连接，较为复杂；而广告、标语等更倾向于使用直截了当、简洁明快的短句，以收到一目了然、易于记忆的效果。此外，对偶、排比、设问、倒装、省略等句式也可让文章别具一格。

④ 修辞。修辞是人们在写作或说话过程中表示强调、渲染气氛、增加色彩等常用的语言手段，可以借助语音、语法、词汇等实现。常用的修辞有明喻、暗喻、换喻、提喻、拟人、对偶、夸张、排比等。例如，排比句的使用，便于表达强烈的感情，突出所强调的内容，增强语言的气势，同时，由于句式整齐，节奏分明，也可以增强语言的韵律美。

⑤ 语篇。王佐良先生曾说过："文体学的贡献之一，是使语言研究者把眼光从单句转移到整篇谈话或文章上面。"（1987：i）在实际交往中，语言的基本单位是语篇，它与句子的关系不是大小关系，而是"实现"关系，语篇是依靠句子来实现的。为了达到某一交际目的，一系列意义相关的句子通过一定的衔接手段连接起来便形成了语篇，而衔接手段、句群关系、段落关系、语篇模式的不同都会起到突显文体效果的作用。如替换和省略可使语言简洁多变；旨在说明的文字往往语义准确、脉络清晰，而旨在审美的小说则可能语义模糊、行文复杂。

⑥ 语相。语相是语相学中的基本概念，语相学也称为字位学（graphology），研究对象是书面语。书写体系包括印刷体和手写体。印刷体的字号、字体和书写体的种种字体都属于字位的变体。字位学还包括语言的视觉中介，亦即书写系统，即标点、拼写、排版、字母和段落结构，以及诗歌中的长短行。此外，图画和图像也属于语相的范畴，语相的再现是翻译必不可少的要素之一。

2 语体

语体学是一门脱胎于传统修辞学和风格学而吸收了现代语言学成果的新兴学科。它又被称为"功能修辞学"，是语言学的分支学科，主要研究语言在运用于人们各种活动领域、交际环境相对应的语言变体时所应遵循的规律，研究由此而形成的不同功能语体的言语特征。

2.1 语体的概念

语体是语言的变体。一个人应能根据不同的会话参与者、不同的场合等语境因素，运用不同的语言形式表达同一意思。多种原因可引起语言变异，如情景、地域、社会背景、题材、时间等。各种语体在用词、句法、语音等方面都有各自的鲜明特征。

程雨民（1989：1）将语体定义为"同一语言品种（标准语、方言、社会方言等）的使用者在不同的场合中所典型地使用的该语言品种的变体"。他进一步指出，"语体的实质是一些在使用场合上有区别的同一变体的选择。"陈国华（1997：48）认为，"文体和语体是两个范畴，前者主要指书面语言的体裁形式，包括散文体、诗歌体、书信体，等等；后者指一种语言的各种变体，包括书面语、口语、地域方言、社会方言、个人特色语，等等。"

2.2 语体的分类

语体类别之间并非泾渭分明，大致有以下的分类：

（1）正式与非正式语体

根据语言环境的不同，可分为正式语体和非正式语体。正式语体礼貌客观但生硬冷淡，非正式语体热情友好但可能粗俗。正式庄重的场合，不太熟悉的或地位有别的人之间用正式语体；宽松随意的场合，熟悉的人之间用非正式语体，如 isn't、won't 等缩略形式就不能用在正式语体中。

根据语言的正式程度，程雨民（1989：2）把语体分为四种：① 正式语体，适用于正式的或仪式性的场合，常用于文件、布告等；② 次正式语体，适用于正式的场合，如公开辩论、电视上的讨论、无讲稿的讲课、陈述事实等；③ 理智性的谈话语体，适用于公开或半公开生活中非正式场合的谈话或写作；④ 家常语体。

（2）书面语体与口头语体

根据使用的媒介，可分为口头语体和书面语体。口头语体的表达形式可以是口头的，也可以是书面的，即写出来的口头语，如文学作品中的对白、听力考试中的对话。书面语体的表达形式可以是书面的，也可以是口头的，即说出来的书面语，如教师讲课、正式会议上的讲话、有准备的演讲等。奥巴马的就职演说、马丁·路德金的演说等都是典型的说出来的书面语。

（3）其他分类

以英语为例，根据使用的地域，可分为以英语为母语国家的英语变体，以英语为第二语言或官方语言国家的英语变体，以英语为外语国家的英语变体。根据语言使用的领域，可分为法律英语、新闻英语、广告英语、科技英语、文学英语等。

2.3 语体特征

语体特征是指在不同语体中出现频次有显著差异的语言现象。如果某个语言现象在某个语体中出现的频次显著超过其他语体，我们将之称为带有某个语体倾向的特征，反之称为带有其他语体倾向的特征。

语体特征的表现形式有：① 音韵学的言语声音形式、音步、韵等；② 句法学的句子结构；③ 词汇学的抽象的或具体的语词、名词、动词、形容词的使用程度；④ 修辞学对形象、语言、想象等的独特运用等；⑤ 功能语体中选择和组织语言手段的规律。

2.4 语体与翻译

语体就是语言的体式，是人们在不同场合、不同情景中所使用的话语在选词、语法等方面的不同所形成的特征。在翻译过程中，译者必须注意译文和社会场合的关系，考虑语体特征和使用场合的匹配，用最能体现原文语体特征的语句建构译文，避免出现"文体失误"。

语体和文体是表达，而翻译也是表达。刘宓庆（2012：23）指出，翻译与语体的关系应该是"原文是什么风格，译文也应是什么风格。译文风格不符合原文风格也会影响译文信度。"翻译之所以借助语体学研究，是因为它们有一致的目的，即如何凭借有效的语言手段进行社会交流。语体与文体的构成既包括表达手法、题材、体裁、结构、语言、格式等，还包括时代精神、民族传统、作家风格、交际境域等。前者是其表层、后者是其深层。翻译者在对文学、应用文等体裁进行翻译处理时，必须展示出原作语体和文体的复杂内涵，再现原作的表达形式以及感情基调。

3 语域

语言总是针对一定的交际目的而使用的。在不同的交际目的、交际场合、交际对象之下，语言会产生许多变体，而语域（register，也称体裁），即是适用于特定语境的语言变体。Trudgill（1983：102）指出，原则上语体和语域是独立的，如足球语域可与正式语体共现（如高级报纸的报道中），或与非正式语体共现（如酒吧里的谈话中），但许多时候二者往往是联系在一起的。

方梦之（2002：35）对"语域"的定义是："在特定的社会环境（如学术界、宗教界、正式的或非正式的场合）使用的语言变体。可以根据题材（话语范围）区分为各种专业语言、行话等；根据正式程度（交谈方式）分为庄重体、正式体、通常体、随便体等。"郭著章、李庆生（2003）指出："语域是由语言使用场合所决定的语言变体：正式的与非正式的，书面的与口头的，礼貌的与粗俗的，方言俚语的与共用核心的，还有各种文体的各类语言。"侯维瑞（2008：23）将"语域"定义为随着使用场合、环境不同而区分的语言变体，是在特定的语言环境中使用的，有一定语言特征的语言变体。而西方语言学家们对"语域"的认识也是多种多样。Hatim 将"语域"定义为"使语言行为适用于某一特定活动类型，正式程度等的一种倾向"（转引自李运兴，2000：88）；而 Halliday（1978：59）则从系统功能语法的角度，指出"语域是由多种情景特征——特别是为了迎合不同的交际需要，产生的许多变体，这些变体所形成的范畴便被称为语域"。语域这个术语专门与按使用者特点定义的语言变体（即地域或阶级方言等）对立，指按其使用的社会情景定义的语言变体，如有科技英语、宗教英语、正式英语等语域，并细分为语场、语旨、语式三个方面。

- 语场（field）指实际进行的整个活动，言谈的主题。
- 语旨（tenor）指活动参与者之间的关系。
- 语式（mode）指交际的媒介与渠道。

语场指话语发生的主题，包括事物发生的时间、地点等信息；语旨反映话语交际的社会因素，如人际间的相互关系、在交际过程中扮演的社会角色等；语式指话语交际的渠道或媒介，也包括修辞方式。语域的这三个变体相互依赖且不可分割。

我们根据使用场合的不同及其规范程度的差异，将语域划分成非正式语（slang spoken, informal familiar languages, regional dialects 等）、共同核心语（common core）和正式语（written, formal, polite, elevated languages）三部分。

3.1 英语语域标志

语域在不同场合的变体有其特定的标识，这种标识被称为语域标志。英语语域标志可以区分英语正式语体和非正式语体，一般从语音层、词汇层、句法层和语篇层四个方面来加以区分。

（1）语音层面语域标志

如果语言中出现：ye（代替 you）、yeah（代替 yes）、feller（代替 fellow）等这类非正规语音形式，或是反复使用 I've、We'll、You'd、They're 等缩略形式时，表明这些语言属于口语、随便语或非正式语，它们发音比较含糊，出现弱读、连音现象较多，这些发音很少出现在法律文件、政府协定或各种合同等正式正规的文体中。而正式文体语调平衡，能产生庄重、严肃的效果。因此，语体越正式，发音越清晰。

（2）词汇层面语域标志

大量的语域标志出现在词汇层面上，众多的同义词形成各种语域。词类、词源和词的搭配的不同，都可以造成不同的语域标志。

从词源来说，英语的词汇来源于盎格鲁-萨克逊语（亦即英语本身的词汇）、法语词、拉丁词、希腊词。人们日常的非正式交谈，主要使用英语本身的词汇，因为其口语化，短小精练，听上去比较自然。拉丁词用于公文、正式演讲、学术文章等书卷气浓厚的材料中。（贾丽梅，2009：15）

（3）句子层面语域标志

这个层面的语域标志也比较明显。非正式语中口头语通常有这样的特点：句子短、句法简单、偶尔有长句，但结构松散、省略句多，常伴有插入语、口头语。这些特点很少或几乎不出现在正式书面语中。正式书面语的特点通常是：句子长、结构缜密、句型复杂，常出现被动句、强调句和虚拟语气。

（4）语篇语域标志

英语的语篇是由语音、词汇、语句组成的，因此语篇语域标志包括语音、词汇、语句三个层面。此外，在英语正式语中，语句之间常常使用过渡词、标点、数词，以使得结构连贯，语气庄重，语义确切。英语正式语有时还会使用修辞，如排比、重复、对偶等，以表达强烈的感情和磅礴的气势。

3.2 语域分析

语域分析是从语场、语旨、语式入手，探讨语言形式与情景语境之间的关系。它把对语言形式的描述与发话人的交际目的联系起来，不仅可以帮助读者认识特定语篇产生的背景，有利于对语篇的深层意义进行合理的而不是主观的推理，还有助于从社会情景角度分析语篇构建的得体性。

译文语篇的构成是在各种语境的引导和制约下以原文语篇为模本的语篇再生过

程。语篇翻译与语境有密切关系，而语境又直接与语域相关联。

每个语篇都产生于特定的语境之中，因此每个语篇直接与其特定的语域相关。所以，识别并分析原文语篇的语域，一方面有助于把握原文语篇的文体特征和行文风格，另一方面则有助于为译文语篇设定与原文语篇相对应的语域，从而使译文语篇尽可能得体合度。

4 文体与翻译

文体探索语言使用的得体性，文体与翻译探索译文的得体性。得体性是翻译学和文体学两门学科互通的桥梁，是两门学科的汇合点。

文体是写作者或说话者对语言规律性选择的结果，这种个性化选择使该文本不同于常规表达方式，其规律性表现出一定的稳定性。在翻译研究中，对文体的关注主要着眼于原文本与目标文本中规律性的语言特征、不同类文本在文体层面的匹配程度，以及目标语文本与目标语语言使用规范的符合度。

语言具有感情色彩，文体学的任务在于探讨表达不同情感特征的各种语言手段以及它们之间的相互关系，并由此入手分析语言的整个表达方式系统。文体学是运用现代语言学理论和方法来研究文体的学科，在某种意义上，它与语言学之间的关系是一种极为密切的寄生关系，新的语言学理论的生成和发展往往会催生新的文体学分支。（申丹，2008）同样地，文体学的蓬勃发展也为翻译研究者提供新的研究视角，重新审视与翻译活动相关的文体现象。

文学作品的语体和文体涉及体裁和题材的语言与结构。语体和文体是表达，而翻译也是表达。寻求原作的表达，并在译文中表达出来，是翻译的核心所在。Tytler 的翻译三原则其中之一就是"译作的风格和手法应和原作属于同一性质"，"翻译就是指从语义到文体在译语中用最切近、又最自然的对等语再现原语的信息"（转引自谭载喜，1999：87）。周煦良先生认为我国传统译论"信、达、雅"中的"雅"即指"和原文的内容和体裁相称，要得体"（转引自方梦之，2002：35）。刘重德先生（1994：67）认为译者在达到既忠实又通顺的程度之后，必须进一步探求风格的切合。

原语的一个词、一个词组、一个句子，甚至一个段落，在译入语里可能有多个同义形式。在翻译思维中有一个同义选择的层次。除了语言结构因素（如词性、词语搭配、上下文）之外，译入语的选择与文体相关。选择的目的是使译文得体——得相应文体之体。得体体现在遣词、造句、组篇的各个层次。

文体分析的重点是分析具有文体意义和美学价值的语言特征，挖掘作者的语用意图和语用效果，从而达到审美和鉴赏的目的。通过文体分析，译者可以对原语的文体以及原文中具体的语言形式所蕴含的文体价值有更好的把握，加深对原语的理解，帮助其翻译工作的进行。另外，在译文检查方面，译者本人或他人可以通过对译文的文体分析及与原文的对比，检查译文是否再现了原语的文体特色，进而帮助保证或提高译文质量。

翻译既要"译意"也要"译体"——既要准确通顺，也要得体合度。当然，翻译活动的目的性、译文的读者对象以及时代的变迁与发展等因素，也无不影响和制约着译者翻译策略的选择。因此，对文体风格的传达还应该具有动态的、辩证的眼光。

翻译文体学研究是通过语言对比这一纽带将文体学与翻译研究结合起来，改变了翻译研究仅仅关注语言转换或文化研究的单一模式局面，将语言对比、文体学研究与翻译研究结合起来，拓宽翻译研究的视野。将文体学研究对象的范围扩大到翻译文本，即以翻译文本为基础，从文体学的视角探究翻译文本所表现出的各类特征的根源。

5 思考题

（1）什么是文体，文体观是否会随时间变化？
（2）文体在翻译理论中的地位如何？
（3）文体在翻译过程中的地位如何？
（4）什么是语域（体裁），它对翻译的文体风格有何制约作用？
（5）译者的独特风格在译本中如何实现？
（6）语域分析对翻译的文体对等有何作用？

第一编 实用文体与翻译

- 导论
- 第1章 致辞
- 第2章 通知、海报
- 第3章 简介
- 第4章 公示语
- 第5章 广告

导 论

实用文体不是一种统一的文体类别，它的体式最为驳杂。诸如公函、书信、通知、请柬、启事、海报等都应属于实用文之列，社会交往、公共活动、工作沟通和商务往来诸方面，都可见这些文本活跃的身影。本编选择实用文体中最常用的五种文体，探讨掌握各类实用文体的翻译要领。

实用文体翻译涉及英汉致辞、简介、广告、公示语、通知、海报等各种社会人际往来和商务活动，它们无处不在、无时不用，而且还具有极大的时效性、直观性、广泛性和告知功能，每一种具体的文体都有其突出特征，都有相应的翻译策略。

凡涉及翻译的所有原则都对实用文体文本的翻译有一定的参考和指导作用。实用文体文本是以传递信息和内容为主要目的，与文学文体有较大区别。翻译中要根据文体的具体变化和需要，做相应的调整和变化。

不同文体需要遵循符合其特点、准确体现其目的和要求的翻译标准。实用文体文本属信息性文本，属普通科技语域，语域层次多，范围广，总体翻译原则采用交际翻译策略。

1 文体特征

实用文体是一个很广泛的范畴，使用的语言也非一成不变。不同类别的实用文，其语言的差别悬殊，根据不同的内容与目的有不同的要求。例如，通知、海报与广告、公示语所使用的语言和格式互不相同，简介、致辞等也各有其特点。因此实用文从内容到形式都很驳杂。但尽管如此，各类实用文体还是有其语言和格式上的相同点和共性的，所以实用文的翻译也有其相应的共同原则和方法。总体上，实用文属于科技语域。其语场是传播科技知识、描写生产过程、说明产品的使用方法等。语旨是内行人员对外行人员写作的文本。语式是采用自然语言，偶尔也会使用人工符号，用词生动，句法简易，文风活泼，多用修辞格。实用文包括：

通知、海报类： 活动、讲座通知等；

致辞类： 社交往来、信函等；

公共服务类： 公示语等；

简介： 企业简介、产品简介等；

商业推销： 广告等。

实用文体常以简明的语言、生动的方式把信息传递给普通民众。

1.1 语言简练 直截了当 条理清晰

实用文的内容有很强的针对性，与实际的工作、学习、生活联系紧密，具有"实用"的特点，语言简练、直截了当、条理清晰。例如，致辞主要在纪实，文体较为正式，不求虚饰，不容自由挥洒，必须使对方一目了然，不存疑问。

1.2 表达准确 用词恰当 明白易懂

实用文的第二个特点就是表达准确，用词恰当，明白易懂。

（1）词汇特征

① 多用小词

实用英语多使用小词、短语。

② 用动词代替抽象名词

较少使用名词化结构；用单个词代替词组。

如：We ask that all employees cooperate. (We ask for the cooperation of all employees.)

③ 多用代词

使用人称代词来拉近作者与读者的距离，增加亲切感。

如：When you choose the Shut Down command from the Start Menu, you see a dialog box that asks, "Hey, what do you mean, 'shut-down'?"

（2）句法特征

① 使用短句

实用文体倾向于用短句，以使文字简洁有力，生动活泼。短句语义明晰，通俗易懂。

② 避免使用形式主语 it 和 there

用 it 和 there 展开句子往往阻碍信息的快速传递，语气弱且使文字呆板和抽象。

③ 多用主动语态

在实用文体中，"主谓宾"句型是最基本的句型，有利于作者与读者的交流，创造一种非正式的语气。如：In order to complete this chapter and our overview of

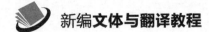

Internet, we need to spend a few moments talking about TCP/IP. As you know, the Internet is built on a collection of network that cover the world. These networks contain many different types of computers, and somehow, something must hold the whole thing together. That something is TCP/IP.

（3）修辞特征

在实用文体中，大多数修辞格都有应用，功能也和文学文体一样，都是为了增强生动性。

例1 Unlike me, my Rolex never needs a rest.

译文 跟我不一样，我的劳力士手表从不需要休息。

例2 Flowers by Interflors speak from the heart.

译文 英特弗洛那，鲜花诉衷肠。

暗喻（例1）和双关（例2）是实用文体中最常见的两种修辞格，其他如押韵、排比、拟声、借代等也时有应用。

2 翻译原则

由于实用文体文本重在纪实，译文总的要求是不求虚饰但求简明、严谨、准确，特别是不应疏漏事实细节（包括日期、数量、代号等），以免产生歧义。

2.1 平易简洁 把握分寸

实用文体目前虽有平易化的趋势，但总的来说仍是一种比较正式的拘谨文体，不容许挥洒自如，文本中情态虽有变化，但一般在表述上都很婉转，翻译时应该把握分寸。

2.2 行文端重 文言词语、套语多

实用文体文本用语和行文都讲究端重，常用文言词语，套语亦多。常用的公函词语，如"收悉、承蒙、祈谅、见告"等现在还可酌情使用。翻译实用文体时需保留英语正式书信程式，不必套用中国传统旧式。

2.3 多种翻译方法并用

实用文体涉及多种文本，可根据实际情况分别采用多种翻译方法。如摘译之应

用于致辞、公函等；交际翻译法之应用于广告、公示语等。

实用文体最大的特点是"实用"，因此其总的文体特点是不求浮华的辞藻和文风，但求把问题和情况表述清楚。实用文体文本都有其约定俗成或者比较规范的格式，因此，翻译时应注意语言简练、直截了当、条理清楚、表达准确、用词恰当、明白易懂。一般就事论事、不求虚饰、不作修饰和自由发挥，避免晦涩难懂的词语，这样才能不仅译出原文的意思，而且还可译出原文的语言文体风格。

第 1 章 致辞

致辞文体与翻译

　　致辞，也称为"致词"（speech 或 address），是指在社交、外事等仪式场合发表的"社交演说辞"。涵盖范围较广，一般包括主宾双方表示勉励、感谢、祝贺、哀悼等的讲话，也指在会议或某种仪式上具有身份的人的讲话：包括欢迎辞、欢送辞、祝酒辞、祝贺辞、新年献辞、告别辞、追悼辞、开幕辞等。致辞可以看作是演讲的一种特定形式。有些"致辞"超出了某种仪式本身的约束，上升到议论，说明更为广泛的问题，就兼具了"演讲"的特点。致辞一般由开场白、正文和结束语三部分构成。

　　根据场合不同，致辞可分为正式和非正式两大类。正式致辞结构比较严谨，语言也比较规范，一般是国家政府人员或高级代表团成员的讲话；非正式的致辞语言比较随和，基调也比较轻松，一般适用于一般团体和个人的讲话。

　　致辞在人际交往中占据着十分重要的地位，在许多的场合都是不可或缺的。一般来说，致辞的言语风格多样，翻译时要注意原文的口吻、语气；致辞中往往有一些固定的套语，运用这些套语对于恰当得体地翻译致辞有一定的帮助作用；致辞兼有书面语和口语体的特征，如何准确把握其文体风格是翻译的难点。

　　本章学习了解致辞的种类和格式规范，熟悉致辞的常用词汇和句型，区分不同文体风格的致辞，以便在翻译实践中能准确得体地翻译好不同种类和风格的致辞。

第1章 致辞

> **1.1 课前实践**

1.1.1 晚宴致辞

Speech at the Fourth Confucius Institute Conference	**第四届孔子学院大会晚宴致辞**
Ladies, Gentlemen, and Friends, 　　Good Evening!	女士们，先生们，朋友们： 　　晚上好！
Today marks the second day of the Fourth Confucius Institute Conference. All delegates have participated in the Conference activities with great enthusiasm and without a break, and contributed wonderful ideas and suggestions in their extensive and in-depth discussions, which ensured successful running of the agenda. On behalf of the Ministry of Education of People's Republic of China and the Confucius Institute Headquarters, I would like to extend my heartfelt thanks to you!	第四届孔子学院大会开幕已经两天了。各位代表不辞劳苦，以满腔的热诚投入工作，积极建言献策，广泛深入讨论，使大会各项议程进展非常顺利。在此，我谨代表中华人民共和国教育部和孔子学院总部，向你们表示诚挚的感谢！
Tomorrow morning, we will hold the Closing Ceremony of the Conference. Conveners of the President's Forum and the Director's Forum will share their fruitful discussions with everyone. After that, Mr. Yuan Guiren, Minister of Education of China, will deliver concluding remarks. The Headquarters will listen carefully to ideas and suggestions from the delegates, for the purpose of improving the work for next year.	明天上午，我们将举行大会闭幕式，校长和院长分论坛的召集人将与大家交流并分享大会的成果。之后，中国教育部部长袁贵仁先生将作总结讲话。总部将认真听取各位代表的意见和建议，把明年的工作做得更好。
Through 5 years of hard work, we have started the Confucius Institutes from zero, facilitated their growth from small to big, and helped them develop. As of now, more than 280 Confucius Institutes and 270 Confucius Classrooms have been established in 88	经过5年的努力，孔子学院从无到有，从小到大，不断发展，至今，已在88个国家和地区建立了280多所孔子学院和270多个孔子课堂。各国朋友都说，孔子学院是一个大家庭，在世界各

countries and regions. Our friends from other countries have all commented that the Confucius Institutes are like a big family and we have brothers and sisters all over the world. Tonight, on behalf of the Ministry of Education of China, and the Confucius Institute Headquarters, I would like to host a family banquet for friends attending the Conference from home and abroad. I hope that everyone enjoys a pleasant trip in China!

The New Year will come in about 20 days. I would like to propose a toast, to the prosperity and greater success of the Confucius Institutes; to a happy and successful New Year, to a happy family and to a year of good luck!

地都有我们的兄弟姐妹。今天晚上，我代表中国教育部和孔子学院总部，在这里设家宴，款待出席大会的中外朋友！希望大家这次中国之行心情愉快，身体健康！

再过20天就是新年了。在此，让我们举杯，共同祝愿孔子学院在新的一年里，蓬勃发展，取得更大成功！祝愿各位朋友新年快乐、工作顺利、家庭幸福、万事如意！

1.1.2 开幕式致辞

Rogge 2008 Beijing Olympic Games Opening Ceremony Speech

罗格2008年北京奥运会开幕词

Mr. President of the People's Republic of China, Mr. Liu Qi, Members of the Organizing Committee, dear Chinese friends, dear athletes:

For a long time, China has dreamed of opening its doors and inviting the world's athletes to Beijing for the Olympic Games. Tonight that dream comes true. Congratulations, Beijing.

You have chosen as the theme of these Games "One World, One Dream". That is what we are tonight.

中华人民共和国主席先生，刘淇先生，奥组委的成员们，亲爱的中国朋友们，亲爱的运动员们：

长久以来，中国一直梦想着打开国门，邀请世界各地的运动员来北京参加奥运会。今晚，梦想变成了现实，祝贺北京！

你们选择"同一个世界，同一个梦想"作为本届奥运会的主题，今晚就是这个主题的体现。

As one world, we grieved with you over the tragic earthquake in Sichuan Province. We were moved by the great courage and solidarity of the Chinese people. As one dream, may these Olympic Games bring you joy, hope and pride.

Beijing, you are a host to the present and a gateway to the future. Thank you!

I now have the honor of asking the President of the People's Republic of China to open the Games of the 29th Olympiad of the Modern Era.

我们处在同一个世界，所以我们像你们一样，为四川的地震灾难而深感悲恸。中国人民的伟大勇气和团结精神使我们备受感动。我们拥有同一个梦想，所以希望本届奥运会带给你们快乐、希望和自豪。

北京，你是今天的主人，也是通往明天的大门。感谢你！

现在，我荣幸地邀请中华人民共和国主席先生宣布第29届现代奥林匹克运动会开幕。

1.1.3 欢送辞

Speech-off Speech

Dear Miss Klein,

All the members of our section here at the ABC Trading Company are before you today to wish you a farewell and good luck in your future marriage.

You have been with this company for six years, and it may seem a long time to you, but the time seems short when we think of the while wonderful friendship we have had with you were here. No one in the company has such a good reputation as you for being always cheerful, willing to help, efficient, and friendly. I, myself, feel that I have a special relationship with you, because it was you who broke me in on my job and taught me to get along here at this company. No one could have done it better.

欢送辞

亲爱的克莱因小姐：

今天，ABC公司我们这个部门的同仁都聚集一堂来欢送你，并祝你即将开始的婚姻美满幸福。

你和我们在这个公司共事6年。6年对你来说或许很长，但对我们来说，一想到你在这里时的友谊，我们感到时间太短。在这个公司，还没有人能像你这样总是令人开心、乐于助人、办事利索、待人友好。我自己对你感受更深，是你教我很快适应新工作和与同事相处，没有人比你做得更好。

> Now you are getting married, and I guess we can say that you will be starting a new career as a wife and mother. I know that you will enjoy this new career and we hope that you have all the happiness and success that you so richly deserve.
>
> Please accept this small gift from us as a token of our friendship and esteem. It is a watch with the names of the section members and the date of your departure inscribed on it.
>
> All the best wishes for you and your family!

> 现在，你就要结婚了，我想说，你一定会成为一个贤妻良母的。你将会热爱你的新角色，从中得到你必定会得到的成功和幸福。
>
> 请接受我们这件小礼物作为我们对你的友谊和敬意的象征。这是一块手表，它上面刻有我们这个部门所有员工的名字和你离开我们的日期。
>
> 谨向你和你的家人表示最美好的祝愿。

1.2 文体特点

1.2.1 行文结构程式化　言辞形象生动

英汉致辞的行文结构基本类似，一般包括称呼、开场白、正文、结束语等部分，表达程式化，以欢送辞为例，一般包括开场时对客人的尊称；正文开头以主人的身份对客人来访任务的圆满完成表示祝贺；正文主体部分回顾客人来访交流的整个过程，列举双方达成的共识和己方的收获；在结尾部分表达美好的祝愿，提出倡议和希望。

致辞虽然是口头表达的艺术，但使用的语言并不单纯是口语。致辞不同于一般的谈话，它实际上是一种书面语言的口语化，或者说，它使用的是一种规范的口语。因此，致辞对语言的要求就更高。它首先要求表达准确、规范、无误；还要求生动形象，使听众有兴趣、受感染。像演说辞一样，正式场合的致辞有时也使用各种修辞格，以使语言生动、活泼，具有强烈的吸引力与感染力。根据统计，最常用的修辞格是排比，其次为明喻、隐喻、重复、反问、头韵法、双关、幽默、引用等手法也经常使用。

1.2.2 语域特征显著　文体风格迥异

致辞的社会语境是社交、外事等仪式场合发表的"社交演说辞"，反映话语交际的社会因素，其"语旨"体现的是致辞者与听话者的人际间相互关系、在交际过程中扮演的社会角色等。其"语场"反映了不同致辞话语发生的主题，包括致辞发生的时间、地点、场合等信息。其"语式"体现的是致辞发生的渠道或媒介，以及其言语表述的修辞方式。因而，致辞文体的语域特征显著。

致辞文体既有口语体的特点，也有书面语体的特点，处于这两种文体之间。但是由于致辞种类繁多，致辞的社会活动的情景语境不同，致辞人的背景（职业、性别、文化程度）不同，致辞的具体目的和对象不同，致辞者所使用的语言形式也就迥异。因此，各类致辞的语言风格有它们的共同点，也有它们的不同点。语言的表达有时庄重典雅，有时慷慨激昂，有时诙谐幽默，有时活泼风趣。这就要求根据场合和具体情况灵活运用各种语言风格。例如，在宗教场合的致辞须引经据典，还要显示出虔诚，所用的语言比较陈旧，也较为正式、严谨。

1.2.3 文化背景差异显著　遣词造句简约质朴

语言是文化的载体，由于社会环境、风俗习惯、思维方式和价值取向的不同，英汉致辞中存在着巨大的文化差异。在欢迎辞中，中国人常用"一路辛苦了！"作为开篇的问候语，但在英语中却不能直译为"You must be very tired."，这样会让远道而来的客人误以为自己一路颠簸面容憔悴。同样，在欢送辞中，中国人常说"招待不周，敬请见谅。"这样的客气话，如果直译为英语"Excuse me for not having served you very well."则不免让客人信以为真，产生误解。中国自古以来就是人口大国，孕育着"多子多孙多福寿"的传统文化，因此"早生贵子"之类的祝福语在婚礼致辞中是必不可少的，主人听到之后也会感到心情愉悦。相反，在英语婚礼致辞中如果以"May you soon have a son!"结尾，一定会让在场的客人感到惊讶，更让主人感到尴尬。

由于致辞多用于社交礼仪场合，所以致辞的文体风格具有平易、简约、朴质的特点，以达到通俗易懂之目的。

总体来说，致辞受场合、事件、受众等的限制比较大，一般不宜太长，还要讲求文采，不能过于口语化，力求简洁朴质。这是英汉致辞的共同点。

1.3 翻译要领

致辞既有书面语的特征，又有口头语的特征，内容广泛，风格迥异，用词富有感情且极具文化性。致辞翻译不但要实现文本意义的对等转换，更要追求与目的语国家读者的感情交流和文化融合。

1.3.1 传递原作情感　语言表述对等

致辞是一种极富人情味的感情交流途径，致辞者运用通俗的言辞、动人的语调、专注的神情向听众阐明观点、传达信息，引起他们感情上的共鸣和心灵上的震撼。

因此翻译致辞同样也要充满深情厚谊，从目的语中选择恰当的词汇和修辞手段再现原作的情感。

1.3.2 保持原作风格　译文通俗易懂

由于致辞场合及致辞者喜好的不同，致辞的语言风格也各异。有些人喜欢言简意赅，有些人则习惯引经据典；有些人喜欢平铺直叙，有些人则喜爱别开生面；有些人喜欢质朴的语言，有些人则偏爱华丽的辞藻。无论是哪一种风格，译者都要耐心琢磨、仔细体会、认真模仿，力求再现原作者的风格而不是展现自己的文风，只有这样才能较好地把握原作的主旨，让目的语读者领会原作的精髓。

一般来说，致辞的目标听众应该是来自社会各个阶层、来自各行各业的人，而且人数越多越好，优秀的致辞者会力求给他们留下清晰、完整、深刻的印象。因此在翻译过程中要想致辞者之所想，尽量运用听众耳熟能详的词汇来表达，避免使用诘屈聱牙的偏词、怪词。例如，"一元复始"是一个极具中国特色文化内涵的成语，所谓"一元复始，万象更新"，而在英文中却很难找到现成的习语表达与之对应，因此译者索性将其译为 at the beginning of the year，虽然缺少了独特的文化韵味，但却得到了外国听众的普遍接受。

1.3.3 灵活处理文化差异　保持交流畅通

语言是文化的载体，英汉致辞在词汇选择、语气语调、陈述方式等方面的诸多不同集中反映了中外社会文化模式的显著差异，也给致辞翻译工作增添了不小的难度。译者应该本着"不偏不倚，力求易懂"的原则，在尽量保持等值效果的前提下，对原作中不符合目的语国家风俗人情和表达习惯的语句或修辞手段进行灵活处理，减少和消除文化差异造成的交流障碍，使致辞产生预期的效果。

1.4 常用词汇句型

（1）欢迎辞

① It is with great pleasure that I extend a warm welcome to...!
我怀着极其愉快的心情对……表示热烈的欢迎！

② I have the honor to welcome... on behalf of...
我很荣幸代表……向……表示热烈的欢迎。

③ It gives me great pleasure to extend a warm welcome to...

能向……表示热烈欢迎，我十分开心。

④ Allow me, first of all, to extend a warm welcome to...

首先，请允许我对……表示热烈的欢迎和问候。

（2）告别辞

① We are very sad to say goodbye to...

要对……说再见了，我们感到非常难过。

② We feel very sad to see... leave...

……就要离开……了，我们很难过。

③ We feel sorry at this moment of parting.

在这离别之际，我们感到非常遗憾。

④ We feel deep regret at parting with our guest.

就要与客人分别了，我们深感不舍。

（3）开/闭幕辞

① I'm very glad to declare this meeting open.（此处 open 是形容词）

我很荣幸地宣布本次会议开幕。

② to declare the commencement of...; to declare the opening of...

宣布……开始；宣布……开幕

③ to deliver a closing speech/address

致闭幕辞

（4）预祝辞

① I wish you success.

祝你成功！

② I wish the conference (a complete) success.

预祝大会取得（圆满）成功！

1.5 译文赏评

1.5.1 典礼致辞

原文

培训部开学典礼讲话

我国政府已明确宣布上海浦东的开发、开放是 20 世纪 90 年代中国改革开放的重点，不仅要求浦东的开发、开放加大力度，加快速度，而且还要承担起长江流域经济腾飞的龙头作用。浦东已经并且还将在中国走向社会主义市场经济的过程中担当重要角色，因而，全国注视着浦东，世界也在注视着浦东；但我们也清醒地看到：历史不仅赋予了我们难得的机遇，同时也带来了艰巨的挑战。我们重返关贸总协定的日子已不再遥远，我们正面临着与国际市场、与世界经济接轨的迫切问题。如何才能面对这些挑战？关键的一条就在于培养、造就一大批既具备各项专业技术知识，同时又具有与世界对话能力的新型人才。

译文

Speech at the Opening Ceremony of the Training Department

The Chinese Government has made it clear that China throws her emphasis of reform and opening-up in the 1990's on Pudong area of Shanghai. Therefore, the development of Pudong will be intensified and accelerated. Besides, Pudong is entrusted with the task of taking the lead in the economic boom of the Yangtze River valley. Pudong has played and will continue to play an important role in the shaping-up of China's socialist market economy. For these reasons, not only the whole country but also the whole world are watching Pudong. However, we must remain sober-minded as history presents us with a real challenge as well as a golden opportunity. The day for China to rejoin the General Agreement on Tariffs and Trade coming near, we are confronted with the pressing problem of bringing China's market and economy with the international market and world economy. What must we do to take up this challenge? The first and the most important is to turn out a large number of well-trained professional personnel in various fields who are also capable of communicating with outside world.

赏评

本篇讲话的语体属于一种正式的口语，更接近书面语的特点，或者称为"书面的口语"，用词和句子结构都比较严谨，又因为毕竟是要让人听懂的口语，所以句子不能太长，以免听众听了后面忘了前面。

译文对长句的处理较为合理。原文中逗号串起来的长句有好几个，但是译者进行了适当的断句，以使译文通顺易懂。第一个长句中"不仅要求……"和"而且还要承担起……"，译文处理为两个短句，符合致辞简约、朴质的特点。

译者对于一些词语进行了恰当的处理。第一句里"开发、开放"出现两次，"开放"共出现三次，如果照原样译出，就会显得非常啰唆，所以译文做了一些适当的调整。"人才"，一般译成 talented people，重在 talented，指具有某种天分。但是汉语中，"人才"这个词的使用很广泛，可以译为 trained、qualified、people of ability 等，但是到底如何翻译还要取决于上下文。该译文把"新型人才"译为 well-trained professional personnel，符合上下文的意思。

1.5.2 会议致辞

原文

在知识产权北京国际会议上的致辞

主席先生，女士们，先生们：

我非常荣幸地宣布，知识产权北京国际会议现在开幕！我代表中国政府和人民，并以我个人名义，向所有与会代表和来宾表示热烈的欢迎。我祝贺这次会议在北京胜利召开。会议组委会的全体成员为这次会议的成功召开付出了辛勤的劳动，我谨向他们表示感谢。

侵犯知识产权是当今世界面临的一个严重问题。仅以计算机软件行业为例，每年世界各地的疯狂盗版行为使这一行业蒙受了巨大的经济损失，进而迫使软件制作人和厂商提高软件的售价，将部分损失转嫁给了诚实使用软件的顾客。保护知识产权成了世界各国日益关切的问题。参加本次会议的各国代表都希望能携手合作，共同打击侵权行为，遏制盗版恶流的蔓延。我深信这次会议将达成意向保护知识产权的协议。

我预祝大会圆满成功！

译文

Speech at Beijing International Conference on Intellectual Rights

Mr. President, Ladies and Gentlemen,

It is my great honor to declare the commencement of Beijing International Conference on Intellectual Rights. On behalf of the Chinese Government and people, and in my own name, I would like to extend my warm welcome to all the delegates and guests. I would also like to extend my congratulations on the successful opening of the conference in Beijing. I wish to thank all the members of the organizing committee for their hard work, which has made this conference possible.

The violation of intellectual property rights has become a serious problem facing the world today. Every year, for example, the computer software industry throughout the world suffers a heavy financial loss from worldwide reckless piracy, a loss that consequently compels the programmers and the manufacturers of the published software to raise the retail prices, thus shifting part of their loss to honest users. The protection of intellectual property rights has become a growing concern among all the nations of the international community. The participating countries at this conference have expressed their hope for joint efforts to wage a war against the violation of the copyrighted property and stop the wicked spread of piracy. I am convinced that this conference will reach an agreement on the protection of intellectual property rights.

I wish the conference a complete success!

赏评

这是一篇关于打击盗版的公开演讲辞。全文用词正式，结构比较严谨，语言也比较规范，是由国家政府人员或高级代表团成员发出的，原文致辞者通过正式的用词、严谨的句式结构以及严厉的语气，表达了对于打击盗版的严正态度。因此，译文也应体现原文语域的正式程度，从用词到组句成篇再到致辞风格，都要与原文一致，以保证论述的严谨。原文致辞的起始句沿用了致辞的套话，"我非常荣幸地宣布，知识产权北京国际会议现在开幕！"铿锵有力，掷地有声。译文忠实地再现了这一套话"It is my great honor to declare the commencement of Beijing International Conference on Intellectual Rights."，表现了致辞的语体风格。原文第二段第一句是一个"是"字句结构，说明当今知识产权的状况。译者考虑到上述状况有不断蔓延的趋势，使用了一个动态词 become，这样整个句子就活起来了：The violation of intellectual property rights has become a serious problem... 原文第二段第四句有"参加""希望""携手""打击""遏制"五个动词，在英译文中若用这么多动词，显然会使动词拥挤不堪，造成阅读不畅。考虑到英语擅用名词和词组短语的习惯，译者应用词性转换等技巧，译为：... hope for joint efforts to wage a war against the violation of the copyrighted property and stop the wicked spread of piracy. 短文结尾也采用了致辞的套语，前后呼应，一气呵成，使致辞完美收官。

 **1.6 课后练习**

（1）东道主的欢迎辞

Ladies and Gentlemen,

It is with great pleasure that I extend a warm welcome to the Chinese Provincial Trade Delegation. I am very happy that you are here to attend the opening ceremony of Canadian Industrial Exhibition. I would like to take this opportunity to convey to our Chinese guests the warm greetings from the Canadian Chamber of Commerce.

This exhibition is a display of recent industrial achievements in Canada, as well as a showplace of our high-tech advances in such areas as aviation, machine tools, electronics, coal mining, power generation equipment, off-shore oil exploration, automobiles, covering all sections of Canadian industry. I am very proud that some of the exhibits are the products from some Canadian-Chinese joint ventures. Although these products are a mere fraction of all our exhibits, they mark the arrival of a new era of the economic and scientific and technological cooperation between our two great nations. Our cooperation is one of great promise. As you know, "A good beginning is half of the battle."

In addition, we are staging business and trade discussions with major Canadian companies. The interested parties may schedule time for business or technical talks with them.

The Chinese Provincial Trade Delegation is the largest visiting group to attend our exhibition and I wish my Chinese friends a most rewarding visit.

（2）在宋庆龄同志追悼大会上的悼词

　　宋庆龄同志鞠躬尽瘁，七十年如一日，把毕生精力献给中国人民民主和社会主义事业，献给世界和平和人类进步事业。她在任何情况下都保持着坚定的政治原则性，威武不屈，富贵不淫，高风亮节，永垂千古。尤其难能可贵的是，她跟随历史的脚步不断前进，从伟大的革命民主主义者成为伟大的共产主义者。……宋庆龄同志逝世前不久，被接受为中国共产党正式党员，实现了她长时期以来的夙愿。这是宋庆龄同志的光荣，也是中国共产党的光荣。宋庆龄同志永远活在中国各族人民的心中，永远活在中国共产党人心中。

　　宋庆龄同志永垂不朽！

第 2 章　通知、海报

通知、海报文体与翻译

无论在英语国家还是在中国，通知（notice）和海报（poster）都是运用十分广泛的实用文本。社会交往、公共活动、工作沟通和商务往来诸方面都可见这些文本活跃的身影。通知和海报具有极大的时效性、直观性、广泛性和告知功能，其实用价值是任何一种电子通信手段都无法完全取代的。

中英文的通知和海报在格式结构和语言表达方面均有相似之处又有不同之处，所以在翻译时要特别注意。

一般来说，通知、海报中往往有一些固定的套语，运用这些套语对于恰当得体地翻译通知、海报有一定的帮助作用。通知、海报兼有书面语和口语体的特征，如何准确把握其文体风格是翻译的难点。

本章学习了解通知、海报的种类和格式规范，熟悉通知、海报的常用词汇和句型，区分不同文体风格的通知、海报，在翻译实践中，能准确得体地翻译好不同种类和风格的通知、海报。

2.1 课前实践

2.1.1 献血通知

自愿献血通知	**Voluntary Blood Donation**
亲爱的同学们：	April 13, 2012
自愿献血不仅利己利人，还是一种善良的行为。校学生会呼吁大家踊跃向红十字会献血！付出即是回报！今天帮助别人，明	Dear fellow students, 　　It is advocated by the Student Union, that students of this college voluntarily donate blood to the Red Cross. Blood donation is a kind

天定能得到别人的帮助。有意者请于明天上午十一点前到校医务室排队。

校学生会
2012 年 4 月 13 日

of charity, which is not only beneficial to the society but also to the donators themselves.

Giving is getting. We help others today and we may be helped tomorrow. Those who are ready to join the line may go to the school clinic before 11:00 tomorrow morning.

Student Union

2.1.2 开会通知

开会通知

本周五（10 月 19 日）下午二时，全体员工在公司会议室开会，讨论如何改进公司管理制度。请准时出席。

经理办公室
2012-10-18

Notice of meeting

Oct. 18, 2012

All staff is requested to meet in the conference room on Friday, October 19, at 2:00 p.m. to discuss measures for improving company supervising system.

Please be on time.

Manager Office

2.1.3 晚会通知

英语晚会通知

兹定于星期六（6 月 15 日）晚上七点在学校大礼堂举办英语晚会。节目包括：英语歌曲演唱、英语故事、英语相声和英语短剧表演。

欢迎同学们和教师们踊跃参加。

校学生会
2013 年 6 月 10 日

Notice of English evening

June 10, 2013

An English evening is to be held in the Grant Hall on Saturday, June 15, at 7:00 p.m. Programs include English songs, English story-telling, cross-talk in English and English short plays.

All welcome.

Student Union

2.1.4　海报

<table>
<tr>
<td>

Go, Go, Go to English Corner!

April 25, 2012

Do you want to speak fluent English? Do you want to make friends with foreigners?

Our English Corner is your best choice. Every Tuesday evening, just beside the gate of our college, near the fountain, we are always waiting for you to practice your oral English. Here all you need to do is to open your mouth.

Many participators have overcome their shyness merely by going regularly and can now speak more fluent English. That's why more and more people are joining us.

Do not hesitate any more. Come along and come on.

School of Foreign Languages

</td>
<td>

英语角开始了！

你想说一口流利的英语吗？你想结交外国朋友吗？到我们的英语角来吧！

我们的英语角是你最好的选择。每星期二晚上，就在学校大门旁边的喷泉旁，我们与你相约。在这里，你只需张口就行了！

我们的英语角已经帮助很多同学克服了羞怯的毛病，提高了他们的英语口语表达能力，所以越来越多的同学正加入我们的行列。

别再犹豫了，马上参加吧！

外国语学院
2012-4-25

</td>
</tr>
</table>

2.2　文体特点

2.2.1　措辞准确　格式固定

通知、海报的发布目的一般是解释或阐明发布者的立场、观点或政策、措施，因此在措辞上必须准确明晰，切忌模棱两可或含糊、晦涩。因此，通知、海报的选词往往会从词义的异同、词义的轻重、词义的时代特征、词义的对象、词义的感情色彩等方面仔细辨析，选出恰当的词语，表达准确的概念。所以，通知、海报的措辞具有准确、明晰的特点。

2.2.2　用词正式　或用古体词

通知、海报作为政府或职能部门所发布的公文式文章，需具有权威性、规范性。因此在用词上一般较为正式，并且不排除使用一些较为古雅的词（如 hereinafter、hereof、herewith，等等）。海报文体既简明扼要又轻松自由，较多地使用缩略语。

2.2.3　义随境迁　句式盘杂

通知、海报因其表达简洁、使用场合特定、接受群体相对固定的特点，在行文中常常使用普通的词，但是赋予其特定的意义。作为公文文体的一种形式，为使其逻辑严谨，表意准确，在句法上常常叠床架屋，以至句式有时显得臃肿迟滞，同时句子的长度也大为增加。

2.3　翻译要领

2.3.1　内容简练　用词正式

通知、海报的主要目的是传递即时性较强的信息，所以必须开门见山、直截了当。根据告知对象和事由的不同，语言可正式，也可随意。发布通知时间还可省去年份。

在措辞上必须使译文的语体与原文相适应。一般说来，通知、海报翻译通常应使用正式书面语体，并酌情使用一些文言连词。翻译中要注意长句的处理。要在厘清句意和各部分之间逻辑关系的前提下恰当使用切分法或语序调整法，以使译文通畅、自然、地道。

严肃的通知要求使用正式的语言，而且句式也要严谨，但无论有多正式，也一定要使用通俗易懂的语言，要避免使用大词和专业术语，要在格式、体例及词义等方面加以提炼，使之符合目的语国家通知、海报的表达习惯。

2.3.2　准确传递信息　用词具有鼓动性

虽然大部分通知不需要称呼语，但对于那些具有呼告功能的通知来说，一般还是需要加上一个可以起到呼告作用的称呼语。

海报常使用描述性语言，既有鼓动性，又要避免夸大其词。海报通常包含以下信息：① 事由（标题）；② 活动时间和地点；③ 鼓动性语言；④ 主办单位。但很多情况下，汉语鼓动性语言也可遵照英语习惯省去不译。

2.3.3　信息简洁明快

翻译通知、海报等公文型文本首先要注意公文特有的形式，包括格式、体例等。对已模式化、程式化的格式，不应随便更改。翻译时要透彻理解原文，特别是要正确把握原文词义，认清一些普通词汇在文本中特有的含义。通知海报的译写主要使用排列法。这种方式简洁明快，能把信息明白无误地传递给读者。

2.4 常用词汇句型

（1）标题

... Notice; ... Lost; ... Party; ... Lecture; ... Poster

（2）正文

① Under the auspices of...; Do you want ...?; Our... is your best choice...

② Name: ...; Time: ...; Place: ...; Fare: ...

（3）落款

School of.... ; ... office; Bureau of...

2.5 译文赏评

2.5.1 广播式通知

原文

女士们，先生们：

欢迎您乘坐中国××航空公司航班××前往××（中途降落××）。由××至××的飞行距离是××，预计空中飞行时间是××小时××分。飞行高度××米，飞行速度平均每小时××公里。

为了保障飞机导航及通讯系统的正常工作，在飞机起飞和下降过程中请不要使用手提式电脑，在整个航程中请不要使用手提电话、遥控玩具、电子游戏、激光唱机和音频接收机等电子设备。

飞机很快就要起飞，现在有客舱乘务员进行安全检查。请您坐好，系好安全带，收起座椅靠背和小桌板。请您确认您的手提物品是否妥善安放在头顶上方的行李架内或座椅下方。本次航班全程禁烟，在飞行途中请不要吸烟。

本次航班的乘务长将协同机上××名乘务员竭诚为您提供及时周到的服务。

谢谢！

译文

Good Morning (afternoon, evening), Ladies and Gentlemen,

Welcome aboard XX Airline flight XX to XX (via XX). The distance between XX and XX is XX kilometers. Our flight will take XX hours and XX minutes. We will be flying at an altitude of XX meters and the average speed is XX kilometers per hour.

In order to ensure the normal operation of aircraft navigation and communication systems, passengers please do not use mobile phones, remote-controlled toys, pocket games and other electronic devices throughout the flight and the laptop computers are not allowed to use during take-off and landing.

We will take off immediately. Now there're cabin crew for safety check. Please be seated, fasten your seat belt, and make sure your seat back is straight up, your tray table is closed and your carry-on items are securely stowed in the overhead bin or under the seat in front of you. This is a non-smoking flight. Please do not smoke on board.

The (chief) purser XX with all the crewmembers will be sincerely at your service. We hope you enjoy the flight! Thank you!

赏评

这是一则广播通知。它是口头通知的一种形式。在旅游业中，广播通知应用范围极广。如在机场、车站、码头、娱乐场所等地方，人们往往通过广播通知有关事宜。

广播通知的对象往往泛指，可为 Ladies and Gentlemen、Boys and Girls 等，目的是让有关人员及时知晓有关事宜。发出通知的单位名称及日期一般均无须播出。广播通知的内容要求简明扼要，措辞要求通俗易懂，力求口语化，而且尽可能多地采用礼貌语言，在人称上多使用第二人称，以示亲切的互动交流，句式上采用祈使句，且句子结构不宜长而复杂，多为平直式的单句或扩展句。如本例。

译文中第二人称与第一人称交叉使用，增强了亲切感，有效拉近了通知发出者与接受对象之间的心理距离；英语译文用词平实通俗、简短的祈使句式增强了通知内容的严肃性和执行效力。

2.5.2 海报式通知

DEAN'S OFFICE NOTICE

A Seminar of Modern English Literature

By

The Language Research Institute

On

Friday, October 12, 2007, at 9 a.m.

In

Room 310, Lecture Hall

All foreign language teachers and students are expected to be present.

October 10, 2007

译文 1

系办公室通知

外语系语言研究所将于 2007 年 10 月 12 日（星期五）上午 9 点在演讲楼 310 室举行现代英国文学研讨会。外语系全体师生务必参加。

2007 年 10 月 10 日

译文 2

通　知

全系师生务必参加

现代英国文学研讨会

时间：2007-10-12（星期五）9:00

地点：系语言研究所

外语系办
2007-10-10

赏评

　　此英文通知的第一句较长，包含内容丰富，读来令人有上气不接下气之感，原文将介词另起一行单列，以不寻常的版面设计，巧妙断句，增加阅读时的间隔和停顿时间，似乎在有意给人喘气的机会。从语相的角度来看，通过语言的视觉中介，即书写系统——标点、拼写、排版、字母和段落结构，产生跳跃的动态感觉，使人耳目一新。在句式结构上，使用直截了当、简洁明快的短句以收到一目了然、易于记忆的效果。译成中文时，可转换为普通通知格式（如译文 1），或保留海报格式（如译文 2）。无论哪种格式，都必须注意英汉语序的差异与调整。

2.5.3　书信式通知

原文

October 12, 1993

　Dear Examinees,

　　As you know, due to unfortunate circumstances, ETS was forced to cancel the scores of the October 1993 TOFEL administration in the People's Republic of China. At that time, you were notified that you would be able to take another TOFEL without charge up through the October 1994 administration. You should be aware that the TOFEL program has a long standing policy of not refunding test fees when administrations are canceled.

We apologize for any inconvenience that this may cause to you.

Russell Webster
Executive Director
TOFEL Program Education Testing Service

译文

各位考生：

如您所知，很遗憾教育考试服务处被迫取消 1993 年 10 月在中华人民共和国进行的托福考试成绩。当时，我方通知您在 1994 年 10 月以前可以免费参加在此期间的任何一次考试。您应该知道托福考试项目长期以来的政策：当考试被取消时，不向任何考生退还考试费。

因此给您带来的不便，深表歉意。

托福教育考试服务中心
经理罗舍尔·韦伯斯特

赏评

此类通知英汉语言都十分正式，英语中多用物称主语、被动语态和祈使句，汉语中多用无主句、主动态，英汉互译时需注意句式转换。如"you were notified that you would be able to take..."，译成汉语时为"我方通知您……"。

2.6 课后练习

（1）学术报告会通知

北京理工大学珠海学院外国语学院院长、资深翻译家宋天锡教授将于 10 月 20 日下午两点整（星期四）在教学楼 B 座 203 教室举办题为"翻译与文化"的专题讲座。欢迎全体师生参加。

（2）球赛海报

×××智能电子有限责任公司篮球队将在公司运动场迎战前来挑战的华威食品公司篮球队。请全体员工前往助威。

（3）会议通知

国际金融与管理学院定于本周五（5月13日）下午三点整在学院会议室召开会议，讨论毕业论文指导与控制论文质量的问题。请学院所有副教授及以上职称教师参加。

（4）紧急通知

电脑服务中心通知：由于受地震影响，连接海外的亚太电缆及其他部分海底电缆出现损毁，中国、美国及日本的网站浏览服务及其他通讯均受到影响。有关运营商正在组织抢修，不便之处，敬请谅解。

（5）商品拍卖告示

星期五鞋包店打算举行清仓大拍卖，所有货物五折销售，欢迎选购！所有商品一经售出，概不退换，请认真挑选。

（6）放假通知

中秋节就要到了，为表示对各位几个月来辛勤工作的感谢，同时也为了能让各位与家人一起尽情享受中秋佳节，公司决定从8月31日当天放假至9月3日（包括在内）。所有员工均享受带薪假期。

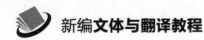

（7）演讲比赛海报

校团委与英语爱好者协会共同主办的第二届非英语专业学生英语演讲比赛将于 2013 年 9 月 20 日（星期五）晚上七点整在教学楼 A 座报告厅举行。演讲主题是"和谐社会，和谐校园"。请各位同学踊跃参加。

（8）遗失启事

本人昨晚九点左右不小心将自己的耐克牌书包遗失在学校图书馆，包内有本人的身份证、学生证、钱包、两本教科书和三个笔记本。请拾到书包的同学速与本人联系。联系电话：138-3459-9***，不胜感激！

第 3 章　简介

简介文体与翻译

简介（brief introduction 或 summarized account）是以简明的文字向公众介绍有关人物或事物的基本情况和特征的实用文体。简介的标题一般由"介绍+简介"构成，如《××大学简介》。有些虽未标有"简介"字样，但也属于简介之列。

作为一种大众传播手段，简介涉及诸多领域，种类繁多，主要包括人物、单位、展品、旅游景观和影视作品等的简介。简介的最大特点就是告诉读者一些实质性的信息，从企业的经营性质到从业人员、产品的相关情况，甚至有时负责人的照片也会被附上，信息涉及面比较广。

由于中西方思维方式和文化的差异，中国和英语国家的简介在侧重点和内容上存在着许多差异，造成了翻译中的困难，涉及的历史渊源、文化特色等是翻译中最难把握的。因此翻译简介时，要求简洁明了、重点突出、层次分明、前后呼应，体现一种简洁明快的美，但同时，它又要求精练准确，还需有艺术性，通过简介本身的艺术性给人以美的享受，同时让读者对介绍对象留有深刻印象。

本章学习简介的文体特点、专业词汇和常用句型结构，掌握不同种类简介翻译的侧重点及其翻译策略；对于简介中的独特文化信息，要学会运用释义、增补、删减、类比或转移、创造性翻译、改译法等，进行灵活处理。

3.1 课前实践

3.1.1 学校简介

广东省外语艺术职业学院于 2001 年 12 月，经广东省人民政府批准，在广东省外国语师范学校的基础上设立。学校前身是广东外国语师范学校和广东艺术师范学校。广东外国语师范学校成立于 1978 年 12 月。广东艺术师范学校成立于 1983 年 6 月。2001 年 5 月经广东省人民政府批准，广东艺术师范学校并入广东外国语师范学校，合并后更名为广东省外语艺术职业学院，是一所由省政府设立的全日制五年制基础和学前教师教育为主的高等职业学校。

学校位于广州市天河区，辖五山和燕岭两个校区。广东省外语艺术职业学院现有 38 个专业，其中英语教育、视觉艺术教育、音乐教育、现代教育技术、以及学前教育（英语）专业被授予广东省品牌专业。

Guangdong Teachers College of Foreign Language and Arts (GTCFLA) was founded in 2001 through the merger of Guangdong Foreign Language Normal School and Guangdong Art Normal School established in 1978 and 1983 respectively, with the approval of Guangdong provincial government. It is a state-owned full-time institute of higher education with five-year primary and pre-school teacher education as its distinctive strengths.

Located in the District of Tianhe, traditional Wushan university area in Guangzhou, it comprises of Wushan Campus and Yanling Campus. GTCFLA offers 38 diploma programs among which English Education Program, Visual Arts Education Program, Music Education Program, Modern Education Technology Program and Pre-school Education (English) Program are accredited as the provincial model programs.

3.1.2 旅游景区介绍

滕王阁是一座具有 1300 多年历史的文化名楼，具有深厚的文化底蕴。自 1989 年重建开放以来，滕王阁作为省会城市南昌的对外接待窗口单位，以其深厚的历史

Tengwang Pavilion is a renowned cultural attraction with a history of more than 1,300 years and very profound cultural influence. Since its rebuilding and re-opening in 1989, Tengwang Pavilion has been serving as a major site to host

底蕴，巨大的文化魅力，完备的服务设施，一流的服务质量，笑迎八方来客。2000年9月被中央文明办、建设部、国家旅游局确定为第三批"全国文明风景旅游区示范点"；2001年1月被国家旅游局授予首批"国家AAAA级旅游区（点）"称号；2002年12月被评为"江西省价格、计量信得过单位"，2004年被国务院批准为国家重点风景名胜区。滕王阁已成为江西南昌的标志而享誉中外。

the receptions for the foreign visitors in Nanchang City, the capital of Jiangxi Province. Its fantastic historical and cultural heritage embodying the charms of Chinese culture, well-equipped facilities and first-class tourist service impressed numerous tourists and visitors from home and abroad. In September 2000, Tengwang Pavilion was honored as one of the third batch of "Demonstration Spots of National Advanced Scenic Tourist Areas" by the Central Spirit Civilization Office, the Ministry of Construction and the National Tourism Administration. In January 2001, it was listed among the first group of sites to be granted the title of "National AAAA Tourist Attraction" by the National Tourism Administration. In December 2002, it was awarded the title of "Reliable Organization in both Pricing and Measurement in Jiangxi Province". In 2004, it was approved by the State Council as one of "National Key Scenic Spots". Tengwang Pavilion has become the symbol of Nanchang City, the capital of Jiangxi Province, winning a great reputation both at home and abroad.

3.2 文体特点

简介的作用在于提供信息、争取顾客、保持需求、扩大市场以及确保质量，因此行文时必须注意语言的感召力。

从本质上看，简介属于广告类实用文体，它虽不如标语式广告简短、醒目，但拥有的信息量更大，有助于在消费者心目中树立良好的企业形象。

3.2.1　句型多变　讲究音韵

中英文简介在文体风格上有着较大的差异，中文的简介基本上遵循一个潜在的语篇模式，尽量将方方面面的信息按照习惯模式罗列出来，不够活跃，但常常会用一些四字结构或排比句来增加其韵律美，从而加深读者的印象。英文的简介则灵活轻松，句型多变，不一定将各方面信息都罗列出来，强调简洁，往往注重给读者留下切实可行的印象。

简介属于"呼唤鼓动型"语篇，同时也兼有"信息型"语篇的特点。为了更好地解释经营宗旨，提高知名度，中国的简介常用一些程式化语言。如企业的简介常用诸如"主要经营……"（engage in...; handle a large range of business including...），"奉行/坚持……原则"（hold/abide by the principle of...; adhere to the aims of...）等用语。为了更好地起到宣传解释的功能，也经常使用一些标语口号式的文字，如"质量第一，信誉第一"（Quality Primacy, High Reputation），"团结、拼搏、务实、创新、奉献"（Unity, Striving, Hardworking, Creation and Dedication）。这些用语和文字，具有简短、醒目的特点，起到画龙点睛的作用。英语简介中这类话语相对较少。

3.2.2　句式自由　结构简单

简介的结构可以根据简介的种类、设计的目的而自由组织，相对来说比较松散，没有固定的模式，呈典型的流散句式。如：新疆古称西域，乌鲁木齐 2000 年前就成为丝绸之路北道上的重镇、东西方经济文化交流中心，而今天是新疆维吾尔自治区的首府。又如波音公司的简介：Boeing has been the premier manufacturer of commercial jetliners for more than 40 years. Through Boeing Commercial Aviation Services, the company provides unsurpassed, around-the-clock technical support to help maintain their airplanes in peak operating condition. 短小的段落和简短的句子使得简介更简洁易懂，达到宣传和广告的双重目的。其次，简介一般使用现在时，多用主动语态。

3.2.3　精练生动　艺术性强

简介语言精练准确，简洁明快，具有艺术性和生动性，给人以美的享受，同时让读者对其留下深刻印象。相对于英语的简介，汉语的某些简介这一文体特点更加显著，如："雕工画意展厅……唐代雕塑一改南北朝'秀骨清像'之风格，形成雄健奔放、饱满瑰丽、意气风发的新风格"；"……这里还展出了许多女佣的美好形象……"，像是一则广告，促使读者去参观访问。简介一般涉及一些专业领域知识，旅游景观类简介涉及历史渊源、文化特色等词语，如"老字号酒店""琼楼玉宇""桥廊轩榭"等。

3.3 翻译要领

3.3.1 用语简洁　直观明快

简介的翻译不同于其他作品的翻译，不仅要供人"欣赏"，更重要的是吸引人们的注意力，以激发人们的购买欲望从而导致购买行为。从汉、英语言的特点来看，汉语突出物象，表现情理，喜欢托物寄情，所以中文的简介一般多含有一些华丽之词和朗朗上口的四字成语或四字结构；与之不同的是，英语更重形式、重写实、重理性，因此英文的简介一般用词简洁自然，叙述直观明快，句式上相对于善用复杂句的中文简介则显得简短。这就要求我们在英译中文简介时，不能过于受汉语原文和汉语思维习惯的影响，往往要根据英语的表达习惯来重新组织行文，删掉那些如果译出反而显得拖沓臃肿的内容。

另外，中文的简介常常以一句寓意深刻而又响亮的口号作开头或结尾，言简意赅，令人难忘。翻译时应注意体现这种简练、通俗、朗朗上口的行文风格。

3.3.2 入乡随俗　文化适宜

文化适宜是简介类实用文体翻译必须注意的一个部分。如果过于局限于原文，而忽略了其他因素，如语言、文化、政治、风俗，等等，翻译出来的东西有时会有悖于译入语文化。

例如，有的中文企业简介中会出现"宾至如归、热诚服务"等为国人所熟悉的四字结构短语，如果直译为"We offer you all-round services with good credit, financial strength, and best quality."，就显得不太得体，因为译文忽视了译文读者的存在，没有迎合人们顾客至上的心理，含有一种高高在上的语气，如改为"A home from home with our cordial service."，这样一口气讲出，语气紧凑，也符合英语表达习惯。

中西方语言文化和认知结构存在差异，为了使译文在译语中达到相应的预期目的，汉语简介中出现的一些人名、地名、朝代名、佛名等文化词，如果直译成英语会使国外读者看来不知所云或者累赘，就有必要采取释义、增补、删减、类比或转译，甚至创造性翻译等方法，使译文符合目的语读者的欣赏趣味和语言习惯。

3.3.3 变译、转译　灵活处理

西方传统的哲学理念为"天人各一"，英语语言表达重形式、重写实、重理性；中国传统比较注重"天人合一"理念，汉语表达追求工整匀称，重意义、重描写、重感性。翻译时就需要运用"改译法"。对于汉语简介中的大话套话、过于浮夸、空洞无物、重复性、形象化的语句，在翻译时遵循"化'虚'为'实'，删繁就简"

的原则，尽量把原文的实质性、关键性内容凸显出来。具体说，就是删去原文中读者不需要了解的信息内容，在变译中表现为对原作的取舍。

3.4 常用词汇句型

（1）产品简介词汇

保质保量 quality and quantity

瑰丽多彩 pretty and colorful

操作简便 easy and simple to handle

花色时尚 fashionable patterns

畅销全球 selling well all over the world

技艺精湛 exquisite craftsmanship

典雅大方 elegant and graceful

加工精细 finely processed

洁白纯正 pure white

洁白透明 pure white and translucence

方便顾客 making things convenient for customers

方便群众 making things convenient for the people; to suit the people's convenience

结构合理 rational construction

经久耐用 durable in use

各式俱全 wide selection; large assortment

久负盛名 to have a long standing reputation

顾客第一 customers first

款式活泼端庄 vivid and great in style

工艺精良 sophisticated technology

款式齐全 various styles

花样繁多 a wide selection of colors and designs

款式新颖众多 diversified latest designs

货色齐全 goods of every description available

美观大方 elegant appearance

美观耐用 attractive and durable

客户第一，信誉第一 clients first, reputation first

品种多样 numerous in variety

品种齐全 complete range of articles; a great variety of goods

规格齐全 a complete range of specifications; complete in specifications

优质原料 superior materials

品质优良 excellent quality; high quality

誉满中外 to enjoy high reputation at home and abroad

巧用原料 to make best use of materials

色彩鲜艳 bright in color

原料精选 choice materials

色泽光润 bright luster; color brilliancy

造型富丽华贵 luxuriant in design

色泽艳丽 beautiful in color

造型新颖 modern design

设计合理 professional design

造型优美 beautiful design

设计精巧 deft design

制作精巧 skillful manufacture

深受欢迎 to win warm praise from customers

质量可靠 reliable quality

式样优雅 elegant shape

质量上乘 superior quality

数量之首 the king of quantity

质量稳定 stable quality

五彩缤纷 colorful

质量最佳 the queen of quality

性能可靠 dependable performance

种类繁多 wide varieties

（2）旅游景观词汇

    庵 Buddhist nunnery

    观景木台 timber deck

    碑文 inscription

    观景台 viewing deck

    避暑胜地 summer resort

    广场 main plaza

    晨跑小路 jogging footpath

    国家公园 national park

    城堡 castle

    旱喷泉 dry fountain

    出土文物 unearthed cultural relics

    皇家园林 royal garden

    丝绸之路 the Silk Road/Route

    庄园 manor; villa garden

    私家园林 private garden

    字画卷轴 scroll of calligraphy and painting

    古建筑群 ancient architectural complex

    景色如画 picturesque views

    园林建筑 garden architecture

    御花园 imperial garden

    水榭 waterside pavilion/house

    竹园 bamboo garden

（3）常用短语

① 表示公司、企业等的创立或建立 be founded/be established/be set up

② 表示某一单位的地理位置 be located/be listed/be ranked

③ 表示公司的生产或经营范围 manufacture/produce/undertake/engage in/involve in

④ 表示单位在同行业中的地位 be named/be listed/be ranked

⑤ 以……为宗旨 follow the tenet; based on the motto of the company; with the enterprise spirit of...

⑥ 行销世界 (products are) sold all over the world; sell well all over the world

3.5 译文赏评

3.5.1 企业简介

原文

北京工美集团

北京工美集团（原北京市工艺美术品总公司）是以生产工艺美术品为主，融科研、生产、经营、教育、出版于一体的多元化经济联合体。集团拥有工商企业50余家，合资企业21家，驻外贸易机构一个，开展"三来一补"业务。特艺、地毯、抽纱共有50多种产品获国际和国家大奖，自营进、出口商品60大类、上万个品种、花色。销往世界五大洲130多个国家和地区。

北京工美集团的宗旨是让世界更美好。

译文

Beijing Gongmei Group

Beijing Gongmei Group specializes mainly in arts and crafts. It is an economic complex combining scientific research, production, marketing, education and publication. Under the group are 50 industrial and commercial enterprises, 21 Sino-foreign joint ventures, and a trade agency abroad. The group manufactures products according to client's samples or designs, or using client's materials, and conducts compensation trade. Over 50 of its products have won international or domestic prizes, including special handicrafts, carpets and drawn work. It imports and exports 10,000 products in 60 categories, and its products are sold to more than 130 countries and regions on five continents.

Beijing Gongmei Group aims to make a better world.

赏评

原文旨在向读者忠实地展现该集团及其产品的特点，具有信息功能、祈使功能和美感功能。原文有四层意思：集团的性质、规模、荣誉与成就、经营范围和宗旨。全文语言简洁、意思连贯、层次分明、重点突出，使读者对该企业及其产品有较为清晰和全面的了解，而且语言朴实无华，加深了企业在读者心目中的可信度。这一切都会促使读者产生购买欲，达到该集团促销的目的。翻译时应遵循原文风格，但在具体词语和句子的处理上，需要做一些调整：原文第一句括号中的集团前身的名称可以省略,重要的是让读者记住现在的企业名称,如果将两个不熟悉且不同的外国企业名字摆在一起,反而会分散读者注意力;同时,集团的名称采用音译加解释的方法译为 Beijing Gongmei Group,以避免误解;"融……于一体"做定语修饰"多元化经济联合体",译为分词 combining 修饰中心词 economic complex;原文第二句"拥有"和"开展"是并列结构,体现了汉语多动词的特点,翻译时可以译为两句;对于简称"三来一补"(来样加工、设计加工、来料加工、补偿贸易),最好译出全称,以免晦涩难懂;译文保留了原文单独成段的集团宗旨,使之特别醒目突出,但根据英语的语言习惯改变了句子的结构。

3.5.2 景点简介

原文

黄 鹤 楼

黄鹤楼位于武昌蛇山之巅,自古与湖南岳阳楼、江西滕王阁并称为"江南三大名楼"。黄鹤楼的神话传说故事给它蒙上了一层神秘的色彩,传说中蛇山黄鹤矶头上原有辛氏开设的一家酒店,一道士经常向其讨酒喝,为了感谢他的千杯之恩,临行前在壁上画了一只鹤,告之辛氏它能下来起舞助兴。从此酒家宾客盈门,生意兴隆。过了十年,道士复来,取笛吹奏,道士跨上黄鹤直上云天。辛氏为纪念这位帮他致富的仙翁,便在其地起楼,取名"黄鹤楼"。

黄鹤楼始建于三国时期东吴黄武二年(公元223年),传说是为了军事目的而建,孙权为实现"以武治国而昌"("武昌"的名称由来于此),筑城为守,建楼以瞭望。至唐朝,其军事性质逐渐演变为著名的名胜景点,历代文人墨客到此游览,留下不少脍炙人口的诗篇。唐代诗人崔颢一首"昔人已乘黄鹤去,此地空余黄鹤楼。黄鹤一去不复返,白云千载空悠悠。晴川历历汉阳树,芳草萋萋鹦鹉洲。日暮乡关何处是?烟波江上使人愁。"已成为千古绝唱,更使黄鹤楼名声大噪。

至唐永泰元年(公元765年),黄鹤楼已具规模,使不少江夏名士"游必于是,宴必于是"。然而兵火频繁,黄鹤楼屡建屡废。最后一座"清楼"建于同治七年(公元1868年),毁于光绪十年(公元1884年),此后近百年未曾重修。

1981年10月,黄鹤楼重修工程破土开工,主楼以清同治楼为蓝本,但更高大雄伟。运用现代建筑技术施工,钢筋混凝土框架仿木结构。飞檐5层,攒尖楼顶,金色琉璃瓦屋面,通高51.4米,底层边宽30米,顶层边宽18米,全楼各层布置有大型壁画、楹联、文物等。楼外铸铜黄鹤造型、胜像宝塔、牌坊、轩廊、亭阁等一批辅助建筑,将主楼烘托得更加壮丽。登楼远眺,"极目楚天舒",不尽长江滚滚来,三镇风光尽收眼底。

新的黄鹤楼,被视为武汉市的象征。

Yellow Crane Tower

Yellow Crane Tower, located on Snake Hill in Wuchang, is one of the "Three Famous Towers" South of Yangtze River (the other two: Yueyang Tower in Hunan and Tengwang Pavilion in Jiangxi). Legend has it that in Wuchang, there used to be a wine shop opened by a young man named Xin. One day, a Taoist priest, in gratitude for free wine, drew a magic crane on the wall of the shop and instructed it to dance whenever it heard clapping. Thousands of people came to see the spectacle and the wine shop was always full of guests. After 10 years, the Taoist priest revisited the wine shop. He played the flute and then rode on the crane to the sky. In memory of the supernatural encounter and the priest, the Xin built a tower and named it Yellow Crane Tower.

It was said that the tower was built for military purposes. In order to achieve the goal of "taking military control (wu zhi) over the country to gain prosperous (chang)" (hence the name of "Wuchang"), Sun Quan built a fortified city, for the purpose of watching out. Till the Tang Dynasty, its military nature gradually evolved into a famous scenic spot. Visitors of men of letters in the successive dynasties had left many popular poems during their visits. The Tang Dynasty poet Cui Hao's famous poem "The ancient people had gone riding on the Yellow Crane, and an empty Yellow Crane Tower had been left. The Yellow Crane was gone forever and the White Cloud was empty throughout the history. The Qingchuan River had seen a history of Hanyangshu trees. Green grass became luxuriant on the Parrot Island. Where is my native land beyond the setting sun, the mist-veiled waves of River Han make me homesick." The poetic masterpiece has become an eternal song through the ages, and it makes the Yellow Crane Tower famous.

Until the first year of Tang Yongtai (AD 765), the Yellow Crane Tower had already become a splendid historic site. Lots of famous celebrities of Jiangxia take it as the only place "for their touring and banquet". However, through years, frequent fighting took place again and again, Yellow Crane Tower was destroyed after building repeatedly. The last "Qinglou Building" was erected in the 7th year of Tongzhi (AD 1868) and was destroyed in the tenth year of Guangxu (AD 1884). Since then, it has not been rebuilt in nearly 100 years.

In October 1981, the Yellow Crane Tower restoration project starts. The main building takes the Tongzhi Building as its blueprint, but is taller and more majestic. It adopts modern construction technology, taking reinforced concrete, wood imitation structure as its frame. The building has 5 layers cornice with pavilion roof and golden glazed tile roof. Its pass height is 51.4 meters high, the bottom edge is 30 meters wide, the top edge is 18 meters wide. Large wall paintings, couplets, cultural relics and so on are scattered along all the flights all over the building. Outside the building, a number of ancillary buildings such as bronze pagoda, wooden pagoda, archway, porch, pavilions and so on are erected as accessory buildings which make the main building more magnificent. Standing on the tower and "Gaze into the distance over Tianshu", the endless Yangtze River comes out of the sky and the scenery of the three towns is full of sight.

The new Yellow Crane Tower is regarded as the symbol of Wuhan City.

赏评

这是一篇旅游景点简介。它的语场是旅游景点,交际目的是吸引游客观光旅游。语旨是旅游公司或有关旅游管理部门对国内游客。语式是用书面语进行旅游宣传。语言采用客观描述手段,可接受程度适中。原文结构合理、清晰,语言比较客观、朴实,涉及内容基本上是围绕"黄鹤楼"的名称和历史古迹来源介绍。

但是译文的语境因素在语言转换过程中发生了一些变化。其语场与原文相同,但是语旨是针对不懂汉语的国外游客,语式是用书面语宣传。语言描述客观,较少使用主观描述,目的是为外国人提供信息,让他们了解该景点。

译文翻译策略采取直白陈述式的方法。如原文第一句的翻译,就采取有意突出其历史位置的方式,使译文读者对黄鹤楼的历史价值有更清楚的了解。运用描述式翻译方法,原文多为景点来源的介绍,如"然而兵火频繁,黄鹤楼屡建屡废。最后一座'清楼'建于同治七年(公元1868年),毁于光绪十年(公元1884年),此后近百年未曾重修。",译文中对这一事实进行描述性翻译,在直译的基础上,对景点的历史发展做出了客观描述,引起外国游客的兴趣,使译文符合译文读者的接受需求。

其次,原文中作者引用了唐代诗人崔颢的诗"昔人已乘黄鹤去,此地空余黄鹤楼。黄鹤一去不复返,白云千载空悠悠。晴川历历汉阳树,芳草萋萋鹦鹉洲。日暮乡关何处是?烟波江上使人愁。",反映了诗作更使黄鹤楼名声大噪、成为千古绝唱的史实。这是典型的汉语式写作方式,中国人熟悉且喜闻乐见,但若按照原文译成英语,国外读者则很难欣赏到其优美意境,因为他们并不熟悉汉语"写景抒情"的诗文风格。这句的译文建议改用一个简洁的陈述句代替原文中的诗句:Cui Hao, a famous poet during the Tang Dynasty (618–907), made the tower well known throughout China with his poem *Yellow Crane Tower*.

3.6 课后练习

（1）

The Sydney Opera House is one of the most famous buildings in the world. It is considered to be one of the most recognizable images of the modern world although the building has been open for only about 30 years. The Sydney Opera House is as representative of Australia as the Pyramids are of Egypt.

6,225 square meters of glass and 645 kilometers of electric cable were used to build the Opera House. It includes 1,000 rooms. It is 185 meters long and 120 meters wide. The building's roof sections weigh about 15 tons. There are one million tiles on the roof. It provides guided tours to 200,000 people each year.

But do you know the Opera House with a roof was designed by a famous Danish architect Utzon? In the late 1950s the Australian Government established a fund to finance the construction of the Sydney Opera House, and conducted a competition for its design. Utzon spent a few years reworking the design and it was 1961 before he had solved the problem of how to build the distinguishing feature—the sails of the roof. The venture experienced cost blowouts. In 1966 the situation reached crisis point and Utzon resigned from the project. The building was finally competed by others in 1973. The Sydney Opera House was opened by Queen Elizabeth on 20 October 1973.

The Opera House reaches out into the harbor.

Seen from the air or a ferry, the skyline of the Sydney Opera House, the blue water of the harbor and the Sydney Harbor Bridge, is beautiful.

（2）

屠呦呦，女，药学家。1930年12月30日生于浙江宁波，1951年考入北京大学，在医学院药学系生药专业学习。1955年，毕业于北京医学院（今北京大学医学部）。毕业后曾接受中医培训两年半，并一直在中国中医研究院（2005年更名为中国中医科学院）工作，期间前后晋升为硕士生导师、博士生导师，现为中国中医科学院的首席科学家。中国中医研究院终身研究员兼首席研究员、青蒿素研究开发中心主任、药学家、诺贝尔医学奖获得者。

屠呦呦多年从事中药和中西药结合研究，突出贡献是创制新型抗疟药青蒿素和双氢青蒿素。1972年成功提取到了一种分子式为$C_{15}H_{22}O_5$的无色结晶体，命名为青蒿素。2011年9月，因为发现青蒿素———一种用于治疗疟疾的药物，挽救了全球，特别是发展中国家的数百万人的生命而获得拉斯克奖和葛兰素史克中国研发中心"生命科学杰出成就奖"。2015年10月，屠呦呦获得诺贝尔生理学或医学奖，理由是她发现了青蒿素，这种药品可以有效降低疟疾患者的死亡率。她成为首获科学类诺贝尔奖的中国人。

屠呦呦是第一位获得诺贝尔科学奖项的中国本土科学家、第一位获得诺贝尔生理医学奖的华人科学家，是中国医学界迄今为止获得的最高奖项，也是中医药成果获得的最高奖项。

第 4 章　公示语

公示语文体与翻译

公示语（public signs/notices）是指设置于公共场合，针对公众，起着提示、指示、限制、命令、警告、呼告等功能的文字，标示/识语（signs）、标志语（indicators）、交通标识语（traffic signs）、标语（slogans）、警示（warnings）、海报（posters）和告示/公示（short notices）等宣传广告性文字（图案）都可视为公示语，是一种给特定人群阅读、以达到某种特定交际目的的文体。其应用范围非常广泛，几乎涉及我们日常生活的各个方面，如街头的路牌、广告牌、路标、商店招牌、警示语、宣传语等。狭义的公示语按照功能划分为标识性、指示性、限制性和强制性四种类型。广义的公示语还包括对地点、人物、事件等的简介。

公示语是国际化都市及国际化旅游目的地语言环境、人文环境的重要组成部分。设立公示语是国际大城市的重要标志，大大方便了外国游客和商人。所以，恰当得体的公示语翻译非常重要。

公示语往往采用精练、简洁、正式的文字或文字加图案，向公众传递某个具体信息，是一种特殊的实用语言文本。

本章学习了解公示语的文体特点；掌握改译、意译、不译和套用等方法；学会通过大小写的变化、正确的表达符号、语句的排列形式、使用不同的背景颜色和图表来凸显公示语所强调的重点。

4.1.1 提示语

Rules for the Library	图书馆规则
[1] Before entering the library, shoes should be taken off and put on the rack outside.	[1] 进图书馆前，脱掉鞋并放在外边的鞋架上。
[2] Silence must be kept in the library; anyone violating that rule will be advised to leave.	[2] 馆内请保持安静，违者建议离开。
[3] Playing in the library is not allowed.	[3] 馆内不允许嬉戏。
[4] Food and drink are not allowed in the library.	[4] 馆内不允许饮食。
[5] Resources of the library are not to be taken away without borrowing process.	[5] 未经办理借出手续，不得随意带走馆内书籍。
[6] School bags and books not belonging to the library are not allowed inside the library. Personal belongings can be put on the school bag shelf in the library.	[6] 不允许带进书包和非馆内书籍。个人物品放在包内，置于图书馆的放包架上。

4.1.2 警示语

Warning for *Terminator 2*	《终结者2》警示
[1] *Terminator 2*: 3D involves loud noise, strobe lights, fog effects and sudden movements.	[1]《终结者2》属于3D影片，有巨大声响、频闪灯光、雾效和强烈的动作。
[2] Due to the intense nature of this attraction, parental guidance is advanced.	[2] 由于本项目动感极强，父母要照顾好孩子。
[3] Person with the following conditions should not experience this attraction: • Heart Conditions • Back, Neck or Similar Physical Condition • Expectant Mothers • Motion Sickness or Dizziness • Medical Sensitivity to Strobe Effects • Medical Sensitivity to Fog Effects	[3] 有以下情况者不要参与本项目： • 心脏病 • 背痛、颈部疼痛和类似情况 • 孕妇 • 晕动症或眩晕症 • 频闪效果过敏 • 雾效过敏

• 对高分贝和突发的噪声敏感	• Sensitivity to Loud or Sudden Effects
[4] 游客可以坐在标准的轮椅中或电动便利车中。	[4] Guest may remain in their standard motorized wheelchair or electric convenience vehicles.
[5] 带有服务犬的客人请向服务人员咨询。	[5] Guest with service animals please see attendant for assistance.

4.1.3 指示语

电梯使用注意事项	Elevator Safety & Usage Tips
[1] 进出电梯要迅速。	[1] Enter and exit the elevator promptly.
[2] 进出电梯时注意脚下。	[2] Watching your steps when entering or exiting the elevator.
[3] 儿童乘梯须由成人陪同。	[3] Children should always be accompanied by an adult when using the elevator.
[4] 切勿让孩子在电梯上玩耍。	[4] Don't allow children to play on or around the elevator.
[5] 儿童应由成人陪同,决不可单独留在电梯附近。	[5] Children should be accompanied by an adult and never left alone in the vicinity of the elevator.
[6] 未经授权者严禁进入电梯井。	[6] No unauthorized person should enter the elevator hoistway.
[7] 发生火灾或其他紧急情况时切勿使用电梯。	[7] Do not use the elevator in the event of a fire or other emergency situations.
[8] 禁止打开电梯紧急逃生出口运载超长物品。	[8] Do not transport any long objects by opening the car top emergency exit.
[9] 电梯运行时不要在电梯里上蹿下跳。	[9] Do not jump in the car while the elevator is running.
[10] 严禁使用物品妨碍红外线探测门传感器的正常运行。	[10] Do not prevent the operation of the infrared door detection-cells with objects.
[11] 切勿用物体或身体的任何部位阻碍电梯门的关闭。	[11] Never wedge an object or any part of the body in the path of a closing elevator door.
[12] 清洁走廊或电梯时应避免将	[12] When cleaning corridors or car interior,

水扫进电梯井。	avoid sweeping water into the shaft.
[13] 紧急时刻使用"停"或"报警"按钮。	[13] Use the "stop" and "alarm" button only when required.
[14] 需乘电梯，只按您需要的"上"或"下"键。	[14] When calling the elevator, press only the button indicating the directions you wish to travel.

4.2 文体特点

4.2.1 用词简洁　准确易懂

公示语最明显的文体特征就是用词简洁明了，准确易懂。公示语语体比较正式，词汇选择非常重视公众化，尽量使用常用词汇，严格避免使用生僻词语，大量使用结构简单的名词或动词短语。

（1）名词中心型

公示语主要针对公众进行指示和提示，其内容自然是对大量基础设施、单位部门名称、功能设施等进行说明和指示，用其明白无误的信息为公众提供生活与工作上的便捷。这类表示指引、说明、告知等信息的公示语都是静态的，所以无论中文还是英语都会使用名词或名词性结构。如：

　　登记处——Registration　　美食街——Food Court
　　咨询台——Information　　消防通道——Fire Engine Access

（2）动词中心型

公示语经常向公众发出一些提示、号召或要求，并期望公众做出相应的行为。这类公示语极富动感，所以无论是英语公示语还是中文公示语，都会使用动词和动词短语，以突出这类公示语的动态性和警示性。如：

　　小心碰头——Mind Your Head　　登记入住——Check In
　　小心轻放——Handle with Care　　推杠报警——Push for Alarm

4.2.2 祈使省略　简洁明了

从语法上看，公示语多使用现在时态，以实现对公众行为的指示、限制和强制；多采用省略的方法，比如省略主语、谓语、名词、介词、冠词、标点符号等，如："节约用水"，就省略了主语"你"和标点符号。英语中的公示语准确体现特定的意义、功能，仅使用实词、关键词和核心词，而冠词、代词、助动词等一概可以省略。从句型上来看，英汉公示语都多使用简单句，以求简洁之目的；大量使用祈使句，特别是限制性公示语，对相关公众的行为提出限制、约束要求，语言直截了当，如使用"请""请不要""严禁"等句型。

4.2.3 词句工整 兼顾意韵

汉语公示语依赖于汉语的特征和习惯，常使用传统的四字结构，表现出词句工整、意韵共存的特点。英语公示语在语言特色和修辞特点上与汉语一样，都讲究结构的对称，强调音韵的和谐，呈现出简洁明快、朗朗上口且极具表现力和感染力的特色。公示语还使用修饰来铺成和拔高，使用夸张的手法来引起受众的关注和情感上的共鸣，以期达到传情达意的效果。但两者在语言表达上也有一些不同之处。

（1）中文公示语大量使用四字对称结构，英语则不然。

汉语的"意合"特征使得汉语里有大量结构对称、音韵铿锵的四字结构，中文公示语也秉承了这一特征；而英语的"形合"特征则要求句子结构之间大量使用介词、连词、冠词等虚词起连接作用（有些在公示语里可省略），这就使得英语公示语很难取得中文公示语外形上简洁匀称的视觉美学效果。如：

游人止步，谢绝参观——Closed to Visitors
注意安全，请勿靠近——Keep away for Safety
提高警惕，注意安全——Security Precaution

（2）中文公示语与英语公示语中对名词中心词起修饰作用的成分的位置不同。

公示语大量使用名词性短语，用来说明所标识事物的性质、目的与用途，以便公众识别。然而，汉英两种语言中这类名词性短语的表达方式不尽相同。汉语公示语都是修饰成分在前，直接修饰名词中心词，是"修饰（名词）+名词中心词"结构，中间没有任何其他成分；而英语公示语则是名词中心词在前，修饰成分在后，之间还需其他词来连接，通常是"名词中心词+介词+修饰词"结构。如：

大客车专用入口——Entrance for Buses　　乘务人员工作守则——Rules for Crew
儿童书籍部——Books for Children　　软卧车厢——Carriage with Cushioned Berth
陈列品——Goods on Display　　库存品——Goods in Stock

（3）中文公示语与英文公示语的表达方式与表达角度不同。

在表达方式上，汉英两种公示语的切入角度有时刚好相反。中文通常采用否定句式来对某个动作或某种行为进行禁止，而英语则直接使用名词来达到这一目的。如：

油漆未干——Wet Paint　　　　　　当心触电——Danger: High Voltage
禁止拍照——No Cameras/No Photograph　禁止摆卖——No Vendors
非公莫入——Staff Only

4.3 翻译要领

4.3.1 用词简洁　文化有别

公示语展示空间十分有限，所以要求用词简洁明了。因此，英语公示语可以省去不影响整体语言效果的词语，比如系动词和冠词等虚词，同时大量使用无主句或短语。汉英公示语虽然有相似之处，但毕竟是两种相去甚远的语言体系，在遣词造句、表达角度、文化背景、思维习惯等方面有很大差异，这些差异必然会影响到两种语言公示语的表达形式和内容。

4.3.2 使用简单句式　避免冗词赘语

公示语的语旨是普通大众，往往使用简单句式，避免复杂冗长的句子和可有可无的字词。公示语具有独特的功能特色和语言风格，其语场为其突出的社会功能，所以其语式主要是用于指示、提示、限制和强制公众的行为和举止。中文公示语还有其自身的特色和特殊性，所以在英译汉语公示语时宜遵循三个原则：

① 统一（Consistency）。即直接借鉴（借译）英语国家现成的惯用公示语，统一使用国际惯例。如："打八折"就直译为 20% off，而不能译为 80% discount；"爱护环境，从我做起，垃圾带走，不要残留"，直接采用现成的英语公示语 Don't litter 或 No littering，即可达到功能对等，没必要直译。如果有的译法已经被人们普遍接受，则英译统一用固定译法；如果既无法借鉴又没有固定译法，则英译可采用权威性的网站、报刊和辞典上的译法。

② 简洁（Conciseness）。即要求译文简单、扼要、表达自然。既要用词简洁，还要措辞精确，仅使用实词、关键词、核心词汇，而一些虚词，如冠词、代词、助动词等，均可以省略。

③ 易懂（Comprehensibility）。即英译文的可读性，易被英语人士理解，尽量避免中式英语。"软席、硬席"，可直接译为 Cushioned Seat 和 Ordinary Seat。这样翻译，虽然不大符合"忠实"原则，但是却达到了"易懂"原则，符合英语表达习惯和思维方式，能够达到对外交流和宣传的效果。

4.3.3 句法形态不同　套用惯用结构

（1）中文多用主动语态，英语多用被动语态。

汉语很少使用被动语态，因为汉语被动语态形式通常用来表示不幸与事故，如"被害""挨骂"，因此有学者戏称汉语被动语态为"不幸语态"；而英语出于强调主语或避免言及动作实施者，频频使用被动语态。这一语言特征在汉英两种公示语中也有体现。如：

　　车位已满——Occupied　　　　　已预订——Reserved
　　禁止堆放——Obstruction Prohibited　　左车道关闭——Left Lane Closed

（2）套用惯用结构。

英语公示语常用 keep... 结构来表示那些提示性质的公示语，汉语公示语没有单独对应的表达方法。如：

　　注意随时关门—— Keep Closed　　勿靠近易燃品——Keep away from the Inflammable
　　请自觉遵守秩序——Keep Order　　怕光，置于暗处保存——Keep in Dark Place

英语公示语还有两个惯用结构：Beware of... 和 Caution...，多用于警醒提示目的，两者都相当于汉语"谨防……""提防……""当心……""小心……"之意。如：

　　谨防恶犬——Beware of Dogs　　小心玻璃——Beware of Glass

（3）套用与创新并举。

由于社会生活的共性，很多英语公示语与汉语公示语的使用目的是完全一致的，所以很多汉语公示语在英译时可套用现成的英语公示语。此外，虽然有些英语公示语与汉语公示语的形式和字面意思都不对应，但只要它们的语用功能是一致的，也可以使用，但要避免生造不符合英语公示语习惯的译文。如：

爱护绿地，请勿入内！ Take care of the green meadow, no entrance.

小草微笑，请你走便道！ Little grass is smiling slightly, please walk on the pavement.

考虑到中文公示语英译的服务对象和其功能的要求，翻译时可采取一些具体翻译方法：

① 意译。对于外国游客无法接受的公示语，宜采取"意译法"。如："司机一滴酒，亲人两行泪"可译为"Drink and drive cost your life."；"宁停三分，不抢一秒"译为"Better late than never."，言简意赅，传意明确。

② 改译。原公示语带有限制、强制语气时，应改译成语气得当的译文，既能达到目的，又不会引起任何不快。如："闲人莫入"（旅游景区的标牌）就不宜翻译成 Tourists Stop，可改译成"Staff Only!"。再如，将中文中的"斤"换算成西方

的度量单位 pound，就不会给译文读者带来理解上的困难。

总之，由于中英公示语在表达方式和语用上的差异，以及中文公示语英译的服务对象及其功能要求，决定了在英译汉语公示语时应该采取各种以目标语言和受众为旨归的翻译方法。

4.3.4 语相调整

汉语一般采用两种手段突出公示语的功能：一是通过字形或者字体的变化表示强调；二是通过字体的颜色、给文字加框或者使用感叹号。英语则通过拼写、标点、语句排列的形式、背景颜色和图表的使用实现强调或突出该公示语的功能。

（1）拼写

在形式上，英语公示语为了醒目，可以把公示语全部大写或句中实词首字母大写，甚至所有单词首字母都大写，汉语则习惯于根据自身的特点，通过改变字号或变换字体等方式达到这一效果；此外，两种公示语都惯于在文字之外加上各种图案或符号，以起到警醒或美化妆饰效果。

（2）标点

中文公示语为了达到警醒提示的效果，往往会在公示语后面使用感叹号（也称惊叹号）以壮声势，但英语公示语一般不用感叹号或其他标点符号，只是在那些提示可能会造成严重后果或极度危险的公示语后面才偶尔使用感叹号。

（3）语句的排列形式

英语公示语通常采用文档排版中居中的排列形式，以使公示语整体紧凑、活泼、浑然一体。如：

    WARNING   注意

  BUILDING UNDER   大楼监控

   SURVEILLANCE   24 小时安保摄像

24 HOUR SECURITY CAMERS

（4）背景颜色和图表的使用

英语公示语除文字外，还采用不同的背景颜色和图表，更加明确和准确地给受众以指引、说明、限制和禁止。如：用"轮椅"表示"残疾人专用"，"⊖"圆圈中间画一白线表示"禁止"，"⊕"圆圈中间画箭头表示方向，等等。

4.4 常用词汇句型

（1）标识性公示语

办理登机区 Check in Area　　　　人行横道 Pedestrian Crossing

机场休息室 Airport Lounge　　　　商务中心 Business Center

列车出发 Train Departures　　　　进港 Arrivals

到达机场 Destination Airport　　　各通道出口 Exit to All

消防通道 Fire Engine Access　　　 消火栓 Fire Hydrant

转机处 Flight Connections　　　　行李寄存 Left Baggage

失物招领 Lost Baggage　　　　　　到港行李 Luggage from Flights

取行李 Luggage Pick up　　　　　 休闲广场 Entertainment Plaza

（2）指示性公示语

安全通道 Emergency access

大型超市 Hypermarket

办证处 Library card application

大型购物中心 Shopping mall

部分商品降半价 Off on selected lines

便利店 Convenience store

残障顾客专用通道 Wheelchair accessible

残障顾客专用坡道 Wheelchair ramp

仓储式会员店 Warehouse membership store

即将驶出高速 Approaching end of motorway

避免交通堵塞 Avoid the jams

弯道危险 Dangerous bend

城郊购物中心 Suburban shopping center

家居建材商店 Home furnishing store

大件垃圾 Bulky waste

配件送货上门 Accessories/Spares delivered to your door

（3）限制性公示语

办公区域，观众止步 Staff only

请保持国道畅通 Please keep gateways clear

别让你的烟头留下火患 Please put out your cigarettes

请保留车票待检 Retain your ticket for inspection

贵重物品请随身保管 Please don't leave your valuables unattended

请将通信工具设置为静音 Please mute cell phones

汽车行驶中，严禁与司机交谈 When the bus is moving, do not speak to the driver

请勿坐靠 Please stand clear

（4）强制性公示语

非演职人员请勿入内 Staff only

禁止黄、堵、毒 Pornography, gambling and drugs prohibited

公众不得入内 No entry for general public

仅供非吸烟者 Non-smokers only

禁止浏览黄色网站 Pornographic website visit prohibited

除装货外，禁止停车 No parking except for loading

门前禁止停车 No parking in front of this gate

禁止未成年人进入 Adults only

禁止通行 No thoroughfare

严禁使用明火 No open flame

止步，高压危险 Danger! High voltage

未经允许，禁止张贴广告，否则追究责任 Unauthorized posters and advertisements will be prosecuted

（5）常用句型

① 各种……有货 All the range of... available

② 建议，警觉 Warning + noun; Caution/Mind + action

③ 提醒注意 Beware of + noun; Beware + sentence

④ 禁止 Danger + sentence

⑤ 严禁 Danger + adj./noun

⑥ 紧急情况 Emergency + noun + only

⑦ 紧急情况 Emergency + 名词构成的紧急设施

4.5 译文赏评

4.5.1 警示型公示语

原文

请不要食用非麦当劳食品和饮料

译文

Consumption of McDonald's foods only

赏评

这是一则典型的转换角度翻译的绝好实例,属于反话正说,既十分巧妙地提醒了消费者,语气又非常委婉,不会对顾客造成心理冒犯,汉语原文里过于直白的语气也被消除了。如果直接译为 "Please do not eat or drink non-McDonald's foods and drinks here.",意思似乎清楚了,但语气显得十分生硬,对读者而言缺少尊重。在翻译警示公示语时,一定要注意语气,既要使用礼貌用语,又要注意英汉两种语言文化心理上的差异。

4.5.2 限制型公示语

原文

鳄鱼伤人,禁止游泳

译文

The last one is delicious, bring me another one.

赏评

这是一块置于有鳄鱼出没水面岸边的双语公示语,提示游客此处不能下水游泳,以免鳄鱼伤人。如果直译,肯定也能找到一个相宜的译文,但是译者没有简单下笔,而是转换了叙述角度,以鳄鱼的口吻来说出这句话,真是妙趣横生,肯定能给读者留下深刻印象。一般来说,公示语也可适度幽默,不会有伤大雅。再如有人把"保持车距,小心撞车"译为"keep distance, don't kiss me",也颇具创意。

4.5.3 提示型公示语(1)

原文

您不来,那是您的错。如果您来了,不想再来,那是我的错。

译文

If you don't come, that's your fault. If you have been here and don't want to come again, that's my fault.

赏评

　　这是一家餐馆墙上的标语，意在说明该餐馆的食物美味，服务优质以及环境舒适，顾客来过之后还能再来第二次。遗憾的是，译文却差强人意，主要表现在以下三个方面：① 译文采用了字对字的直译，使译语受众感到莫名其妙，颇令人费解。难道我不去这个餐馆吃饭就犯错误了吗？是谁要求我必须去呢？顾客有选择去何处就餐的自由，如果顾客不再去这家餐馆就餐，餐馆的服务管理人员又何错之有呢？译文没有考虑到译语受众的接受习惯，忽视了礼貌原则，用词造句生硬古板。② 译文忽视了公示语的功能，没有体现出这条公示语应该起到的宣传和召唤功能。③ 译文没有遵循以译语受众为旨归的翻译原则，忽略了东西方的思维差异。

　　对这种内容的公示语，可采取意译的方法，译出餐馆鲜明的个性特征，比如食物口味地道、风味独特、服务卓越、环境优雅等，以此来实现召唤顾客再次光临的目的，体现公示语的功能。可以考虑改译为：

Come on

A Wonderful Restaurant

DELICIOUS and AUTHENTIC

　　这一译文具有强烈的召唤意味，尤其是 Come on 的使用，相当具有亲和力，使客人感到热情和真诚；而 DELICIOUS and AUTHENTIC 又说明了该餐馆食物的特征，再加上两个词全部大写，体现出强调和突出的意义，实现了该公示语的功能。

　　此外，还可以参照餐饮业的其他公示语，如：TASTING CLASSIC, FEELING CHINA；You Will Eat Till Last Meat；Meet Your MOUTH, Keep Your Health。

4.5.4　提示型公示语（2）

原文

教师休息室

译文

Teacher's Rest Room

赏评

　　"教师休息室"应该是教师课后休息之处，而这则英语提示却容易让人误会为是"洗手间"，因为 rest room 虽然也作"休息室"解，其更常用的意思却是指大楼内的"洗手间""公共厕所""卫生间"。"教师休息室"应译为 Teacher's Lounge 或 Teacher's Office 更为恰当。

4.6 课后练习

（1）

① Air quality improvement area

② All visitors must report to office.

③ Anyone caught using this lift will be removed from this list.

④ Hot work in progress

⑤ Passengers Pick Up At Red Tram Stop Only

⑥ Demonstration available

⑦ The performance runs 2 hours 30 minutes including an interval.

⑧ Floor cleaning in progress

⑨ Peace of mind from the minute you buy

⑩ We apologize for any inconvenience caused during building operation.

（2）

① 中央暖气全部开放。

② 本长途汽车专为持全程票者乘坐。

③ 安全出口，保持畅通。

④ 再次选购商品请填单，然后到收款台付款。

⑤ 票上的价格包括票价和服务费。

⑥ 票不可交换，也不能按购买价退票。

⑦ 请保存好收据，作为交款凭证，并享受保修。

⑧ 打电话询问开放时间和门票价格。

⑨ 取车时需交押金。

⑩ 为确保准时发车，此门在发车前两分钟关闭。

第 5 章　广告

> **广告文体与翻译**
>
> 　　广告（advertisement, ad.）是明确的特定行为主体出于某种目的、支付一定的费用、为让公众广为知晓而采用的一种传播手段。文体学上一般将广告分为书面广告语体和口语广告语体。根据内容，广告可以分为商品广告、劳务广告、求购广告等；以传播媒介划分，广告可以分为印刷品广告、广播媒介广告、电视媒介广告和网络媒介广告等。而广告语的翻译，就是把这种传播手段进行语言间的信息传递，其目的就是为了推销商品、服务或者推广某种理念。
> 　　广告类文体是一种形式独特的文体，属应用文之列。广告作为一种特殊的文体在当今的商品经济中无处不在，也越来越多地影响着人们的生活。如何正确地理解和运用广告，是摆在广告参与者面前的一个重要问题。在翻译实践中，正确分析广告文体的语言特点、不同语言间的文化差异，在译入语语境中实现广告所追求的效果是广告人的基本素质。
> 　　本章学习广告的文体特点，掌握不同种类广告的翻译要领；在大量的翻译实践和译文赏析的基础上培养学生翻译广告的能力。

5.1 课前实践

5.1.1 商品广告

Adidas Sports Shoes	阿迪达斯运动鞋
Twenty-eight years ago, Adidas gave birth to a new idea in sports shoes. And the people who wear our shoes have been running and	28 年前，阿迪达斯创造了全新的运动鞋概念。从此以后，脚穿阿迪达斯的人们健步如飞，并

winning ever since. In fact, Adidas has helped them set over 400 world records in track and field alone.

Maybe that's why more and more football, soccer, basketball, baseball and tennis players are turning to Adidas. They know that whatever their games are, they can rely on Adidas workmanship and quality in every products we make.

So whether you are pounding the roads in a marathon, or just jogging around the block, Adidas should be on your feet.

You were born to run. And we were born to help you do it better. You will find us anywhere smart sports people buy their shoes.

Adidas—for all sports people.

在运动场上频频夺奖——仅在田径场上，阿迪达斯就帮助运动员们创造了400多项世界纪录。

这或许就是为什么越来越多的橄榄球、足球、篮球、棒球和网球运动员选择阿迪达斯的原因。他们知道，无论从事哪项运动，阿迪达斯精湛的工艺和优异的质量都值得他们信赖。

不论是在马拉松赛道上飞奔，还是在小区周围慢跑，您都可以穿上阿迪达斯。

奔跑是您的天性，让您跑得更快则是我们的天职。哪儿有优秀的运动员，哪儿就有阿迪达斯。

阿迪达斯——运动者的代名词！

5.1.2 招聘广告

招 聘	Wanted
工程管理助理	**Project Management Assistant**
责任：	**Responsibility:**
——为重庆的工程提供服务。	—Provide service for the project in Chongqing.
——辅助工程经理的日常工作。	—Provide assistance to the project manager for everyday work.
——负责文件管理，为学员和家长们提供客户服务。	—Responsible for file management, customer service for students and parents.
要求：	**Requirements:**
——大学及以上学历。	—College degree and above.
——英语和计算机技能良好。	—Good English and computer skills.
——在国际机构中有过相关的	—Related working experience in the international

工作经验。 ——耐心, 仔细, 能辅助工作。具有强烈的团队工作精神。	organization. —Patient, careful, supportive. Has strong team work spirit.

5.1.3 销售广告

Tomorrow Will be a Reflection of Tonight	**明天是今夜的映像**
Night is a special time, a time of rest and renewal. Your body begins to relax to unwind from the activity of the day and to slip into the softer rhythm of the night. It is the time when your body turns the energy needed for the smiles and laughter of the day into the magical replenishment of the night. This is the time your skin needs special care.	夜晚是一段特别的时间——休息和更新的时间。您的身体开始放松,从白天的紧张活动中松弛下来,转入夜晚轻柔的旋律。白天您的笑容和笑声所消耗的精力要由夜晚魔术般地来补充。这时您的皮肤需要特别护理。
Night of Olay is special night care cream, created to make the most of magic of the night. It is greaseless and remarkably light to touch, a sheer pleasure on your skin, allowing it to breath naturally while it absorbs this special nighttime nourishment.	Olay 晚霜是一种夜晚使用的特别护肤霜,能充分发挥夜晚的魅力。无油脂、轻柔、舒适,让皮肤一面自然呼吸,一面吸收 Olay 晚霜的特殊营养。
"Hour after quiet hour all through the night." Night of Olay enhances your skin's own natural renewal by bathing it in continuous moisture, easing tiny dry wrinkle lines and encouraging the regeneration of softer younger looking skin.	"一夜之中,每时每刻。"Olay 晚霜使您的皮肤始终保持湿润,增强皮肤的自然再生能力,舒展细纹,让您的皮肤显得更柔软,更年轻。
Night of Olay tonight will be reflected in your youthful radiance tomorrow. Night of Olay.	今夜用了 Olay 晚霜,明天您将青春焕发。 Olay 晚霜。

5.2 文体特点

广告语言的基本特点"一方面是语法简单,句子短小,单词、短语、从句独立成句;另一方面是构思精巧,匠心独运,佳句、妙语、新词层出不穷"(曹明伦,2007:87)。

5.2.1 用词简洁 突显效果

为了达到"推销"的目的,广告的用词力求简洁明快。广告英语用词有以下特点。一是大量使用单音节词、普通名词和形容词的比较级,以增强广告的魅力。二是杜撰新词或错拼词,可以增强对消费者的感召力,突出产品的新、奇、特,如:Kodak 世界闻名,却起源于按动相机快门的"咔嚓"声;饮料广告 The Orangemostest 这个词,是由 orange + most + est 组合而成,强化饮料品质绝对上乘,堪为极品。三是使用人称代词增强效果,第一人称突显正式,第二人称突出消费者的主体性,第三人称则是肯定性的描述,如:We are at the heart of Asia; now you are really flying(国泰航空)。最后,使用缩略语节省篇幅,降低成本,如:For rent; single,这是非常明显的出租广告。

5.2.2 句式独特 利落有力

独特的句式结构可以让读者产生积极反应和共鸣。在句式层面上,广告通常句式简短、松散、易懂易记;为了说服消费者,激发其购买欲望,广告还多采用祈使和感叹等句式。广告英语的句式特征:一是多用简单句或省略句,因为社会上的每个人都是潜在的消费者,因此句式要力求大众化,读起来亲切自然,令人玩味,如:Things go better with Coca-cola(可口可乐,万事如意)。二是多用疑问句或祈使句,此类句式能够激发读者的好奇心,缩小与读者间的距离感,如:"What is so special about such butter? Well, can you remember what butter used to taste like? Do you remember how you used to enjoy it when you were young?",问句迭起,环环相扣,能迅速抓住读者心理。三是时态上多用一般现在时,语态上多用主动。一般现在时和现在进行时的选择,取决于广告主的利益需求:过去的事与他们无关,将来的事太遥远,眼前的利益最重要。

5.2.3 修辞灵活 多策并举

广告的创作要符合引起注意、产生兴趣、激发欲望和采取行动的原则。为了迅速激发消费者的购买欲望,广告商不仅注重选词和句式,而且还会使用各种修辞手法,以比喻、拟人、双关、重复为多。利用各种修辞手段,意在将语言艺术与商业心理成功地融合在一起,呈现出艺术感染力和愉悦性,强化广告的诱导功能。如:

Light as a breeze, soft as a cloud（服装广告）；I'm More satisfied（More 牌香烟）；A new way to build it; A new way to buy Escort（福特汽车广告）。难怪有人称广告语为"半文学体"。这些广告或把产品、服务人格化；或以比喻使语言生动；或以双关达意，经久难忘。

5.3 翻译要领

5.3.1 经济节俭 对等新颖

广告翻译既要遵循经济原则，又要让读者产生共鸣。归结到词汇、句法结构的翻译上，应该做到：

① 熟词新译。如上海牌电视机广告：Shanghai TV—Seeing is believing（上海电视，有目共赏）；全球通信广告：Talk global, Pay local（全球通信，付款就近）；swatch 手表广告：Time is what you make of it（天长地久）。除此之外，创造一个好记的新词，也是广告商的手法，如七喜汽水广告：Fresh up with Seven-up（痛饮七喜，神清气爽），其中 seven 的使用则是迎合了西方的文化习惯，因为他们将得"七"视为赢家的代名词。

② 动态对等。如：Elegance is an attitude（优雅态度 真我性格），这个浪琴表广告中的系动词（is），最能通过一个简单的陈述告诉受众深刻的道理，达到广告的效果。翻译时，如果拘泥于原文的语义和形式，译文读起来则味同嚼蜡，不会给受众留下太深的印象。如果采用汉语四字对仗的对偶句（如浪琴表广告的译文），则会达到醍醐灌顶的效果。此外，类似句子还可以采用扩译策略，译成汉语常见的四字成语、八字一对的对称句，以增强阅读效果，实现和原语读者相同的反应。

5.3.2 修辞巧妙 灵活传达

广告翻译中可以应用的修辞手段很多，文学创作中所用的任何一种修辞手段几乎都可以巧妙地应用到广告写作和翻译中，如对偶、比喻、双关、排比和夸张等。如何翻译这些修辞手法，并没有一个理论上的框架，译者可以遵循以下几种原则：

① 最大趋同原则。恒生银行广告语 Your Finances—Your Way 被译为"理财自在，任你发挥"，这一对偶的翻译策略就体现了最大趋同原则。中国传统文化中的对偶是极其讲究的，所谓"天对地，上对下，东对西"。但现在广告中没有这么严格的对仗，只是把意识连贯或语气递进的成语、短语、四字词等任意组合在一起，即为佳句。翻译时，几乎任何英文句式的广告语都可以译成汉语的对偶句，但汉语的对偶句不一定能够成功地译成英文的对偶句。尽量使头韵、尾韵、意义三者之间达到

最大平衡，如帝舵表的广告语 Tong as a Tiger 可译为"坚毅犹如虎威"，虽没有保持原广告的头韵，但运用了比喻的修辞手段，使其意义得以较充分地传达。总之，只要满足了广告的推销目的，让受众对产品印象加深，效果增强，翻译时可以"不择手段"，不必拘泥于原文的辞格。

② 创译原则。在广告的跨文化传播中，创译基本脱离了翻译的范畴，属于重新创造，但又不是全新的创作。此类译文受原文内容的制约，只是意境比原文更深远，句子的精辟程度和可读性更胜一筹。如：Asking for More（More 香烟，多多益善），是一个双关修辞，就体现了创译的原则。

5.3.3 信息传递 视域融合

广告是一种面向大众的重要宣传手段，是一种重要的社会文化。它不仅要遵循社会文化习惯，迎合大众审美心理，而且对于社会文化的形成具有重要作用。如果不知文化间的差异，翻译时不做文化转换，译文就不能达到"信息传递，视域融合"的效果。因此，译者要遵循以下原则：

① 归化原则。要熟悉外族文化，了解异域文化心理。如美国的 P&G（Procter and Gamble）公司中 P 和 G 取自公司创始人的名字，和其中文译名"宝洁"公司没有任何联系。但为了迎合中国文化，将之译为"宝洁"，取"实用"以及"干净"的意思。

② 异化原则。使译文读者忠实地接收到原文信息。如："月宫玉兔"英文译成 Moon Rabbit 而不是 Jade Rabbit，其原因就在于"玉兔"是我国神话故事中的形象，是陪伴吴刚生活在月桂树下的兔子，有特定的文化意象。译成 Moon Rabbit 不仅体现了我国古典文化的风采，又不会让外国读者产生误解，认为是玉做的兔子。

③ 直译原则。使在英语文化和汉语文化中具有相同意思的信息能成功传递。如日本的汽车品牌英文的 Crown，中文为"皇冠"。两种译文都能显示日本车的豪华和霸气。音译是直译的一种重要形式，最为常见。有一种电池的商标叫"白象"，英文译成 White Elephant 应该没有问题，但是文化差异造成此译文的语用错误，因为 a white elephant 是英文的固定短语，译为"无用的东西，沉重的东西"，所以译为 Baixiang Battery 为妥。

5.4 常用词汇句型

① 熟悉……市场 familiar with... market
② 为人正直，良好的职业道德 strong personal integrity and professional ethics
③ 须懂数据库，具备网络知识 Database programming and network knowledge desired

④ 须有……的经验，尤以……为佳 Experience in... preferable in the field of... products.

⑤ 有……的能力尤为重要 Excellent... are considered important.

⑥ 熟悉……优先 Familiarity with... will have an added advantage.

⑦ 主要必备素质是…… The main qualities required are...

⑧ 被授予……称号 entitled it to many honorable titles

⑨ 欢迎批发零售 Wholesale and retail are welcome.

⑩ 坚持以……为中心 Focusing on...

⑪ 目前规模最大、实力最强的企业之一 ... is now among the biggest and strongest companies.

⑫ 性能无与伦比 unequal performance

5.5 译文赏评

5.5.1 促销广告

原文

岁月的小皱纹不知不觉地游走了！（"美加净"护肤霜）

译文

Maxam erases years from your skin.

赏评

这是国产化妆品名牌"美加净"的广告词及其英译。中英文俱佳，但中文在意韵方面更胜一筹。译文没有表示出"皱纹"和"游走"等意思，而是直截了当地使用了 erase（抹去）和 skin（皮肤）字样，同样显而易见地表示出了这种化妆品的功能。erase（抹去）的不就是 years（岁月）吗？这则广告词翻译得相当成功，生动地说明了商品的特征，能引发美好的联想。

5.5.2 公益广告

原文

登革热的传播主要靠白纹伊蚊，这种蚊虫在香港随处可见。要防止该疾病的传播，就必须对蚊虫滋生的地方进行清理。空饮料瓶、空午餐盒等可以装水的物品，必须得到妥善处理。空地上的废弃轮胎应该用针戳穿或包起来以免积水。

让我们一起动手清除污水、消灭蚊虫，关爱健康。

译文

Dengue fever is transmitted by aedes—a mosquito commonly found in Hong Kong. To prevent local transmission of the disease, mosquito-breeding must be eliminated. Containers that can hold water, such as empty soft-drink cans, and empty lunchboxes, must be disposed properly. Disused tires must be punctured or wrapped up to avoid water accumulation.

Let's remove stagnant water to eliminate mosquito for healthy living.

赏评

这是有关政府部门发布的一则关于预防登革热的公益广告文案。其汉语文本语言简单平实，毫无夸饰成分，英语译文在这一点与汉语文本基本做到了对应，是一篇好译文。

5.6 课后练习

（1）A White Shirt

What's in a name?

It sounds ordinary on paper. A white shirt wins a blue check. In fact, if you asked most men if they had a white shirt with a blue check, they'd say yes.

But the shirt illustrated on the opposite page is an adventurous white and blue shirt. Yet it would fit beautifully into your wardrobe. And no one would accuse you of looking less than a gentleman. Predictably, the different white and blue check shirt has a different name, Vivella House. It's tailored in crisp cool cotton and perfectly cut out for city life. Remember our name next time you are hunting for a shirt to give you more than just a background for your life.

On women and children's wear as well as on men's shirts, our label says—quietly but persuasively—all there is to say about our good quality and your good taste.

Our label is our promise.

（2）

茅台酒的广告语：茅台一开，满室生香；国酒茅台，源远流长。

钻石广告：A diamond lasts forever.

美食指南广告：Gourmet Lover? Indulge you appreciate with "Restaurant Guide".

理光复印机广告：We lead, others copy.

太平人寿广告语：Hand in hand, future in your hand.

第二编　商贸文书文体与翻译

- 导论
- 第6章　合同
- 第7章　产品说明书
- 第8章　标书

导 论

商贸文书文体包括商务合同、协议、产品说明书、标书等。随着科学技术的不断发展，信息技术的推广，电子商务的应用，经济越来越全球化，进而表现为贸易的全球化，金融的全球化，投资的全球化，消费的全球化。各企业、公司为了使自己的产品获得更多的消费群体，不少产品的名称和说明书也开始被翻译成其他语言，可以让更多的人去了解、认识、购买。在这个过程中，企业与企业、公司与公司之间也发展了越来越多的商务关系，需要缔结合同、标书等形成贸易关系，因而产生了商贸文书文体。商贸文书的英文文本采用的是商务英语，商务英语是英语的一种社会功能变体，是英语在商务场合中的应用。商务英语除具有普通英语的文体特征外，又有其独特的语言特征。商务文体的语言特征，首先通过其词汇的选择表现出来，对这类文本的翻译，便是商贸文书文体与翻译。不同的文本形式翻译时的要求也略有区别。

1 文体特征

1.1 词汇特点

商贸英语词汇具有"含义范围比较宽泛、丰富多彩，词义对上下文的依赖性比较大、独立性较小"的基本特点。

1.1.1 专业化

商务英语是在商务场合中使用的英语，其内容的高度专业化要求专业词汇的大量使用。专业术语是指适用于不同的学科领域或专业的词，是用来正确表达科学概念的词，具有丰富的内涵和外延，专业术语要求单义性，排斥多义性和歧义性，且表达专业术语的词汇都是固定的，不得随意更改。商务英语拥有数量可观的专业术语词汇。要真正读懂商务英语文章，译者必须懂得商务英语所涉及学科领域的相关知识，避免专业术语词汇普通化，如：encryption（加密），letter of intent（意向书），stockholding（库存），free on board（船上交货价），remittance（汇付）等。这些专业术语国际通用，无歧义，不带有个人感情色彩，因此一般不需要借助上下文来理解。

1.1.2 简洁化

与文学语言不同，商务英语言简意赅、简洁明确。因此，在商务英语中，修饰语使用较少，甚至达到惜字如金的程度，如：Free From Average（一切海损均不赔偿）；Owner's risk（损失由货主承担）；Return if Undelivered（投递不到，退回原处）。

在外贸业务信件、金融行情报价和机构发布的财务信息中，通常使用简短词汇代替词组，行文亦有约定俗成的特征（省略手段）可循。

① 功能词类（function words），如冠词、助动词或系动词、介词等，经常省略，保留实义词（content words），如：Spare parts sold（备件售罄）代替 "Spare parts have been sold."。

② 用词缀将多个词转化成一个词。词缀如：un-、in-、mis-、dis- 等可以代替否定词 not，如：discontinue（终止），dishonor（拒付），U/M（unscheduled maintenance）（不定期维护）。

③ 用单词代替词组，如：expedite 代替 hurry up；despite 代替 in spite of；because 代替 on account of。

简洁精确是商务英语的词汇特征，但同时商务英语中也会使用模糊词。如：

原文 The Contracting Parties undertake to adopt all appropriate measures to create the most favorable conditions for strengthening in all aspects, economic and trade relations between the two countries so as to promote the continuous long-term development of trade between the two countries.

译文 协议双方同意采取一切适当的措施，为在各方面加强两国经济贸易关系创造最好的条件，以促进两国贸易持续和长期的发展。

本句中的 appropriate 是出于礼貌的考虑，实际上包含了国际仲裁在内的一系列国际争端调节手段。因此，上例中模糊语的使用是礼貌原则的最好诠释。

1.1.3 古朴化

在商务合同和法律条文中，常会使用一些古体词以示严谨。Leech（1981）指出，专业英语、古体词及外来词等术语具有正式用语风格的词汇，符合商务英语行文准确、正式严肃的文体风格，比如常用 commence 代替 begin；terminate 代替 end；hereafter 代替 from this time 等。如：

原文 The party hereto shall, first of all, settle any dispute arising from or in connection with the contract through amicable negotiations.

译文 合同双方首先应通过友好协商，解决因合同而发生的或与合同有关的争议。

1.1.4 广泛使用缩略词

商务贸易注重实效和时效，简洁明了的商务语言会节省双方大量时间，提高交易效率。因此缩略词是商务英语词汇的重要组成部分。其特点是语言简洁凝练，使用方便，信息量大，而且容易书写，易读易记。缩略词最早用于电报电传中，以减少商务成本，提高效率，但目前商务英语缩略词数量日增，形式多样，意义广泛，涉及经济、贸易、财政、金融等各领域。主要有四种形式：

① 首字母缩略词。由短语中每个实词的第一个字母构成，多用大写字母，可以拼读或用字母读。这是一种常见的缩写法，如：APEC（Asia-Pacific Economic Cooperation，亚太经济合作组织），CBD（Central Business District，中央商务区），IAG（International Auditing Guideline，国际审计指南）等。

② 截短词。截取自然词的一部分字母，可以是词尾、词腰、词首，从而形成缩略词，如：pro（professional，专业人士），cap（capital，资本），phone（telephone，电话），memo（memorandum，备忘录）等。

③ 以辅音为核心组成的缩略词。这类缩略法主要用于单词的缩写，可用大写字母，也可以用小写字母，一般用字母读，也可以拼读，如：Frt.（freight，运费），gds.（goods，货物），hdqrs（headquarters，总部），mkt.（market，市场）等。

④ 利用同音或近音字母组成缩略词。这种缩略词相对较少，常用于单音词和少数双音节词转化为同音字母的缩写词，按拼写或字母读音，如：biz（business，商业），oz（ounce，盎司），ozws.（otherwise，否则）等。

1.1.5 措辞规范

商务英语的用词明白易懂，正式规范，简短达意，语言平实。在用词的明白易懂方面，尽量多用较为常用的词语，如多用 approval 而不用 approbation，要保证所有用词具有国际通用性，保证能为普通大众所理解，但与此同时又不能过于口语化。也就是说，商务英语所使用的语言不能过于非正式，而且也不使用短语或者粗俗用语。

商贸文书涉及信函、合同协议、广告、说明书等，在语言表述方面要求准确清楚，措辞方面更要规范严谨。

1.2 句式特点

1.2.1 结构复杂

商务文体行文严谨，逻辑严密。因此，句子结构一般都比较复杂，常使用短语、从句来限定说明成分，形成较冗长的句子，有时甚至一个句子就可单独成段。

1.2.2 多用被动语态

被动语态虽然是语法范畴的一个重要概念,却能够在语篇中体现特殊的修辞效果,发挥特殊的交际语用功能。当商务活动各方之间产生冲突、矛盾、抱怨等令人不快的情况时,应当采取合适的、礼貌的语言策略让各方能够心平气和地接受、理解并解决出现的问题。被动语态可以将陈述的重心从"人"转移到"事",这样既可以将问题的症结表述清楚,又可以避免把矛盾的焦点集中在造成过失的"人"身上,保护了对方的面子,从而使商务活动得以顺利进行。

1.2.3 名词化倾向

为了使商贸文书更加正式、客观,商贸文书文本中通常倾向于使用名词,或使用名词性结构代替动词性结构。如:

原文 As it is certain that the market is in great need of miniskirt, we wish to book with you a repeat order for the following items.

译文 市场急需大量迷你裙,我方希望再次订购下列产品。

在这个例句中,使用了 in great need of 的介词短语,而没有用动词 need。再如:

原文 Your first priority to the consideration of the above request and early favorable reply will be highly appreciated.

译文 若贵方优先考虑上述要求,并且给予有力答复,我方将不胜感激。

在这个句子中主语使用了名词性词组,不但信息量大,句子的表达也较为简洁。

1.2.4 使用固定句型结构

商贸文书中有不少套语或惯用的句型结构,这些用法是在长期的商务活动中逐渐形成的,已为人们所接受使用。常见句型有:

① The contract is made by and between the seller and the buyer..., whereby...

② The underdesigned buyer and seller have confirmed in accordance with the following terms and conditions.

③ Party A and Party B hereby agree to conclude the contract in accordance with the following terms and conditions.

以上句型都可译为:买卖(甲乙)双方依据/特立约如下。

除此之外,商贸文书中还有很多固定条款,其句法结构和表达方式也在商务实践中逐渐固定了下来。这些固定句型在表达意思时更为准确,在合同中经常会用到,如:subject to, without prejudice to, for the purpose of, by and between, on and after, or other, similar or dissimilar, causes 等。

1.2.5 条件句式的应用

商贸文书，尤其是商务合同，是用来约定合同各方应享有权利和应履行义务的书面文件。由于这种权利的行使和义务的履行均需要各种条件，所以商务合同中存在大量的条件句式。条件句多采用现在时态，体现了合同文体的严肃性。商务合同中的条件句多由下列连接词引导：if, in case (of), in the event of/that, provided (that), should, 等等。

1.2.6 状语从句的使用

商贸文书中常常使用状语从句，精确地指出在何种情况下、在何时、何地、以何种手段接受和完成商务业务。如：

原文 I am sure you will think it fair on our part when we suggest that the total value of the parcel should be reduced by 50%.

译文 我方建议这批货从总价中削减 50%，相信你方会认为这样对我方是公平的。

1.3 篇章结构特点

商贸文书的行文格式虽较为固定，但在体裁上大致有商务报告、商务合同、产品说明书和标书等不同类型之分，因此其篇章结构有不同的行文特点。商贸文书的篇章结构逻辑合理，意义连贯。所谓逻辑合理包括句子结构合理、段落安排合理、语篇思维合理。所谓意义连贯包括句与句之间语义连贯，段与段之间内容连贯，上下文之间思路连贯，而且通常遵循先综合后分析的思维模式。

2 翻译原则

2.1 术语精确

商务材料涉及经济、贸易、法律等很多方面，因此不可避免地要牵涉很多术语。要精确传达原文的信息，使译文读者准确理解原文，译者必须使用标准的、对等的术语，如："不可抗力"不可译为 force that can not be resisted，而应该是 force majeure。

此外，还有一些缩略语因简洁高效而被广泛使用，这也是翻译中不可忽视的问题。

2.2 语气恰当

在商务活动中,礼貌是非常重要的。在商务交往及商务文本中,双方都尽量措辞严谨,语气温和。中西方都有一些固定的表达方式可以使商务文本严肃可信。因此,译者在准确传达原意的基础上,可采取归化翻译手段使译文更容易接受。

2.3 地道专业 严谨规范

商贸文书翻译标准除应遵循"忠实通顺"外,还应注意"地道"原则。商贸文书格式固定,语体庄重,措辞婉约,行文严谨,因此,其翻译要兼顾"条理性、规范性、严谨性"。商贸文书翻译不仅要求译者要精通商贸英语语言特点,了解商务文化,还必须熟悉商务方面的专业知识,了解商务文体各个领域的语言特点和表达方法。商贸文书翻译不同于文学翻译和其他文本的翻译,它必须强调语义对等或等效,做到"地道",让读者有专业化的感受,而不只是一般的语言描述。

"地道"即是指译文的语言和行文方式都要符合商贸文书的语言规范和行文规范,也就是说译者所给出的译文读起来应该像是内行的人用译语写成的文章,其中的术语、表达都应该符合商贸文书的要求。其次,商贸文书采用的译名、概念、术语等在任何时候都应保持统一,不允许将同一概念或术语随意变换译名,符合商务英语翻译的"同一律"原则。

2.4 常用翻译方法和技巧

商贸文书翻译的最高标准是功能对等。功能对等就是从商务语篇去把握商贸文书翻译的内涵。译者在努力达到这一目标的同时,首先必须考虑的是词语的选择,尤其是专业术语词汇的选择。词语的选择与译作存在着非常紧密的联系。恰当、得体的词语选择可以为译文的准确、通顺、流畅铺平道路。

在商贸文书翻译实践中,根据具体情况,有一定的处理方法和技巧,包括转换、颠倒、增补、省略等。

(1)转换

汉语属分析型语言,英语属分析综合参半型语言。在语序上汉语和英语均属"主谓宾"语言,但也存在差异。转换是指商务文本翻译中语言的词性和表现方法的改变。由于英语和汉语的表达习惯、句子结构和词的搭配关系均有差异,在翻译中往往难以做到词性和表现方法一致。为了适应译文语言的表达习惯和语法规则,在商务文本翻译中必须运用此类转换技巧。

① 词性的转换。动词和名词的转换，如：

原文 The "Events of Default", as used in this Contract, shall mean the occurrence, from time to time, of any of the following circumstances.

译文 合同中使用的"违约事项"是指发生以下情形。

本句的 occurrence 本为名词，但在译成汉语时，转换成动词，译成"发生"更通达。

名词和形容词或副词转换，如：

原文 The fair price connected with the superiority of varieties of our products will be able to guarantee our competitive edge in the international market.

译文 我方各种各样的产品价格公平，品质优良，能够确保在国际市场的竞争优势。

② 词义转换。在正常的情况下，译者只需按照原文中各个词的词典含义就能准确而地道地把原文翻译成中文。然而，在一些特殊情况下，尽管按照词典含义意思对等地翻译，但在母语者看来，这种译文总让人觉得别扭，表达总是很不妥。在这种情况下，译者就必须按照译文的表达习惯，改变词典含义来表达原文的真正含义。如：

原文 Each Party shall have the right to change its legal or authorized representative and shall promptly notify the other Party of such change and the name, position and nationality of its new legal or authorized representative.

译文 双方有权撤换其各自的法定代表人或授权代表，并应将新法定代表人或授权代表的姓名、职位和国籍及时通知另一方。

在原文中 change 的原意为"变化"，但为了符合中文的表达习惯，将它翻译成"撤换"。再如：

原文 The company may establish branch offices inside China and overseas with the consent of the Board and approval from the relevant governmental authorities.

译文 合营公司经董事会决议并经有关政府机关批准可在国内外成立分支机构。

原文中 consent 的原意为"同意"，但根据中文商务语言的表达习惯，在译文中将其翻译为"决议"。

③ 句型转换。由于英汉语表达思想、遣词造句的方式和所用的形象均有不同，因此，我们在翻译时应该按照习惯用法决定是否改变表现方法。最为常用的方式是将英语中某些肯定和否定形式的句子在汉译时作句式转换处理。如：

原文 They were very few, fewer than at the last meeting of the board of directors. The chairman didn't say much at the meeting, but every word was to the point.

译文 他们没有几个人到会，比董事会上次到会的人还要少。董事长在会上说话不多，但每句话都很中肯。

④ 语态的转换。英语惯用被动语态，而汉语则多用主动语态。因此，英译汉时宜按照汉语的表达习惯作改组，这样的改组常见于那些以人的动作和活动为主语、且已表明或暗示动作的执行者的句子里。如：

原文 Everything possible has been done to save their enterprise and to carry on the entire reform of their management and control.

译文 他们已采取了一切可能的措施，以挽救他们的企业，并对他们的经营进行彻底的改革。

（2）增补

增补也是商务文本翻译中不可忽视的重要技巧之一。所谓增补，就是要根据上下文的意思、逻辑关系以及目的语的表达习惯，增加词量，以表达原文字面没有出现但已经包含的意思。增补主要是因为英汉两种语言在遣词造句以及思维方法上的不同造成的。商务语言的表述，失之毫厘，谬以千里。某些商务语言的表述虽然简单，但丝毫不会影响其内容的准确性。因此，在翻译时，为避免引起误解，就需要根据英汉语言的习惯和语法规则对这些词或句子予以重述。

① 增加实义词。鉴于商务语言的严谨性和规范性特点，在商务英语汉译过程中需要适当添加一定的词汇，以限定范围，提高表达的准确性。如：

原文 This Agreement is made by and between _____ Company having its registered office in _____ (place) and _____ Company, address of which is _____ (house number, street, city).

译文 本协议由 _____ 公司（注册营业地在 _____）和 _____ 公司（法定地址是 _____ 市 _____ 街 _____ 号）之间达成。

地址有多处，在通常的商务语言环境下，address 即表示"法定地址"，因此翻译成汉语时，需在"地址"前增加"法定"一词。

② 增补连词。汉语多偏正复句，很多时候不出现连词，如果文中有表示"时间""假设""条件""让步""目的""原因"等关系的"偏句"，可以用相应的英语连词表示上述各种关系。商务语言中最为典型的是"的"字结构的假设句，英译时必须添加显示主句和从句逻辑关系的连接词。如：

原文 合同对科技成果的使用权没有约定的，当事人都有使用的权利。（民法第88条）

译文 If the contract does not contain an agreed term regarding rights to the use of scientific and technological research achievements, the parties shall all have the right to use such achievements.

③ 增补同义词。英语有一词多义的特点，同一个词可以同时与若干个词进行搭配，语言仍自然流畅，如下文中的 decrease，翻译时应该将其多义性表述清楚。如：

原文 The innovation of products is one of the reform measures of the state-owned enterprises because it can decrease loss, cost and budget.

译文 产品的革新是国企改革的措施之一，因为它可以减少损失，降低成本和递减预算。

④ 增补主语。英语和汉语中的主语均是句子的主体，但按照汉语的表达习惯和文体特征，省略主语的情况较多，而英语句中的主语则通常不能省略。因此，在汉译英时运用增补技巧，可以补充汉语句中省略的主语。

原文 如蒙尽快慧告美国电脑详情，不胜感激。

译文 We should be grateful if you would give us further details of American computers at the earliest time.

原文中，收信人是卖方，询问电脑情况的人是买方，译文中增补"我方"和"你方"，不仅使英语的句子结构完整，而且表明了卖方与买方的关系。

⑤ 增补宾语。汉语和英语的及物动词后面都有宾语，表示动作的对象，动作关系涉及人或事物。在某些情况或一定的上下文条件下，汉语句子中的宾语可省略，而英语及物动词在任何情况下都须带宾语。运用增补技巧，可以补充汉语中省略的宾语。如：

原文 我们觉得在这个时候延长信用证和更改卸货港口是不恰当的。

译文 We don't think it proper to extend the validity of L/C and amend the discharging port at this time.

译文中增补宾语 it 形成复合结构中的"不定式"，使英语句子结构完整无缺。如果不采用增补技巧，则上述两个英语句子不能成立。

⑥ 省略。省略就是把原文中的某些冗余成分略去不译，或去掉不符合译文表达习惯的无用之词，以保证译文内容准确，文字简洁，结构规范。具体有以下几种。

• 省略表示重复、多余概念的词汇。如：

原文 Within... days after the effective date of this contract, the Owner shall pay the contractor as full and complete compensation for accomplishing the works and assuming all obligations under this contract.

译文 在本合同生效后 ×× 天内，业主应向承包商支付完成该工程及承担本合同规定的所有义务的全部报酬。

full and complete 如直译为"全部和所有的"，则与汉语表达习惯不符。汉语中这两个概念几乎没有区别，因此只要译出一个词即可。

• 省略修饰词。如：

原文 By a loan agreement dated _____ made between _____ Co. (Borrower) and _____ Co. (Lender), the Lender has agreed to make available to the Borrower a loan facility of up to $_____.

译文 根据_____年_____公司（借款方）和_____公司（贷款方）签署的贷款协议，贷款方同意向借款方提供_____美元的贷款。

up to 在句中表示"直到，多大"之意，为使译文更加精练，翻译成汉语时可以省略。

• 省略连接词。如：

原文 The parties must act in accordance with the principle of good faith, no matter in exercising rights or in performing obligations.

译文 当事人行使权力、履行义务应当遵循诚实信用原则。

原文中的 or 在翻译成汉语时用顿号代替，可以达到简练的目的。

• 省略介词。如：

原文 The contract is made by and between the Buyer, _____ Co. and the Seller, _____ Co.

译文 本合同是由买方_____公司和卖方_____公司签订的。

between（在……和……之间）在这句中用来限定范围，以表明合同是在特定的买卖双方之间签订的，但在译文中，其意思已经由于汉语内在的逻辑关系而得到明确体现，因此可以不译。

• 省略"here/there/where + 介词或副词"的表达。如：

英语商贸文书中有一套惯用的副词。严格地说，这类副词并不是商务术语，但从修辞和文体的角度来看，这类词的广泛使用既可以使句子简练严密，又使句子严肃庄重，具有商务文体风格。因而商务条文和文本中大量运用，在翻译成汉语时有时可省略不译。如：

原文 In accordance with the Law of the People's Republic of China on Chinese Foreign Equity Joint Venture and other relevant PRC laws and regulations, party A and party B hereby agree to set up a joint venture limited liability company.

译文 根据《中华人民共和国中外合资经营企业法》和其他相关的法律法规，甲方和乙方同意组建合资经营有限责任公司。

此句中的 hereby 即 in accordance with the Law of the People's Republic of China on Chinese Foreign Equity Joint Venture and other relevant PRC laws and regulations，可理解为"据此"。而汉语表达的连贯性已经使得译文忠实地再现了原文的含义，所以 hereby 可省略不译。

• 省略时态。如:

原文 Where the seller sells the subject matter which has been delivered to a carrier for transportation and is in transit, unless otherwise agreed by the parties, the risk of damage or loss is born by the buyer as from the time of formation of the contract.

译文 出卖人出卖承运人运输的在途标的物,除当事人另有约定的以外,易损、灭失的风险自合同成立时起由买受人承担。

英语时态区分细致,动作的进行过程通过时态表述得非常精确。相比之下,汉语的时态则模糊表达,在保持句意流畅的同时也忠实地反映了原文的意思。

⑦ 拆分。英语商贸文书中长句多,直译的汉语句子拉得较长,结构松散,内容杂乱,眉目不清。如果采用拆分技巧译出,情形就不一样。如:

原文 In order to facilitate business in consideration of the present monetary stringency, the corporation, on behalf of which I am studying this proposition, is willing to the base transaction on trade by barter and would import any articles, which you would ship to the United States.

原译 为便于交易,考虑到最近银根很紧,本人正在研究这笔交易所代表的公司希望以易货贸易为基础进行交易,并进口你方能运到美国的任何商品。

拆分 最近银根很紧,为谋求达成交易,本人代表公司正在研究如何做成这笔交易。我们希望以易货贸易为基础,进口你方能运到美国的任何商品。

把原文拆开译成两个汉语句子,并将并列连词 and 前面的短语"以易货贸易为基础"调整到第二个汉语句中,译文准确流畅,搭配恰当。原文的最后部分是一个结论性分句,拆成两个句子后,译文的层次分明,概念清楚。

⑧ 调整语序。由于英语语序和汉语语序并不完全一致,所以在翻译时,有时需要对语序做出调整,以使译文符合译入语的表达习惯。如:

原文 The Parties hereby agree to establish the Company promptly after the Effective Date in accordance with the EJV Law, the EJV Implementing Regulations, other Applicable Laws, and the provisions of this Contract.

译文 双方特此同意在本合同生效后依照《合资企业法》《合资企业法实施条例》、其他相关法律以及本合同的条款及时成立合营公司。

尽管原文中 in accordance with the EJV Law, the EJV Implementing Regulations, other Applicable Laws, and the provisions of this Contract 等词作为状语被放在后面,但在译文中,按照中文的习惯被放在了谓语的前面。

商贸文书的翻译不仅要求译者了解英汉语言的特点和基本翻译技巧,也要熟悉两种语言文化及商务语言的特性。

第 6 章　合同

合同文体与翻译

合同（contract）是当事人之间设立、变更、终止民事关系的协议，是指双方或多方之间为了实现某项特定的目标——商品买卖、技术合作或转让、合资经营或合作开采、工程承包、涉外劳务、涉外信贷、国际投资等，用文字的形式，明确订立具体的权利和义务，确定债权债务关系的文书。它是检验合同当事人履行合同行为的准绳，也是合同当事人之间建立和终止关系的协议书。合同亦称契约，是具有法律约束力的承诺，表示当事人愿意承担权利和义务，一经签订，当事人各方均须严格执行。凡违约者应对由于其违约所造成的损失承担责任。一旦发生合同纠纷，可经友好协商解决或通过仲裁解决。

合同作为契约具备以下三个特征：条理性——包括逻辑及语体的条理；纪实性——言而有物、言之有实；规范性——约定俗成、有条不紊。

商务合同一般分为销售或购货、技术转让、合资或合营补偿贸易、国际工程承包、代理协议、来料加工、多种贸易方式相结合的合同（如：涉外信贷合同、国际 BOT 投资合同、国际租赁合同、国际运输合同、聘请雇员合同、保险合同）等。

本章学习商务合同的文体特点以及翻译要领。合同翻译一般是指对国际贸易中的合同、章程、条款的翻译。翻译合同时，要理顺句子之间的逻辑结构，注意行文的条理性及严谨性。此外，根据语法分析译文的结构，根据目的语的表述习惯安排条款的排列顺序，可以考虑采用拆分长难句、省略法、断句法、重组法等翻译方法。

6.1 课前实践

6.1.1 赔偿合同

Provided the Buyer has not altered the Goods or the packaging of the Goods in any manner before sale, the Seller will defend any suit for damage brought against the Buyer based on a defect in the materials, design, or manufacturing of the Goods or on patent or trademark infringement in connection with the sale or use of the Goods. If any action is brought against the Buyer, it will promptly notify the Seller. The Seller will indemnify the Buyer against any liability, damage, or expenses incurred in connection with any such suit and will pay any judgment entered against the Buyer in such suit.	如果买方在销售之前未曾变动货物或其包装,那么卖方应对任何因货物的材料、设计、制造方面的缺陷或专利/商标侵权行为,对买方在销售或使用中在此的损害而面临起诉的情况负责。如果买方被提起诉讼,应立即通知卖方。卖方应对买方与该诉讼有关的任何责任、损失和费用予以赔偿并支付买方判决的费用。

6.1.2 保密合同

[1] Within twelve years after the signing of the Contract the Buyer shall not disclose in whole, or in part, the know-how Technical Documentation and other information of the Process obtained under the Contract. However, the Buyer shall have the right to disclose such information to those who work for or have connection with the Contract Plant.	[1] 在合同签订后 12 年内,买方不得全部或部分地披露合同所获得的专有技术、技术资料和其他情况。但买方有权将上述内容提供给本合同工厂或与本合同工厂有关的人员。
[2] In case the Seller is responsible to remove the defects the Buyer shall supply to the Seller on his request necessary personnel, erection tools, cranes, etc. for performing the removal of the defects. The cost thus incurred shall be borne by the Seller. The removal of defects shall be	[2] 若由卖方负责消除缺陷,买方应按卖方要求,向卖方提供必需的人员、安装工具和吊车等。由此产生的费用由卖方负担。消除缺陷应尽快进行,卖方应

performed as quickly as possible and the Seller shall do his best not to affect the progress of the construction of the Contract Plant.

尽最大努力使合同工厂的建设进度不受影响

6.1.3 知识产权合同

The Buyer understands that the Seller owns the exclusive rights in the designs, patterns, trademarks, trade names, and company names (the "Intellectual Property") used in connection with the Seller's Goods. The Buyer is given no rights in any of the seller's Intellectual Property. The Buyer will not use the Seller's Intellectual Property as if it were the Buyer's own property, nor will the Buyer register the Seller's Intellectual Property in any country as if it were the Buyer's own. The Buyer acknowledges that its unauthorized use of deceptively similar to the Seller's Intellectual Property will be deemed an infringement of the Seller's exclusive rights.

买方理解卖方拥有所售货物的设计、图案、商标、贸易名称和公司名称的专有权（"知识产权"）。买方不拥有任何卖方的知识产权。买方既不会使用，也不会在任何国家注册卖方的知识产权。买方理解未经授权使用或注册卖方的知识产权或具有迷惑性和欺诈性的类似知识产权，都将构成对卖方专有权的侵害。

6.2 文体特点

合同是一种法律文书，依法订立的合同一经各方签字，即具有法律效力，并对合同各方当事人都具有约束力，未经一方同意，不得随意变更合同内容，否则就算违约。因此，起草、翻译合同时各方都应慎之又慎，对合同语言必须仔细推敲、反复琢磨，避免因语言模棱两可而产生歧义。

6.2.1 用词简练　语体正式

合同的用词造句具有准确、简练、明晰和正式的特点。合同语言严谨，言简意赅，内容完整。如：In the event of a single arbitrator being unable to be agreed upon by the two parties...（一旦一个仲裁员不能被双方同意……），按照合同语言应改为：If the two parties fails to agree on a single arbitrator...（如果双方不能就此仲裁达成协议……）。

合同行文具有意思明晰、戒含糊其辞和模棱两可的特点，因此用词要规范，比如，"在乙方的要求下，甲方同意派遣技术人员帮助乙方安装设备"，对应的英译文是"At the request of Party B, Party A agrees to send technicians to assist Party B to install the equipment."。原句中"帮助"用的是 assist 而不是普通词 help，表达上更为正式。

6.2.2 用词专业 惯用长句

考虑到合同的语场需要，有时会对一些关键术语的定义做出明确的限定和说明，一般可分为扩张性解释和限缩性解释两种。如："'Patent' in this contract shall mean registered invention rights, registered utility model rights, right of registered industrial design and any technical applications listed in the attachment herewith."（本合同中的"专利"系指注册发明权、注册实用新型权、注册外观设计权及本合同附件中所列明的技术应用。），该例句中的"专利"一词已作了扩张性解释，超出了一般专利的范围。我们常见的知识产权法中的"专利"一词通常仅指"发明、实用新型及外观设计专利"，而此处的"专利"还包括该合同项下"任何技术应用"。又如："'Trademark' here means registered trademark."（本合同中的"商标"系指注册商标。），此处的"商标"则作了限缩性解释，它排除了普通商标，即非注册商标。

（1）词汇特征

① 多用词语并列形式。合同中的词语并列往往分为两种情况：词语并列结构和成对同义词结构。为使商标条约表意明确和规范严谨，合同制定者在行文中大量使用词语并列结构，用 and 或 or 把两个或多个短语并列起来。这种并列结构有更强的包容性，同时也更加有弹性。如：

（合同）项下或按照（合同）	under or in accordance with
按总体或部分来讲	in whole or in part
在欧盟内部或外部	within EU or elsewhere
撤回、停止或强制接受	revocation, suspension or imposition

另外，英语合同中使用较多成对的同义词，同样也是由 and 或 or 连接并列使用，是通过两个或多个词语的共同含义来限定其唯一词义，从而排除了一词多义可能造成的歧义，体现了合同作为法律文书的严肃性和用词的严谨性，确保了原文意思高度完整、准确，避免合同意思被曲解。如：

make amendments to and revision of	修改
fulfill or perform	履行
null and void	无效

② 多用情态动词。与所有的法律文件相同，合同在情态动词的选用上很慎重。may、must、will、shall、should 各司其职，不可混淆。如：shall 在合同中并非单纯表示将来时，而是用来表示一方应尽的义务，表示强制性责任和履行义务，与中文中"应该""必须"的意义相同，表达力度比 will 要强。在合同中，在向对方提出要求时总是倾向于使用带有强制性含义的 shall 或 must，而在谈到己方的义务或责任时，总是避免使用 shall 或 must，而较多选用 will 或 should，甚至选用 may，以淡化语言强度。如："The bidder shall bear all costs associated with the preparation and submission of its bid."（投标人须承担用于编制和提交其投标书而引起的一切费用。）

③ 频现缩略词。缩略词在合同中出现的频率很高，主要为首字母缩略词和截短词。国际经贸合同中的价格、支付及保险方式大多以首字母缩略词形式出现，例如：FOB（Free on Board，离岸价格）、T/T（Telegraphic Transfer，电汇），等等。此外，还有一些计量单位及相关名称则通常以截短词形式出现，如：CTN（carton，纸箱）、No.（number，号），等等。要准确翻译此类缩略词，关键在于平时的积累，并在此基础上熟知缩略词的全称，领会其含义，这也是起草、翻译合同所应具备的基本条件。

④ 古英语及特殊用语的使用。英文合同中常出现古英语词汇，最为突出的是用 "here/there/where + 后缀 in/after/by" 等的介词。这类古英语词汇能避免重复，使句子结构紧凑精练。如：

hereafter = after this time	今后
hereby = by means of	特此
thereto = to that	此外
thereupon = then	随后
whereof = of what; of which	关于那里
wherein = in what; in which	在哪里

合同中还有一些特殊用语，翻译时应特别注意，如：

whereas	鉴于（在约首用于引出签约的背景和目的）
witness	证明（在约首中用作首句的谓语）
now/therefore	兹特（常用于开头，接于 whereas 条款之后引出具体协议事项，并和后面的 hereby 结合。）
in consideration of	以……为约因
hereinafter referred to as	以下简称

（2）句法特征

在句法特征上，合同作为法律文书，规定了各方当事人之间的权利和义务，合同文字所表达的意思必须完整、明确、肯定，所以合同对句子类型的选择存在明显的倾向性，陈述句的使用频率比较高。陈述句用于阐述、解释、说明、规定和判断，语言比较客观、平实。此外，合同句法的另一个明显特征是较多使用长句和惯用句型。

① 多用长句。与普通英语相比，英文合同的句子较长，结构也复杂得多。长句的使用主要是为了准确地界定各方当事人的权利和义务，排除被曲解、误解或出现歧义的可能性。

② 惯用句型。英文合同中有不少套语或惯用句型结构，这些用法是在长期的贸易实践中逐渐形成的，已被普遍接受和使用，此类套语或惯用句型主要出现在合同的前言、结尾、保险、支付以及检验、索赔、仲裁等一般性的条款中，如：

a. The undersigned buyer and seller have confirmed… in accordance with the following terms and conditions.

b. Party A has agreed that Party B shall… under the following terms and conditions.

c. In consideration of the premises and covenants described hereinafter, Party A and Party B agree as follow.

d. The expiry date of the L/C is to be the 15th day after the date of shipment.

e. The L/C shall remain valid until the 15th day after the shipment.

a 大多出现在销售或购货确认书中；b 和 c 则通常在加工、代理及合营企业合同中使用；d 和 e 经常在合同的支付条款中出现，也是规定信用证付款方式时所采用的惯用句型。翻译此类套语或惯用句型时，切忌照原句字面直译，尽可能采用套译法，也就是采用中文合同中的相应套语或惯用句型，如："买卖双方依据……特立约如下"或"信用证有效期至……后的第……日"。

6.2.3　措辞婉约　得体讲究

合同措辞十分讲究分寸、得体，避免刺激对方，即使是向对方抱怨，甚至索赔，也是彬彬有礼，十分婉转。如："We wish to advise you that the relative L/C has been established."（兹通知，有关信用证业已开出。）；又如："You must deliver the goods on board the S.S "East Wind" within the time limit as stipulated in your contract, otherwise dead freight, if any, should be borne by you."（你方必须按合同规定的期限将货装上"东风轮"，否则，空仓费将由你方负责。）。第一句使用 advise，而译文用"兹通知"，使得句子语气比较委婉，如果逐词译为"我们愿意告诉你有关信用证已开出"，让人感到语气生硬；第二句使用了 if any，语气较委婉。

6.3 翻译要领

目前，我国涉外经济交往中所采用的合同大多为英文文本，而英文合同对语言有严格的要求，因此，把握合同语言的特殊性，是准确理解、翻译合同的关键所在。合同作为一种具有法律约束力的契约文本，其文本有用语正式、措辞准确、结构严谨、格式规范等特点。翻译合同这类文体的具体标准通常有以下三个方面。

6.3.1 术语准确 译文完整

合同行文严谨，措辞确切，译文严谨准确是合同翻译的基础，这样既可以避免产生误解和歧义，又可以明确和保证合同各方的权利和义务。翻译时尤其要注意合同中的专业术语和关键词语的准确性。合同文本有自己的一整套术语，有其独特性，应避免简单的字面翻译。如：accept 在一般情况下译为"接受""认可"，但在涉外合同中，这个词可能要译成"承兑"。另外，翻译合同时也要注意译文的完整性，决不能只求保持原文与译文在词语表面上的对等。

6.3.2 译文通顺 条理清楚

合同译文的通顺着重体现在"条理清楚"上，特别是在处理长句、复杂句时更是如此。合同的句式结构一般为复杂的长句，这是因为合同的撰写者希望一句话里尽可能多地容纳完整严密的信息，从而不给他人曲解或误解之机。所以译者首先要清楚了解主句的内容，然后逐步分析其他限定、修饰成分，译文尽量用规范的译入语表达，尽量使译文明确清楚，通俗易懂。如：

原文 One third of the total amount shall be paid with the order when the Contract is signed, one third by documentary bills when shipment is effected and the balance by clean bills when the goods have arrives.

译文 合同签订时先预付货款总额的三分之一，装船后凭跟单汇票再付三分之一，剩余的三分之一在货物抵达时凭光票一次性付清。

原条款陈述的是分期付款的三个阶段：交货前、交货时、交货后。译文通过在每一个具体阶段前分别添加"先预付""再付"以及"剩余的三分之一"，使整个条款层次清楚，意思明确。

6.3.3 符合契约文体特点

与其他商务文本相比，合同文本是正式程度最高的契约文体。所以，翻译合同时所使用的语言应尽量体现出契约文体的这一特点，选词要正式，所采用的句式也应符合译入语合同的格式特点。实际上，合同文本一般都有其相对统一的格式，具有程式化、条款化的特点，特别是首、尾处和正文中的某些必备条款，都形成了一套固定的格式和套语，因此翻译时应尽量符合译入语合同的规定格式，符合译入语的契约文体特点。如："因为"一般用短语 by virtue of 来翻译，很少用 because of；"在……之前"一般用 prior to，而不用 before，等等。再如：

原文 本合同于 2006 年 5 月 30 日在中国上海签订，一式两份，每份用英文和中文写成，两种文本具有同等效力。

译文1 This Contract was signed in Shanghai, China on May 30, 2006. Each copy was written in English and Chinese with two copies in each, and the two texts have the same effect.

译文2 This Contract was signed in Shanghai, China this 30th day of May, 2006, in duplicate in English and Chinese languages, both texts being equally authentic.

译文 1 用语不够地道，如用 effect 来翻译"效力"，不符合合同英语的特点。除此之外，句式采用的是简单句，没有反映出英语契约文体的句式风格。而译文 2 则通过采用介词短语 in duplicate in English and Chinese languages 和分词的独立结构 both texts being equally authentic 译成英文的复杂句，译文规范严谨，符合英文契约的文体特点。

6.4 常用词汇句型

① 本合同于_____年_____月_____日由_____公司，地址：_____（以下简称甲方）与_____公司，地址：_____（以下简称乙方）签订。

This contract is made and entered into this _____ day of _____, _____ by and between _____ Co., at _____ (hereinafter referred to as Party A) and _____ Co., at _____ (hereinafter referred to as Party B).

② 这是我们的一份包括……条款的合同样本。

This is a copy of our specimen contract in which... are contained.

③ 合同的任何更改变更均应得到……许可才有效。

Any modification alteration to the contract shall be made with the consent of...

④ 不经……同意，合同不能做任何更改。

No changes can be made on this contract without the consent of...

⑤ 我们必须确认你方必须在……内完成货物装运。

We must make it clear in the contract that you are obliged to complete the delivery of the goods within...

⑥ 如果不能在……装运，则合同视为无效。

If the shipment can not be made within... as stipulated, the contract will become void.

⑦ ……的一切活动必须受中国的法律、法令和有关规章条例的管辖。

All activities of... shall be governed by the laws, decrees and pertinent rules and regulations of China.

⑧ ……委托……为其在……的独家销售代理商。

... hereby appoints... as its exclusive sales agent in...

⑨ 当有……发生，……提前……天向……发送书面通知后，可以终止合同。

... may terminate this Contract... days after a written notice thereof is sent to... upon the happening of one of the following events.

6.5 译文赏评

6.5.1 购货合同

原文

Purchase Contract

This contract is made on the _____ day of _____ 20 _____, by and between _____ Ltd. (hereinafter referred to as the Seller) and _____ Company (hereinafter referred to as the Buyer). Through friendly negotiation, both Parties have hereby agreed on the terms and conditions stipulated hereunder:

1. Contract Products: _____
2. Specification: _____
3. Quantity: _____
4. Unit Price: _____
5. Total Value: _____
6. Country of Origin: _____
7. Shipping Marks: _____
8. Shipment: _____

To be shipped on or before _____ subject to acceptable Letter of Credit (L/C) reaches the Seller before the end of _____, and partial shipment allowed, transshipment allowed.

9. Grace Period:

Should last shipment have to be extended for fulfillment of this contract, the Buyer shall give the Seller a grace period of 30 days upon submitting evidence by the Seller.

10. Insurance:

To be effected by the Buyer.

11. Packing:

In new Kraft paper bags of _____ kg/bag or in wooden cases of _____ kg/case, free of charge.

12. Payment:

The Buyer shall open a 100% confirmed, irrevocable, divisible and negotiable and partial shipment permitted Letter of Credit in favor of the Seller within 5 calendar days from the date first presentation of the following documents:

(1) Full set of Seller's Commercial invoices;

(2) Full set of clean, blank, endorsed Bill of Lading;

(3) Inspection Certificates of quality and weight.

13. Notice of Readiness:

The Buyer shall advise the Seller by telex the scheduled time of arrival of cargo vessel at least seven days prior to the arrival of the vessel at the loading port.

14. Performance Guarantee:

(1) Upon receipt of Buyer's Irrevocable L/C by the Advising Bank, the Seller shall perform a Performance Guarantee representing _____% of the L/C.

(2) The Performance Guarantee shall be returned in full to the Seller after completion of shipment and delivery of the contracted goods. In case of non-delivery of (all or part of) the goods for reasons other than those specified in clause 12, the Performance Guarantee shall be forfeited in favor of the Buyer in proportion to the quantity in default.

(3) Should the Buyer breach the contract or fail to open the L/C in favor of the Seller within the period specified in clause 9 (except for clause 12), the Buyer has to pay the Seller the same value as the Performance Guarantee.

(4) The Letter of Credit must fulfill all the terms and conditions of this contract. The terms of the L/C should be clear, fair and made payable to the Seller. Upon acceptance of L/C by the Advising Bank, the Advising Bank shall send the Performance Guarantee to the Issuing Bank.

15. Force Majeure:

The Seller or the Buyer shall not be responsible for non-delivery or breach of contract for any reason due to Force Majeure incidents.

译文

购 货 合 同

本合同由 _____ 公司（以下简称售方）和 _____ 公司（以下简称购方）于 20_____ 年 _____ 月 _____ 日签订。双方通过友好协商特此同意下列条款：

1. 合同货物：_____

2. 规格：_____

3. 数量：_____

4. 单价：_____

5. 总值：_____

6. 原产国：_____

7. 唛头：_____

8. 装船：_____ 年 _____ 月 _____ 日前装运，但要以售方 _____ 年 _____ 月 _____ 日前收到可接受信用证为条件，容许分批装运和转运。

9. 优惠期限：为了履行合同，最后一次装船时发生延迟，售方提出凭证，购方可向售方提供 30 天的优惠期限。

10. 保险：由购方办理。

11. 包装：用新牛皮纸袋，每袋为 _____ 公斤，或用木箱装，每箱为 _____ 公斤，予以免费包装。

12. 付款条件：签订合同后 5 天（历日）内购方通过开证行开出以售方为受益人，经确认的、全金额 100% 的、不可撤销的、可分割的、可转让的、允许分期装船的信用证，见票即付并出示下列单证：

（1）全套售方商业发票；

（2）全套清洁、不记名、背书货运提单；

（3）质量、重量检验证明。

13. 装船通知：购方至少在装货船到达装货港的 7 天前，将装货船到达的时间用电传通知售方。

14. 保证金：

（1）通知银行收到购方开具的不可撤销信用证时，售方必须开具信用证_____% 金额的保证金。

（2）合同货物装船和交货后，保证金将原数退回给售方。若出于任何原因，本合同规定的第 12 条除外，发生无法交货（全部或部分），按违约的数量比例，没收保证金支付给购方。

（3）若由于购方违约或购方不按照第 9 条规定的时间内（第 12 条规定除外），开具以售方为受益人的信用证，购方必须按照保证金相同的金额付给售方。

（4）开具的信用证必须满足合同规定的条款内容。信用证所列条件应准确、公道，售方能予以承兑。通知银行收到信用证后，通知银行应给开证行提供保证金。

15. 不可抗力：售方或购方均不承担由于不可抗力的任何原因所造成的无法交货或违约责任。

赏评

原文中使用了大量的并列短语和词语，如：by and between（由……和……间）；terms and conditions（条款）；confirmed, irrevocable, divisible and negotiable（确定的、不可撤销的、可分割的、可转让的）等，使意思的表达更为正式严谨，充分体现了合同文本的语言特征。

原文中也大量使用了古词来增强文体的正式程度，如：hereinafter、hereby、hereunder 等，这些词在英文法律文本中经常出现，它们不仅能使句子结构紧凑，增强了语意的逻辑衔接和连贯，而且增强了表达的正式性。

这篇短文中出现了一些缩略语，如 L/C（信用证——一种付款方式），国际经贸合同中的价格、支付及保险方式大多以首字母缩略词形式出现，这是经贸合同的惯例，在翻译时也尽量采用缩略形式。

should 引起的假设状语从句，相当于 in case 从句，一般翻译成"若……（发生）"。

在情态动词选择上，原文中选用了 shall、must、will 等。shall 用来表示一方应尽的义务，表示强制性责任和履行义务，与中文中"应该，必须"的意义相同，其表达力度比 will 强。

6.5.2　经营合同

原文

中外合资经营合同（节选）

甲乙双方本着"长期合作，互惠互利"的原则，就共同合作生产新型民用住房建筑材料的有关事宜达成如下协议：

1. 甲方的权利与义务

（1）甲方负责向乙方提供具有国际领先水平的新型民用住房建筑材料的专利技术资料及相关专用设备，并出具相关专利技术证书。

（2）甲方负责指导乙方掌握生产设备安装维修操作与新型建材的安装、修缮专用技术，并负责完成乙方职工的上述技能培训工作。

（3）甲方负责向乙方提供厂房建设设计图纸资料及新型板材环保证明材料，并为乙方提供生产厂房的安装技术培训。

（4）在正式投产后，甲方协助乙方降低成本，并包销该项目全部产品，包销时间由双方另行商定。

2. 乙方的权利与义务

（1）乙方付款 300 万美元购买甲方提供的生产设备。

（2）乙方负责提供生产流动资金 5000 万元人民币。

（3）乙方负责提供生产场地、厂房。

（4）待双方合作项目正式签约后，乙方同意甲方以专利技术入股，占该项目纯利润的 35%。

（5）自本协议签订之日起至正式合同签订期间，甲乙双方各自承担本方发生的费用。

（6）董事长、总经理由乙方选派，会计、审计由甲方选派。

上述条款经协商一致，签订正式文本后生效。

Contract of Sino-Foreign Joint Venture (Excerpt)

In accordance with the principle of "permanent cooperation and mutual benefits", Party A and Party B have reached the agreement on the joint manufacture of new-type building material for residential house as follows:

1. Rights and Obligations of Party A

(1) Party A shall provide Party B with internationally advanced patent technology and corresponding special manufacturing equipment of new-type building material for residential houses as well as present relevant certificates for the patent technology.

(2) Party A shall offer Party B the instructions about the installation, maintenance and operation of manufacturing equipment and know-how about the installation and repairing of new-type building material as well as provide the employees from Party B with the training in the about-mentioned know-how.

(3) Party A shall provide Party B with factory site layout and the certificate about environmental protection as well as training in installation technology of the factory facilities.

(4) Party A shall help Party B to reduce cost and be in charge of the exclusive sale of all products of the project after the production is officially launched. The period of exclusive sales shall be determined through consultation between two parties.

2. Rights and Obligations of Party B

(1) Party B shall pay US $3,000,000 to buy the manufacturing equipment from Party A.

(2) Party B shall provide RMB 50,000,000 Yuan as the circulating funds for products.

(3) Party B shall provide the factory site and building.

(4) Party B shall, after the official signature of the joint project contract, agree to Party A's shareholder-ship through the investment of patent technology, accounting for 35% of the net profit.

(5) From the day on which this agreement is signed to the day when the official contract is signed, all expenses of either party arising out of this period shall be assumed by the party itself.

(6) The chairman of the board and general manager shall be designated by Party B while the accountant and the comptroller by Party A.

This Agreement shall come into force upon the official signature by both parties.

赏评

根据英文的表达特点，上面的译文措辞委婉、得体，动词几乎全部使用情态动词 shall，准确反映了合同的语言特征以及跨文化商务交际原则。如：Party A shall provide...；Party B shall pay US $3,000,000 to...；Party B shall, after... agree to Party A's shareholder-ship...

译文动词多使用被动语态，以保持合同语言的客观性和正式语体的特点。如："在正式投产后，甲方协助乙方降低成本，并包销该项目全部产品，包销时间由双方另行商定。"（Party A... is officially launched. The period of exclusive sales shall be determined...）；再如："自本协议前签订之日起至正式合同签订期间，甲乙双方各自承担本方发生的费用。"（From the day on which this agreement is signed to the day when the official contract is signed, all expenses... shall be assumed by the party itself.）。

一般来说，英语重"形合"，汉语重"意合"，在汉译英时需要增加关联词来连接。例如，"甲乙双方本着……就共同……达成如下协议"，"待双方合作项目正式签约后，……纯利润的35%"，两处译文使用了长句，并增加了连接词，以便反映英语这种"形合"语言的基本特征。

本译文基本保留了原文的语体特征，较为准确地再现了合同的文体特征，是一篇不错的合同翻译范本。

6.6 课后练习

（1）

Where the Contract provides for payment in whole or in part to be made to the Contractor in foreign currency or currencies, such payment shall not be subject to variations in the rate or rates of exchange between such specified foreign currency or currencies and the currency of the country in which the Works are to be executed.

（2）专利权和专利使用费

承包商应全力保护业主在使用其提供的工厂时免遭因侵犯第三方的专利、设计或版权而面临的诉讼、索赔、要求和各种费用。如果承包商提供的工程设计、工厂设备的制造和供应以及在工程建造中实施的工作或使用的方法涉及第三方的权利，他也应向第三方支付按许可证或许可证条款规定支付的所有费用、专利使用费和其他款项。但是，如果业主在经营或使用该厂或其中任何部分时涉及了第三方的专利，他应向第三方支付按许可证或许可条款规定应支付的所有费用、专利使用费和其他款项。

第 7 章　产品说明书

产品说明书文体与翻译

产品说明书（instruction、manual 或 specification），又称商品说明书，是生产厂家向消费者介绍说明商品的性质、性能、结构、用途、规格、使用方法、保养方法、注意事项、质量保证、销售范围和免责声明时使用的商贸文书。产品说明书虽然内容较简单，但却有着非常重要的作用，除了向消费者介绍相关产品知识外，还担负着推销产品，扩大企业知名度和品牌影响力的重任。产品说明书在文体上既具有一般性，又具有特殊性。

产品说明书的覆盖范围很广，从工业装置的说明，到一般机械或家用器具的操作简介，以及其他商品使用说明、服务须知等，均属此范围。

产品说明书为读者提供使用产品的说明、指南和要求，准确、明晰的翻译显得尤为重要。成功的译文能够准确地将原文的信息传递出来，从而激起读者的购买欲望；反之，则会让人感觉不知所云，甚至误导消费者，造成不必要乃至无法挽回的损失。

本章学习了解产品说明书的文体特点，熟悉不同类型的产品说明书中的常用词汇和句型结构；在翻译异域文化较为浓厚的信息时，学会灵活变通，运用适当的翻译方法和策略，从而达到预期目的。

7.1 课前实践

7.1.1　药品说明书

冰王鳄油冻疮消

ICEKING Crocodile Chilblain Distinguisher

[1] [介绍] 冻疮是由于肌体较长时间受寒冷和潮湿刺激，使局部血管痉挛，组织缺氧，

[1] **[Introduction]** Chilblain, usually seen in winter or spring, comes

细胞损伤所致的一种冬、春季常见皮肤病形态。

[2] [症状] 冻疮初起为局部发生水肿性紫红斑,继而肿胀,感觉瘙痒,受热后加剧。严重时发生水泡和充血性大疱,疱破后可形成糜烂或溃疡,导致冻疮祛除后肤色加深,甚至留下永久性疤痕。

[3] [产品功能] 鳄油冻疮消选用鳄鱼脂肪中精炼油脂与多种植物萃取物组合而成,属冬季理想的御寒护肤佳品。

[4] [适用范围] 轻度冻疮:皲裂、红肿、瘙痒。中度冻疮:充血、皮肤变紫、起水泡。重度冻疮:红肿、严重溃烂、流水。

[5] [用法与用量] 外用,涂擦于洗净的冻疮部位,每日2~3次。涂擦时轻轻按摩,使渗透吸收。如局部已严重破裂、流水,则只需涂抹表层即可。

with stimulation of cold and damp for quite a period and partial vessels turn spasmodic, tissue anoxic, cells bruised.

[2] [Symptom] Chilblain onset displays purple oedema here and there. Then the oedema swells especially after heating. The serious condition could be water blister and congestive lump. If the blister or lump breaks, there will be ulceration and erosion growing to be future darkened skins or scars even after chilblain cured.

[3] [Product Function] ICEKING Crocodile Chilblain Distinguisher is prescribed with refining grease from fattiness of Thai crocodile as well as extracted Chinese medicine. This product dispels cold elements from existing human essence, warms human channels, distinguish pains or itches of chilblain, dissolve gores and flatten swollen lumps, helps new muscles burgeon and wound heal. It is very effective in evading darkened skins or scars remained after chilblain.

[4] [Eligible for] Shadow Chilblain: chaps, rubefaction, turgidness, pain and itches. Medium Chilblain: congestion in affected parts, purple skin, blistering. Serious Chilblain: rubefaction and turgidness, sad erosion, water infiltration.

[5] [Usage and Dosage] External use only. Past this medicine on the affected parts after washing and cleaning, 2 or 3 times a day. Try giving mild massage to the affected parts to help tissue absorb the medicine. In

	case the affected parts displays chap and water infiltration, it is sufficient to paste the medicine on the surface.
[6] [配方成分] 鳄鱼精油脂、当归浸膏、干姜粉、樟脑、冰片。	[6] [Ingredients of Prescription] Refined crocodile fattiness, angelica cream for dipping usage, ginger powder, camphor, borneol.
[7] [注意事项]	[7] [Cautions]
（1）不可与其他外用产品混合使用；	(1) Mixture of this medicine with others on the affected parts is forbidden.
（2）注意防寒保暖，经常用40℃以上的热水或姜汤浸敷；	(2) Keep patient warm from any cold hurts. Dips the affected parts in warm water over 40℃, or in the boiled water with ginger serves better for therapy.
（3）冻疮消除后请持续使用数日以防再生；	(3) Keep therapy for a couple of days after chilblain cured in case of relapse.
[8] 用后密封,置于儿童不易拿到处。	[8] Keep tight capping from children's reach.

7.1.2 食品说明书

NESCAFE	雀巢咖啡
[1] 雀巢100%纯咖啡，精选上等咖啡豆，悉心烘焙，萃取纯正咖啡精华，香气馥郁，味道丰润醇厚。搭配雀巢咖啡伴侣使用，令咖啡更香浓，口感更幼滑。	[1] High quality coffee beans carefully selected and blended, delicate roasting and extraction, NESCAFE 100% pure coffee brings you rich aroma and full flavor, for an original and rewarding coffee experience. NESTLE Coffee-Mate enhances the aroma and the smooth taste of your coffee. The perfect match for a perfect cup!
[2] 雀巢咖啡礼盒长久以来被消费者认为是时尚、大方、高档的礼品，每一款礼盒中搭配赠送不同的珍藏礼品，是消费者馈赠亲朋好友的理想选择。	[2] The NESCAFE Gift Box has become a reference for high quality in China. Each box includes a unique special gift. It's the ideal way to your love and appreciation at a time of joyful festivity.

[3] 雀巢100%纯咖啡（速溶咖啡）　　[3] NESCAFE 100% Pure Coffee (Soluble Coffee)

[4] [净含量]100克　　[4] [Net Content] 100 g

[5] [配料] 咖啡豆　　[5] [Ingredient] Coffee Beans

[6] 雀巢咖啡伴侣　　[6] NESTLE COFFEE-MATE

[7] [净含量]200克　　[7] [Net Content] 200 g

[8] [配料] 葡萄糖浆, 食用氢化植物油, 稳定剂（E340ii, E452i, E331iii）, 酪蛋白酸钠（含牛奶蛋白）, 乳化剂（E471, E472e）, 食用香料/调味剂, 抗结剂（E551）。　　[8] [Ingredients] Glucose syrup, hydrogenated vegetable oil, stabilizer (E340ii, E452i, E331iii), sodium caseinate (contain milk protein), emulsifier (E471, E472e), flavouring, anticaking agent (E551).

[9] [保质期] 见瓶底　　[9] [Best Before] see bottom of jar

[10] [生产日期] 见瓶底　　[10] [Manu. Date] see bottom of jar

7.1.3 化妆品说明书

佰草集清肌养颜太极泥

Herborist T'ai Chi Detoxifying & Nutrient Clay

佰草集清肌养颜太极泥，分黑、白二泥，蕴含赤芍、白芍等本草精华，先清后补，给肌肤带来全新的体验。第一步——清：黑泥蕴含的赤芍能帮助促进肌肤活力和代谢机能，增强肌肤的抵抗能力，同时搭配草药相互作用，能有效清洁肌肤表面和毛孔内部，如污垢、彩妆残留和过度老化的肌肤角质等，使肌肤达到一个清的境界；第二步——补：白泥蕴含的白芍能发挥其滋润的主要作用，配合其他草本精华，给肌肤提供所需营养，同时在肌肤表面给予养护，从根本上令肌

Herborist T'ai Chi Detoxifying & Nutrient Clay contains extracts from several Chinese herbs, including Peony Root extracts. It is composed of the Detoxifying Clay (black clay) for deep cleansing as well as the Nutrient Clay (white clay), one to cleanse and then the other to reveal the radiance on the face, which brings a whole new experience to skin care. The Detoxifying Clay is an effective cleanser that removes impurities from the surface of the skin as well as from inside of the pores, such as dirt, makeup residue and aging skin cells. The Nutrient Clay soothes and softens the skin, for restoring its radiance and balance. All the harmonious ingredients bring a fresh and fair

肤焕发光彩，恢复平衡状态。

用法：

先清：首先使用黑泥，清洁双手并擦干，用面膜调棒取适量黑泥，涂抹薄薄一层于面部，至掩盖肤色均匀即可，注意避开眼部周围；加以轻轻按摩，使黑泥中的本草成分渗透并作用于肌肤。约5分钟后，用洁面棉擦去黑泥，再用温水洗干净。

后补：接着使用白泥，洗去黑泥后，在面部半湿状态下，用面膜棒取出适量白泥，均匀涂抹于面部，用食指和中指以划圈的方式轻柔按摩面部2~3分钟，按摩后，再使白泥在脸部停留8分钟左右，使肌肤充分吸收营养成分。最后用洁面棉擦去白泥，再以温水洗净。

注意：黑白泥不可相混，在黑泥洗净后，请立即使用白泥，并盖紧置于阴凉干燥处保存；使用时可能有冷、热、微微刺痒等感觉，属正常现象。

complexion.

Direction:

T'ai Chi Detoxifying Clay: Use the mixing stick to scoop an appropriate amount and apply a thin layer over the entire face evenly. Massage gently for about 5 minutes, then remove it with sponge pad enclosed and rinse face with warm water.

T'ai Chi Nutrient Clay: After washing off the black clay, apply immediately the white clay while the face is still damp. Massage with circular motions by using the index and middle fingers for about 2-3 minutes. Leave the clay for about 8 minutes to allow a better action of the product. Then remove it with the sponge pad and rinse face with warm water.

Attention: Do not mix the two clays. Use T'ai Chi Nutrient Clay immediately after using T'ai Chi Detoxifying Clay and save in a cool, dry place. It is normal that cool, warm or slight tingling sensations may be experienced during use.

7.2 文体特点

7.2.1 用词专业　体例固定

产品说明书是一种非常专业的商贸文体，因此会出现大量的专业术语。由于说明书的描述对象（包括产品和服务）覆盖面很广，涉及各行各业，因而常会在某技术领域阐述其特有的"行话"或者称为"半专业词"，例如，anti-age（抗衰老）、

nutritive/nourish（滋养）等。产品说明书承担着向消费者介绍产品的性能、作用、生产工艺、使用方法等多种信息的重要作用，因而它的体例相对比较固定。例如，工艺产品说明书一般由安全使用、工作原理、结构、技术参数、安装、调试、操作和故障排除等几个部分构成；医药产品说明书中一般包括药品名称、成分、性状、作用类别、功能主治、用法用量、注意事项、规格、有效期、生产日期等。产品说明书有以下三个特点：

（1）说明性

产品说明书是介绍产品的性能、构造、特点、使用方法、保养方法等知识的文书，因此采取说明的手法，直接、全面、准确地介绍产品。产品说明书一般很少用议论性的语言，无须具体分析该产品"为什么这样构造""为什么这样使用"等。叙述方法也很少使用，除非有必要简述该产品的发展史。

（2）知识性

这是产品说明书的重要特点，也是根本价值所在。产品说明书中介绍的产品知识偏重于实用性。随着人们环保意识的加强，不少产品说明书除了对产品性能、使用方法、维护方法等进行说明之外，还对将来该产品的废弃处理方式给予指导和说明。

（3）客观性

产品说明书中的介绍必须是对产品本身的客观性说明，要体现科学的、实事求是的精神，不能随意夸大。

7.2.2 词汇特征丰富　句法语篇独具特色

（1）情态、能愿动词使用频率高

中英文说明书中，这一类动词的适用范围都较为广泛，但在众多的英语情态动词及汉语能愿动词中，英语情态动词 can 及与之相对应的汉语能愿动词"能（够），可（以），会"的使用频率最高。然而，总体而言，汉语的能愿动词在说明书中的使用频率要远远高于英语情态动词的使用频率。

（2）修饰性词语丰富

中文说明书中的修饰性、评价性词语非常丰富，且习惯于使用同义或者近义的词语，甚至同义、近义词语相互叠加，如"独特和特别""完全和全面"。中文说明书中这类词语远远高于英文的使用频率，反映出中文说明书的语言更富于夸张性，能给人留下更深刻的印象，而英文说明书中的措辞更近于客观性的描述，反映出对产品性能的自信。

（3）少用人称指示词

中英文产品说明书一般都较少使用人称指示词。若使用人称指示词，中英文说明书都存在第一人称和第二人称并用的现象，以突出语体的亲切性及与读者的互动性，但不同之处在于：中文里的第二人称存在着"你"与"您"的显著差异，且更倾向于使用敬称"您"，以示对读者的尊重与敬意；英文里第二人称 you 并无简称与敬称之别，且人称指示词的使用频率远高于中文，反映出英文说明书更加人性化，读来更具有亲切感。

（4）过程名物化多

产品说明书语言简洁、意思高度浓缩的特点也反映在过程的名物化上。名物化是指将过程（特别是物质过程）名词化、小句子转化为名词词组，经常将句子浓缩为名词（或词组），而其他成分则作为修饰成分。

（5）句法特征独具特色

产品说明书讲究言简意赅，通俗易懂，应避免繁杂冗长，这些文体特征不仅反映在用词上，更体现在句法结构上。

① 多用感叹句和祈使句。感叹句和祈使句在中英文说明书中都很常用，且都被赋予了说明文体独特的功能，即：感叹句除了抒发强烈的情感之外，还可以用来强调产品的性能，仿佛优越到出乎厂家或者商家意料的地步，才会由衷感叹；祈使句与其说是用来表达传统意义上的命令或者请求，不如说是用来以更加恳切的方式传达产品的信息，能拉近与消费者之间的距离，让消费者感觉像在专门为自己介绍，从而产生亲切感，因而被广泛使用。

在疑问句式的使用上，中英文说明书却存在差异。中文说明书倾向于板着面孔作"严肃讲解"状，因而，为了正式、庄重的文体效果，很少采用疑问句式；英文说明书里，疑问句式的使用频率相对而言则要高出许多，其语言较为亲切友好、富有热情。

② 被动语态。在被动语态的使用上，中英文存在着显著的差异。中文说明书很少用被动，而英文说明书中却很常见。由于产品说明书的说明对象是各种产品，读者通常关注的是事物的发生和存在，而并不是谁使其发生或存在。这样，施事者在产品说明书中是弱项，在英文中常以被动语态或者非人称形式等语法手段被"隐藏"起来，但在中文里常以主动语态的无主句式表达。

英文说明书中还有两个常见的句型，极具文体特色：

① 情态动词 be + 形容词（或过去分词）+ 目的状语。这种句型常见于说明书的产品描述部分，说明产品的用途、构造、提示，等等。句子的主语往往是产品名

称。这样的安排主要是为了突出产品的特性（功能或注意事项等），以引起读者的注意。如：

原文 本装置仅限由接受过导管插入诊断及治疗培训的医生使用。

译文 The device should be used only by physicians trained in diagnostic and therapeutic catheter procedures.

② 现在分词（介词）+ 名词（非谓语动词形式）。这种非谓语动词（non-finite verb form）结构往往用于解说维护或操作程序，常常伴有图解。因为这种文字具有十分强烈的实际操作性，类似现场讲解。如：

原文 When cleaning the Control Panel, leave oven door open to prevent oven from accidentally turning on.

译文 擦拭控制板时请将炉门打开，以防不小心启动烤箱。

（6）语篇特征

① 雅俗互现。中英文说明书的措辞都是或雅或俗，正式与非正式用语混杂，典雅如某茶叶中文说明"清香唇齿间，禅心天地外；茶凝崂山绿，涧深水自甜"；通俗如高露洁牙膏中文说明"想要牙齿清洁健康，建议您：每天至少用高露洁双氟加钙牙膏刷牙两次"。但两种语言相比较，中文更加倾向于措辞雅致与凝重。

中英文说明书都倾向于使用简单句，此外，也都常省略某些成分，使用不规则句、独词或短语句。这一语言特色反映出说明书简洁明快的文体特点。

② 环保意识强。中英文说明书都很重视环境保护，或渲染产品的环保特性，或在产品的废弃处理环节上突出环保措施。

③ 权威昭示。中英文说明书同样注重产品的权威性昭示，如"专利产品""……指定（推荐）产品""patented"，等等。不过，由于科技、经济发展的差距，中文说明书在这方面常会标榜"进口"，而外文说明书一般不会。

④ 交际角色差异。交际角色方面的差异可说是中英文说明书在语篇特征方面的最大差异。中文说明书倾向于采取单一的、以局外人为中心的交际角色，注重信息的传递，在对产品的优、特点宣传方面大做文章。英文说明书采取以说话人、听话人或局外人交替为中心的交际角色，除了承载信息传递功能之外，还相当重视其劝说功能，通过人称指示词的使用，增进与读者的心理距离，从而达到销售产品的最终目的。

（7）修辞特征独特

产品说明书的主要功能是传播知识和引导消费，有助于消费者更好地了解产品的特点，熟悉产品的性能，掌握产品的使用方法，进行合理的消费，避免因选择或使用不当造成不必要的损失。当然，产品说明书在介绍产品的同时，也宣传了企业，因此，它也往往具有广告宣传的性质。从这种意义上说，产品说明书是在推销产品，扩大品牌知名度，因此，往往也大量使用修辞手段，达到推销的目的。但是，值得注意的是，尽管产品说明书与广告有相似之处，但是，后者重在宣传号召，说明书则强调解释说明。从销售的先后顺序而言，广告在售前，说明在售后。广告重在唤起购买欲，说明书重在解释如何使用产品。

7.2.3 惯用省略

产品说明书中存在大量的省略句，这跟其简洁明了的文体特征息息相关。省略句具有言简意赅、直截了当的特点，能够突出重点，缩小交流间隔，简化表达程序，增加语言效果。鉴于消费者对产品已有一定的了解，因此，产品名称等信息也常常会被省略。如：药品说明书上有些部分往往只标注 indication（适应症）、contraindication（禁忌症）、side effect（副作用）等即可。

7.3 翻译要领

7.3.1 保留原文的技术性特点

产品说明书属于技术性文本，涉及的专业面甚广，往往包含相关产品的专业技术知识。因此，在翻译之前，译者应该首先参考有关的专业书籍，弄懂说明书的全部内容。而专业术语的准确翻译是确保技术性特点得以保留的关键所在。这就要求译者要有广博的知识，甚至要比原文作者的知识面更广。因为原文作者没有提到的，或认为不言自明的，正需要译者向读者做出解释和说明。为了达到译文的交际目的，译者在翻译过程中应根据原文的内容和语境，尽可能使用与原语等值、恰当的表达。

因产品说明书大多涉及某方面专业知识，即便是一般家用电器的使用说明书也颇带技术性，工用机械说明书的技术性更强。因此，在翻译时要求措辞准确，如有差错就会引起严重后果。尤其是在翻译药品说明书时，首先要特别注意一些术语的翻译，如：composition（成分）、description（性状）、packing（包装），等等。其次，对药品名称的翻译也要慎重，一般有四种译法：音译、意译（为使读者更明白其化学性质）、音意兼译（如将 kanamycin 译为"卡那霉素"）、谐音意译（如将 miltown 译为"眠尔通"，使服药者一看便知其功能和作用）。

7.3.2 客观真实　准确无误

产品说明书的作用是生产厂家向消费者传递相关的产品信息，因而它是连接厂家与消费者的桥梁与纽带。企业若想将产品成功地打入国际市场，说明书的译文必须客观、真实。倘若译文"失真",不仅会给消费者留下不好的印象,还会直接影响产品的形象与销售。所以,我们在翻译时,应该确保相关概念、定义准确无误,避免歧义,避免带有浮夸成分,实事求是地反映出产品的实际情况。

一切说明都是为了要求读者遵循而编写的,因此都具有直观效果,使读者见文如见物。然而直观效果的产生只能凭借有效的、生动的描述才能办到。好的说明是对某一客体的完满描述。所谓"完满描述"是指描述中要包含科学的思维逻辑,使文字具有层次感、程序性和说服力。

准确是对产品说明书用语的基本要求。因此,翻译时一词一句都必须认真推敲其确切的含义,译文要内涵清晰,外延明确,不能有歧义,一般不使用"大概""可能""估计"等模糊词语。同时,语句要符合目标语的语法和逻辑。

7.3.3 言简意赅 通俗易懂

产品说明书的目标读者是消费者,而消费者阅读说明书的目的是要了解与产品相关的各种信息,从而指导产品消费。可见,实用性也是产品说明书的一大特点。由于消费者并不是专业人士,往往对产品所属的领域不是非常了解。因此,产品说明书的翻译除了要忠实地传达原文信息外,还要力求译文简明扼要、通俗易懂,采用平实的语言和简洁的措辞,使之易于被消费者所接受,达到扩大销售的目的。

产品说明书的翻译要求浅显易懂,运用最精练的句子,选择最好的表述形式,言简意赅,其特点为:第一,广泛使用祈使句;第二,广泛使用复合名词词组,以代替后置定语;第三,尽量省略冠词、介词及无关紧要的形容词、副词、连词等;第四,文字要求明了通俗,句子结构简单,避免不必要的修辞手段。

总之,产品说明书的翻译是一个看似简单实则复杂的过程。产品说明书肩负着比广告更重要的使命。毕竟,译者在翻译前,必须首先对说明书原文中所包含的信息进行分析,尤其是要剖析各类信息的可传达度和读者可能的接受情况,然后再采取相应的翻译方法和策略,以确保译文的可读性。

7.4 常用词汇句型

① 表示药品的构成、来源、制备方法 be prepared from/be composed of/be derived from
② 表示药品与其他药物合用 be associated with/in association with/be combines with/in combination with/together with
③ 表示药品对……有效 be effective against/in/for; be active against
④ 表示产品用途 be used for/be designed to/be suitable for/be adopted for (to)

⑤ 表示食品不含…… free of/be certified to contain no...

⑥ 表示产品适用于…… be recommended for...

7.5 译文赏评

7.5.1 销售说明书

原文

1. Open back Inclinable Power Press

This press is of up-to-date design and fine in appearance, compact in construction, safe and reliable in operation and high in rigidity.

It is generally used for cutting-off, blanking, piercing, shallow drawing, bending and other cold operations on sheet or strip metals. It is suitable for tractor, agricultural machinery, automobile, electrical devices, meters, bearing and daily necessities manufacturing plants.

　The frame of the press is inclinable to 30° maximum for gravity removal of workpieces and scraps. If mounted with an automatic feeding device, the press can be operated semi-automatically.

2. Room Air Conditioner (Window Type)

With the advanced level of the 1980's, it adopts the modern Rotary Hermetic Compressor and the unique cross fin coil type with high efficiency super slit fins. Characterized by compact, it is safe for use and automatic in adjusting the room temperature as well as in dehumidifying. It is suitable for the rooms of hotels, hospitals and homes where comfortable environment is needed. It wins a high reputation and is widely trusted at home and abroad.

3. Furniture

Jiangsu furniture is made of selected wood of superior quality, exquisite in workmanship, easy to fix and unfix, elegant and decent in patterns, tight in structure and durable in use. In addition to crafts as carving and inlaying on, thus successfully showing traditional native features, characteristics of modern fashion have been adopted in recent years, both economically and practically, so that it is suitable for various residence and, wins high popularity among consumers.

Here are our main products: bedroom suits, dining room suits, bookshelves of various designs, etc. Buyers and businessmen from all parts of the world are welcome to make their choices and orders, and we also accept orders for processing supplied materials.

译文

1. 开式双柱可倾压力机

本压力机设计新颖，外形美观，体积小巧，操作安全、可靠，刚性高。

本压力机属于薄板冲压的通用压力机，适用于各种冷冲压工艺，如剪切、冲孔、落料、弯曲和浅拉伸等，可供拖拉机、农业机械、汽车、电器、仪表、轴承和日用品制造厂使用。

压力机的机身可以倾斜（最大倾斜度为30°），以便于冲压成品或废料从磨具上滑下。安装自动送料装置后，则可进行半自动冲压工作。

2. 窗式房间空调器

窗式房间空调器，具有20世纪80年代先进水平，它采用了先进的滚动转子式全封闭压缩机和独有的高效率涤翅式散热片。具有体积小、使用安全、能自动调节室内温度、并有一定的除湿能力的特点。适用于宾馆、医院及家庭等要求舒适环境的房间。本空调器享有盛誉，深受国内外用户的信赖。

3. 家具

江苏家具系选用优质木料制作。做工精湛，拆装便利，造型美观大方，结构坚固耐用。辅以雕刻、镶嵌等工艺，具有传统的民族风格。近年来又吸取了现代家具的特点，适合多种居住条件，经济实用，更受广大消费者的欢迎。

主要产品有：卧房套装家具、餐厅家具，各类书架。品种繁多，欢迎各地客商选购，也承接来料订货。

赏评

"This press is of up-to-date design and fine in appearance, compact in construction, safe and reliable in operation and high in rigidity."（本压力机设计新颖，外形美观，体积小巧，操作安全、可靠，刚性高）。此句中，原文用并列短语 fine in appearance, compact in construction, safe and reliable in operation and high in rigidity 来使意思的表达更加清晰，在翻译成中文时也要注意中文译文的对称性，在平时应留心这种中英对照的译文表达方式。

"With the advanced level of the 1980's, it adopts the modern Rotary Hermetic Compressor and the unique cross fin coil type with high efficiency super slit fins." （窗式房间空调器，具有20世纪80年代先进水平，它采用了先进的滚动转子式全封闭压缩机和独有的高效率涤翅式散热片。）在产品说明书中，经常会提及产品是采用何种先进技术的，此时用译文表达式"It adopts..."（适用于）。

Characterized by... 译为"具有……的特点"，是产品推销说明书中经常出现的表达方式。

"It wins a high reputation and is widely trusted at home and abroad." （本空调器享有盛誉，深受国内外用户的信赖。）译文"享有盛誉，深受国内外用户的信赖"体现了原文的意图，措辞符合汉语表达习惯。

7.5.2 药品说明书

原文

【药品名称】感冒清胶囊

【成分】南板蓝根、大青叶、金盏银盘、岗梅、山芝麻、穿心莲叶、对乙酰氨基酚、盐酸吗啉胍、马来氯苯那敏。

【性状】本品为胶囊剂，内为灰绿色至灰褐色粉末；味苦。

【功能主治】疏风解表，清热解毒。用于风热感冒、发烧、头痛、鼻塞流涕、喷嚏、咽喉肿痛、全身酸痛等症。

【用法用量】口服，一次1~2粒，1日三次。

【注意事项】用药期间不宜驾驶车辆、管理机器及高空作业等。

【规格】每粒装0.5 g（含对乙酰氨基酚24 mg）

【贮藏】密封

【包装】铝塑包装，12粒/盒。

凡举报假冒伪造我厂产品地下工厂者,我公司给予重奖,并对举报者身份绝对保密。

译文

[Name] Cold Clear Capsule

[Ingredients] Prepared from isatis root, dyers woad leaf, holly root, all-grass marigold, narrow-leaf screw tree, green chiretta, paracetamol, moroxydine and chiorpheniramine maleate.

[Property] Greenish or brownish powder capsule with a bitter taste.

[Functions & Indications] Smooth wind and resolve the exterior; clear heat and resolve toxin. Used of wind, heat, common cold, fever, headache, congestion and running nose, sneezing, sore swollen, sour pain of whole body, etc.

[Usage and Dosage] Oral use; 1-2 capsules 3 times a day.

[Precautions] Not recommended for use before driving, operating machinery or working high above the ground.

[Specifications] 0.5 g/capsules (including 24 mg paracetamol).

[Storage] Keep it airtight.

[Package] Box of 12 capsules in blister.

Those who report the counterfeiting of our products will be highly rewarded without disclosure of identification.

赏评

药品说明书作为产品说明书的一个分支，是选用药品的法定指南。中药说明书的语言表述介于古汉语和白话之间。在翻译中，如何让外国消费者读懂带有浓厚异域文化的文字介绍，从而正确选择购买，是当今中药国际化亟待解决的问题。此外，由于客观存在的语言、文化障碍，译者在忠实于原文的基础上也需要进行适当地增删和改译，才能更好地向外国消费者介绍中药产品的性能、疗效，从而达到对外宣传和促销的目的，使中药真正走向世界。

翻译中药说明书的目的就是让外国消费者了解和熟悉药品的药理作用、用法、用量、适应症及禁忌等，从而激发他们的购买欲。所以，译者最好按照外国人熟悉的药品说明书格式进行对等翻译。本例的译文中，一些专业术语的表述不够规范，需作修改。例如，"药品名称"较为规范的表达应该是 pharmaceutical name 或 drug name；property 通常用来表示事物的特性、性质以及财产和资产等，但"药品性状"主要是指化学结构、物理和化学性质及成分，比如颜色、味道和气味等，因此建议用 description 或 characteristics 来表示，这也是一般进口药品说明书的通行写法。

译文的 [Functions & Indications] 中，一些描述病症的专业术语基本属于字对字翻译，过于机械，完全没有考虑到外国消费者的理解程度。如，"疏风解表"是中医术语，"疏"指"疏通"，"风"指"风邪"，"解表"指消除感冒所引起的咳嗽、头痛、发热和流涕等症状。而原译文 smooth wind 和 resolve the exterior 显然风马牛不相及，必定会让消费者不知所云；"风热感冒"翻译成了 wind, heat, common cold, 完全是几个单词的机械相加，恐怕连懂英文的中国消费者看后都一头雾水。此外，把"全身酸痛"译为 sour pain 更是无稽之谈，sour 表示食物"有酸味的，馊的"，而 sore 才有"疼痛的"或者"（肌肤的）痛楚"之意。原译文 [Functions & Indications] 项的内容可改为：Effective in resisting pathogenic factors, eliminating the symptoms, easing fever and resolving toxin, used for common cold, fever, headache, nasal congestion or a runny nose, sneezing, sore throat and whole body sore pain, etc.

7.6 课后练习

(1) NEUTROGENA DEEP CLEAN(er) FOAMING CLEANSER

Thorough cleansing with long-lasting oil control for the deepest feeling clean.

Neutrogena Deep Clean(er) Foaming Cleanser is a refreshing facial cleanser that thoroughly removes dirt, oil and dead skin cells while providing long-lasting oil control to improve the look and feel of skin. This clean-rinsing cleanser lathers to an impurities that can build up ports. Oil control formula helps reduce surface oil to keep skin fresh. Skin feels completely clean and refreshed, soft and smooth.

- Oil
- Non-comedogenic
- Dermatologist tested

Direction: Use twice a day. Squeeze a small amount into hands and work into rich lather. Massage onto wet face. Avoid contact with eyes. Rinse thoroughly.

Caution: For external use only. Avoid contact with eyes. If product gets into eyes, rinse thoroughly with water. Keep out of children. Discontinue use if discomfort occurs, seek professional assistance. Not suitable for children under 3 years of age. Do not leave in contact with skin for long periods of time.

Also available:

Neutrogena Deep Cleansing Lotion

Neutrogena Deep Clean(er) Facial Cleanser

（2）长城干红葡萄酒

该产品是精选中国著名葡萄产区沙城地区（怀涿盆地）所产葡萄为原料，严格依照国际葡萄酒 AOC（产地命名酒）标准，采用法国陈酿酒专用酵母橡皮桶发酵、陈酿八年以上等先进工艺精酿而成的鉴赏型高档红葡萄酒。该葡萄酒呈棕红色，酒体澄清、果香，酒香沉馥优雅，橡木香细腻，酒体丰满，长城干红葡萄酒风味独特。

第 8 章　标书

标书文体与翻译

标书（bidding document 或 tender），是招标工作中采、购当事人都要遵守的具有法律效力且可执行的投标行为标准文件。标书实质上是一种商业合同，具有法律约束力，招投标文件措辞要精当，结构要严谨，术语要专业，思维要缜密，文体要正规，语意要明确，排除一切歧义的可能。

按招标的范围，标书可分为国际招标书和国内招标书；按招标的标的物（即当事人双方权利义务指向的对象）划分，标书又可分为三大类：货物、工程、服务。国际招标书，按照国际惯例，运用招标方式采购货物、工程和服务时，与招标采购活动有关的一切文件资料，均须用英文编制，即使允许用非英文的语言编制，也须随附一份英文译本备案，当发生分歧时以英文版本为准。因此招投标文件相关资料的理解和翻译就成了竞标的基础工作，贯穿着整个竞标过程，必须予以足够的重视。

由于标书翻译是法律翻译和商贸翻译的结合，涉及的专业领域纷繁复杂，如机械、电子、化工、医药、食品、石油等，而每个专业领域都有其特定的要求和规范，加之标书翻译是整个投标过程的核心环节，也是投标人编制投标书的依据，这就对译者提出了更高的要求。翻译标书时，译者应该严谨负责，准确把握和传递相关的信息，对相关的知识进行针对性的处理。

本章学习了解标书的作用及其文体特点，掌握基本的术语和句法结构；对于标书中的特有规范，要学会运用相应的翻译策略，进行灵活处理。

8.1 课前实践

8.1.1 投标书

GUARANTEES AND TECHNICAL PARTICULARS

Output Guarantees

The vertical shaft, synchronous Generator, with a combined thrust&lower guide bearing below the rotor, and conforming to the latest edition of standards, shall be capable of delivering a guaranteed rated output without exceeding a temperature in the stator and rotor windings of 130℃ for rated output conditions.

Efficiency Guarantees

The efficiencies at various loads at the rated voltage and power factor, the weighted, average efficiency and temperature rise of the machine shall be guaranteed which shall be subjected to be penalties, tolerances, rejection limits and bid evaluation as defined below. The guarantee shall be without bonus in case of temperature rises being less than those specified.

保证和技术细节

输出保证

结合推力与下导轴承转子下方的垂直轴和同步发电机，应符合最新版本标准，能提供一个保证额定输出不超过额定输出条件下定子和转子绕组温度130℃的输出条件。

效率保证

在各种负荷、以额定电压和功率因素、机器加权平衡和温升下的效率应予以保证。此效率应根据以下所述罚金、公差、废标限制和评标条件确定。如果温升低于规定，该保证不应收取额外费用。

8.1.2 许可证

作业许可证

承包商应建立作业许可程序，规定危险性工序和高风险作业必须由授权人员进行。向授权人员签发作业许可证时，必须向其介绍职业安全分析结果和有关

Work Permit

The Contractor shall maintain a work permit procedure to limit the hazardous processes and high-risk tasks to authorized personnel, who shall be informed of the job safety analysis and the job specific safety precautions, on issue of

其职业的安全事项。按程序签发的作业许可证，其有效期仅可持续某一特定时限。作业许可证的发放，必须在全面满足各种安全要求，并经过安全代表/安全人员或授权进行安全认证的专家签字后，方可发放。作业许可证应适用于许可证所针对的目的。作业许可证的类型有：

安全作业许可证（SWP）

高空作业、石棉板等易碎屋面或其他类似屋面上作业、钢结构安装、水上作业、变电站带电作业或开关站作业（即使作业面未送电）、拆除作业、爆破作业及业主认为有潜在危险的合同工程等，均应办理安全作业许可证，作为强制性规定。

高温作业许可证（HWP）

凡在易燃材料储存库、易燃或易爆材料设备和管道搬运等场地（无论是当前正在作业，还是以前曾经有过类似作业）进行有潜在危险的高温作业（如电焊或气焊、气割、燃烧或其他涉及加热、明火或电弧、研磨和电气作业等），或上述作业的同时还在开展其他新的作业，而业主认为存在危险隐患的地方，必须使用高温作业许可证。

a work permit. The work permit issued under the procedure shall be valid for a specified period and shall be issued only after all safety precautions are fulfilled and duty verified by SR/SA or specialists who are authorized for safety certification as a prerequisite for issue of a work permit. The work permit shall be appropriate for the purpose for which it issued. The different work permits are:

Safety Work Permit (SWP)

SWP is mandatory for working in heights, on fragile roofs such as asbestos or such roofing works, steel erection, work over water, a live substation or switch-yard even if section of work is not electrically charged, demolition, blasting and such potentially hazardous Contract works in the opinion of the Employer.

Hot-Work Permits (HWP)

HWP shall be used where hot working (like electric or gas welding, gas cutting, burning or any other operation involving heating, open flames or electrical works, etc.) is potentially dangerous in areas such as inflammable materials storage, plant and pipe lines handing inflammable or explosive materials either presently or in the pasts, or where new works which in the opinion of the Employer are potential risks. A HWP shall be deemed mandatory in all such potentially dangerous areas.

8.1.3 招标书

招标邀请函	Invitation for Bids
日期:	Date:
贷款号: 1313-RPC	Loan No.: 1313-RPC
合同号: CMCA956105	Bid No.: CMCA 956105

（1）中华人民共和国已得到亚洲开发银行的一笔美元贷款。这笔贷款将用于大连供水项目（南段工程），部分贷款的资金将用于C2钢管线制造与安装合同下的合格支付。本次招标面向全部亚投行合格的成员国的投标人。

(1) The People's Republic of China has received a loan from the Asian Development Bank (ADB) in US Dollars towards the cost of Dalian Water Supply Project (Part Ⅱ) and it is intended that part of the proceeds of this loan will be applied to eligible payments under the contract for C2 Manufacture and Installation of Steel Pipeline. Bidding is open to all bidders from eligible source countries of ADB.

（2）中国工业机械进出口公司（中国机械进出口总公司子公司）与中国沈阳机电设备招标公司（两公司以下简称C＆S）受大连市自来水公司的委托，作为本项目招标代理，现在邀请资格预审合格的投标人对大连供水项目（南段工程）C2钢管的制造与安装工程的承建和完成进行密封投标。

(2) China National Industrial Machinery Import/Export Corporation (a subsidiary of CMC) and China Shenyang Machinery&Electric Equipment Tendering Corporation (hereinafter called C&S), authorized by the Dalian Water Supply Company to be the tendering agent, invites sealed bids from prequalified eligible bidders for the construction and completion of C2 Manufacture and Installation of Steel Pipeline.

8.2 文体特点

招投标文本具有一般法律文本以及商业合同的基本语言特征，如措辞精当、结构严谨、术语专业、思维缜密、文体正规、语意明确。

8.2.1 用词精确专业 情态动词丰富

标书属于商务文件，其措辞力求规范、严密，避免因词义不确定或多义而引起误解。招标文件多用正式词语、并列词语,以突出其严肃性和约束性,并且多用陈述句、多用长句、多用圆周句,以保证其结果的严谨性、逻辑的缜密性。例如,"如果评定的报价最低的投标书在澄清后仍包含有雇主/工程师无法接受的偏差,则通知投标人,给予其书面撤回此偏差的机会。只有在投标人书面确认撤回偏差,并不对标价做出修改,他才真的撤回了偏差。如果雇主/工程师没有收到此类确认,则将该投标书拒绝,而考虑下一个在澄清问题后被评为报价最低的投标书,依此类推。"上述例证包含两个圆周句,这样的句式使文章显得庄重,同时用词准确,极具说服力。

英文招标文本中,大量使用情态动词与命令词。招标方在对投标人提出要求时总倾向于使用带有强制性含义的情态动词与命令词,如 shall 或 must。shall 不是简单的助动词,不是日常生活的"应当""适宜"或"应该"(should),而是"必须""要"等。但是,招投标双方的文本对情态动词使用有别,招标方对自己应履行某种义务时,总是极力轻描淡写,淡化语气强度,较多选用 will 和 should,甚至用 may 表"愿意"或"可以"。

8.2.2　多用大词、古词　采用外来词语

英文招投标文本多使用书面语,包括大词、古语词和外来词(尤其是拉丁语),以体现其权威性和严密性。用复杂短语代替简单介、连词;用笨重动词代替轻灵动词,如 encourage—urge;用冷僻词代替日常用词,如 prior to—before,expiry—end;大量使用(here-, there-)复合词,如 hereinafter、hereby、hereto、hereof、therefrom、therein、thereafter、thereinafter、thereby;大量使用古语词、外来语,如 null and void(无效)、nota bene(注意)、visavis(面对面)、assumpsit(承诺履行)等。

8.2.3　句式结构严谨　长句使用频率高

在日常英语中,主动句式可以自由地改成被动句式,陈述的基本事实不变。在招投标文件条款中,主动句式和被动句式却不能随意转换,尤其在涉及招投标双方的义务和权利方面,不宜随便选用被动句式。若采用被动句式易引起语气弱化,意义含糊,甚至责任、权利不明。

招投标文本在陈述具体条款的时候,总是在把重要的事情说出来的同时,不忘把例外的和次要的事情一并说明。这类文本注重逻辑联系,不允许有联系上的缺环,有什么后果必须探究产生此后果的原因和条件。因此,招投标文件语言结构严谨,长句使用频率颇高。

8.3　翻译要领

招投标文件的翻译要求准确严谨,标书中的专业术语和关键词语都有着严格的

法律含义，绝对不可信手拈来。标书翻译要求"忠实"和"通顺"结合，要尽可能地将"信"与"达"在翻译过程中完美地统一起来。

8.3.1　术语翻译规范　含义传递正确

招标投标已成为一种通行的、具有强制性规范的贸易形式，已经形成了一些专业术语，其意义往往与字典中的释义不同，翻译时应当予以注意。由于标书翻译涉及领域广泛，而每个领域都有其特色的行业规范，有其各自的专业术语，所以在翻译的时候，务必谨慎细致，因为相同的词在不同的专业背景下会产生不同的含义，应该根据具体的语境确定选词的准确含义，避免产生误解，引起纠纷。

如：Pre-qualification 是对投标人的投标资格预审；Pre-qualification documents 是投标资格预审文件；Invitation For Bids 应译为"投标邀请函"，而不是国内常说的"招标邀请公告"；Force Account 意为"自营工程"，是指借款人因项目邀请，先自行完成经批准的土木工程，然后再由贷款银行对该工程费用进行归垫；International Competitive Bidding，尽管国内出版物已约定俗成将之译为"国际竞争性招标"，更准确的译法应为"国际竞争性投标"，因为互相竞争的是投标人而不是招标人；Pre-bid meeting（标前会）是招标人在投标人提交投标书以前组织投标人参加的项目介绍会、调研会议，国内有些出版物将之译为"预标会"属措辞不当，容易产生误导；Negotiating Bids，尽管国内出版物常常将其译为"议标"，实质上，它不属于招投标范畴，因为此种采购不具备招投标活动的最基本特征，应改译为"谈判采购"。

8.3.2　用词正式古朴　翻译准确达意

英文标书经常使用并列的同义词或相关词语、情态动词及复合副词，以突出文件的正式和规范程度，强化当事人的义务和责任，因其各司其职，意义不可混淆，翻译时应当挖掘深层次的含义，准确传递相应信息。

在招标文件中有同义词或相关词语并列的情况，同义词或相关词语往往由 and 或 or 连接，通过两个或多个词汇的共同含义来限定其唯一词义，从而排除由于一词多义可能造成的歧义，体现了招标文件的严谨性和正式性。这类词汇虽然形式复杂，但是意义简洁，翻译一般只需译出基本意思即可。如：amplify or update 更新；update and augment 更新和扩充；revise or augment 修改或增加；administration and execution 执行；responsible or liable 负担；reasonable and responsive 合理的；stipulations and provisions 规定；complaints and claims 声明；null and void 无效的；furnish and provide 提供；fulfill or perform 履行；in full force and effect 完全有效。

① 情态动词。在招标采购过程中，招标方处于居高临下的地位，在对投标人

提出要求时总倾向于使用带有强制性含义的 shall 或 must。显然此 shall 并非日常生活的"应当""适宜"或"本来应当"（should），而是"必须"，非此不可。而招标方在说到自己须履行某种义务时，却总是极力轻描淡写，淡化语气强度，避免使用 shall 或 must，较多选用 will、should，甚至选用 may，表"愿意"或"可以"，此时语气已弱化到模棱两可的选择。翻译时一定要挖掘情态动词的深层内涵，注意将情态动词的语气准确地传达出来。如："The Technical Tender shall include a detailed and point by point response to the Technical Specification, together with the requested reference and other material specified in the Invitation to Tender documents."（技术标书必须包含对技术规范的详细的、点对点的应答，同时提供招标文件所要求的相关内容和其他素材。）

② 复合副词。英文标书中常用复合副词，引导从句时可以起到加强语气或让步的作用。翻译中文标书时，若使用这些词可使译文结构严谨、逻辑紧密、言简意赅。如：hereafter = after this time 从此以后，今后；hereby = by means/reasons of this 特此；herein = in this 此中，与此；hereinafter = later in this contract 在下文；thereinafter = afterwards 以下，在下文；thereby = by that means 由此，因此，在那方面；therein = from that 在那里，在那点上；whereby = by what/by which 由是，凭那个。

8.3.3　句法结构复杂　灵活变通处理

由于标书翻译兼备商贸文书翻译和法律翻译的典型特征，因而在将中文标书英译过程中，为了体现标书文件的严肃性、规范性和准确性，往往采用复杂冗长的句式结构，以准确界定参加投标各方的权利和义务，排除被曲解、误解或出现歧义的可能性，避免今后可能发生的争端，以维护各方的利益。汉语多用短句，环环相扣，层次分明，逻辑关系隐含在句与句之间。英译时若照字面直译原文会令人感到非常别扭，有时甚至行不通，因而需要做必要的变通，即翻译时应对句法做必要的改动和调整，从而使译文符合译语规范和习惯，以准确再现原文。

8.4 常用词汇句型

① 除非上下文中另有要求 except where the context requires otherwise

② 根据上下文而定 as the context requires

③ 视情况而定 as the case may be

④ 视情况指其中之一 any of them as appropriate

⑤ 如果可行 if or when applicable

⑥ 但不限于 among other things

⑦ 自行决定 at his sole discretion
⑧ 合同规定 / 条款 contractual specifications/terms
⑨ 本合同由买卖双方签订。The contract is made by and between the buyer and sellers.
⑩ 本合同一式两份，自双方签字（盖章）之日起生效。
This contract is in two copies, effective since being signed by both parties.
⑪ 本合同未尽事宜，可由双方增补作为合同附件。
What is left unmentioned in contract may be added there as an appendix.

8.5 译文赏评

8.5.1 招标书

例 1：

原文 合同履行后，承包人须将全部合同图纸归还工程师。

译文 At the completion of the Contract the Contractor shall return to the Engineer all Drawings provided under the Contract.

赏评 上句中，"合同履行后"一般译为 after the Contract was completed，但在标书翻译中这样翻译则是欠妥的，有违标书的正式性。译文中为 at the completion of the Contract，较为妥当。

例 2：

原文 兹以招标方式在青岛市四方区兴建一个假日旅店，欢迎参加投标。

译文 We invite tenders to take part in the tender for the construction of a Holiday Inn in Sifang District, Qingdao.

赏评 上句中的译文使用了名词化结构 for the construction of 而没有用动词结构 to construct，体现了标书的正式性特征。

8.5.2 投标书（1）

例 1：

原文 In order to be considered further by the Employer in the process of tender evaluation, each alternative shall be accompanied by a detailed price breakdown indicating the tender's estimate of the additional or reduced cost in present (discounted) value to the Employer compared with the basic Tender Sum, if the alternative offer were to be accepted by the Employer and incorporated into the Contract.

译文 为了让业主在评标过程中作进一步的考虑，每一项备选方案应附有详细的标价细目分项，应指出如果备选方案被业主接受并列入合同后，投标者关于备选方案价格与基本投标金额相比，对业主按现值计算增加或减少的估计费用。

赏评 翻译时，首先确定原文的主句是"each alternative shall be accompanied by..."，其前的"in order to be considered..."是个目的状语从句，"indicating the tender's estimate..."是个定语从句，修饰 a detailed price breakdown，其中又包含了一个条件状语从句"if the alternative offer..."。厘清句子各部分关系后，根据汉语表达习惯，调整从句顺序，转换句子结构，进行翻译。本例译文处理得很恰当。

例 2：

原文 Firms of a country or goods manufactured in a country may be excluded if, (i) as a matter of law or officially regulation, the Borrower's country prohibits commercial relations with that country, provided that the Bank is satisfied that such exclusion does not preclude effective competition for the supply of goods or works required, or (ii) by an act of compliance with a decision of the United Nations Security Council taken under Chapter VII of the Charter of the United Nations, the Borrower's country prohibits any important of goods from, or payments to, a particular country, person, or entity.

译文 一个国家的公司或在一个国家制造的货物，如果属于下列情况，则可以被排除在外：（ⅰ）根据法律或官方规定，借款国禁止与该国有商业往来，但前提是要使世行满意地认为该排除不会妨碍在采购所需货物或工程时的有效竞争；（ⅱ）为响应联合国安理会根据《联合国宪章》第七章做出的决议，借款国禁止从该国进口任何货物或对该国的个人或实体进行任何付款。

赏评 疏通上下文关系，灵活处理长句。在翻译英文标书的长句时，最好的解决办法就是将这些长句在适当关节处断开，分解为意义完整的组件，让每个意群单独成句，然后按照从普遍到特殊、从主要到次要的顺序对各个组件重新排列组合，先叙述要点，再补充细节，最后提示可能发生的误解。本例译文做到了这一点。

例 3：

原文 可向假日旅店筹备处索取一般交易条件、规划蓝图与技术要求，每册 80 美元。

译文 General terms and conditions together with the blueprints and technical requirements can be obtained from the Preparatory Department of the Holiday Inn against payment of $80 for each copy.

赏评 上句中，中文原文省略了主语，而英译文中则把原句中的宾语"一般交易条件、规划蓝图与技术要求"转换成了主语，避免了提及动作的执行者，形成了被动态，更显客观。这一处理非常恰当。

8.5.3 投标书（2）

原文

现地监控方式

风电机组的现地监控系统主要包括风电机组电气控制系统、偏航控制系统及变桨控制系统以及塔筒底部的现地控制柜，可以自动控制发电机组的启停，完成正常运行时的检测和控制。同时可以与风电机组集中监控系统实现数据通信，上传风电机组的运行状态和运行参数，并接受风电机组集中监控系统的控制、调节命令，实现远方手动开/停机操作等。

运行人员可以通过现地控制柜实现对风电机组进行手动开机、手动停机、电动机启停、风电机组向顺时针方向旋转或向逆时针方向旋转。风电机组在运行过程中，控制单元持续监测风电机组的转速，监视制动系统的完整性，使风电机组的制动维持在安全水平上。通过控制单元还可调节风电机组的功率因数等参数。在风电机组塔架上部发电机机舱里的相应位置配有对应的一些运行方式切换开关和现地手动操作的开关和按钮。

现地控制系统可保证风电机组的正常并网发电和安全运行，具备紧急停机功能、故障报警功能，能够操作风电机组启动、停机、偏航和复位，能够记录并显示发电量、发电时间、并网时间等数据。具有后备不间断电源，在停电或电网故障时，保证不丢失运行数据及记录。

现地控制系统不依赖于集中监控系统，在集中监控系统发生链接故障时，现地控制系统能够继续控制风电机组并保证风电机组的正常运行。

译文

LCU Monitoring Mode

LCU control system of the wind turbine mainly comprises electrical control system, yaw control system, pitch control system and local control cabinet arranged at the bottom of the tower. LCU control system can automatically control the startup and shutdown of the wind turbine and perform monitoring and controlling under normal operation, meanwhile, the LCU monitoring system can realize data communication with the centralized monitoring system. The LCU monitoring system can upload the operation parameters of the wind turbine and can be controlled and regulated by the centralized monitoring system to achieve remote manual startup and shutdown, etc.

Startup and shutdown of the wind turbine, electromotor, clockwise rotation or counter-clockwise rotation of the wind turbine can be manually operated by operator through LCU control cabinet. During operation of the wind turbine, the control unit shall continuously monitor the rotation speed of the wind turbine and integrity of the braking system in order to maintain the safety level of the braking system. The control unit shall also be able to adjust the power factor of the wind turbine. Switches corresponding to certain operation mode and buttons for LCU manual operation shall be furnished at relevant position in the wind turbine component on top of the tower.

The LCU control system shall guarantee the combination of the power grid connection and safe operation of the power grid. The system shall have the function of emergency shutdown, malfunction alarm and be capable of operating the startup, shutdown, yawning and restoration of the wind turbine, recording and displaying the power output, generating duration and grid connection duration, etc. The system shall be provided with UPS which shall be capable of storing data and record in case of power failure.

The LCU control system shall be independent of the centralized monitoring system. In case of fault of centralized monitoring system, the LCU control system shall be capable of non-stop control of the wind turbine and guarantee the normal operation of the wind turbine.

赏评

这是某风电工程投标书中对招标文件中（设备）参数要求的回应，也就是说明投标产品性能能否满足招标方的技术需求。同时，这类产品参数的说明还兼具产品简介和宣传的作用。因此，上述这段文字的翻译就包括了标书翻译和产品简介翻译的共同特点。

① 术语翻译准确。LCU全称为Local Control Unit（现地控制单元），原文"现地监控方式"意为"现地控制单元的监控方式"，"现地控制系统"指的是"现地控制单元的控制系统"，"现地控制柜"是"现地控制单元的控制柜"，因此上述三个术语的对应译文LCU Monitoring Mode，LCU control system和local control cabinet是准确和恰当的，并非冗余。只是在标书正文中首次出现LCU时应该给出全称Local Control Unit（现地控制单元）。

② 准确地传达出情态动词的语气。译文中使用了9个情态助动词shall，在法律文本中，shall主要用于施加性义务，即强制当事人应当这样行为。在合同文本中，

担保条款或者承诺条款中用于表述承诺内容的名词性从句如果包含了 shall，其作用就在于强调担保人或承诺人的决心，而不是向当事人施加义务。

③ 并列名词短语的处理较为恰当。译文中并列名词短语的使用也是特色之一，如 the rotation speed of the wind turbine and integrity of the braking system、switches corresponding to certain operation mode and buttons for LCU manual operation 等，这说明译者能够熟练运用目标语言，翻译功底扎实。

总而言之，这是一篇相当不错的标书译文。

8.6 课后练习

（1） INTERPRETATION

Language

Unless the Contractor is a national of the Employer's country and the Employer and the Contractor agree to use the local language, all Contract Documents, all correspondence and communications to be given and all other documentation to be prepared and supplied under the Contract shall be written in English, and the Contract shall be construed and interpreted in accordance with that language.

If any of the Contract Documents, correspondence or communications are prepared in any language other than the governing language under GCC Sub-Clause 3.1. above, the English translation of such documents, correspondence or communications shall prevail in matters of interpretation.

Singular and Plural

The singular shall include the plural and the plural the singular, except where the context otherwise requires.

Headings

The headings and marginal notes in the General Conditions of Contract are included for ease of reference, and shall neither constitute a part of the Contract nor affect its interpretation.

Persons

Words importing persons or parties shall include firms, corporations and government entities.

（2）

承包商应对现场进行实地考察，检查并获取其所需的各种信息，并充分确认现场出入条件、须改建的现有构筑物的出入条件、业主所供设施、通信条件、运输条件、通行权利、工程所需设备设施的类型和数量、本地人力、建筑材料等及其价格、本地社会经济工作条件、气象、洪水位、勘测数据、地基土条件、基岩条件、自然排水、政府及地方主管部门规定的规章制度、税费、赋税、关税等各种相关事宜均能满足其工程需求。承包商对现场条件的忽略，不得作为向业主索要补偿或延时的理由，施工用水及其他用水可免费从喀辅埃河抽取。承包商应配备必要的抽水设备，并自行承担费用。投标人向本项目投标即应视为投标人已进行过上述考察；凡后期因上述原因提出索偿/争议的，业主均不会接受，也不予以考虑。

第三编 专用科技文体与翻译

导论

第 9 章　摘要

第 10 章　科技论文

第 11 章　报告

导 论

专用科技文体是一种重要的文体形式，可以泛指一切论及科学和技术的书面语和口语体，包括：科技著述、科技论文和报告、实验报告和方案；各类科技情报和文字资料；科技实用手册（包括机械、仪器、工具等的结构描述和操作规程）；有关科技文体的会谈、会议、交谈；有关科技的影片、录像等有声资料的解说词。

科技文体的语场包括基础科学理论、技术性法律条文，涉及科学试验、科学技术研究、工程项目、生产制造等领域。语旨为各科技专业领域的专家、学者。在语式中，抽象程度很高的基础科学理论，如数学、力学等的论著以人工语言为主，辅以自然语言，不是行家的翻译工作者难以理解，通常由专业人员自行阅读，无须翻译。

科技文体的一般特点是表述客观、逻辑严密、行文规范、用词正式、句式严谨。科技文体的意义系统是由其交际功能所决定的。专家与专家或科学家之间交流科技的发现与发明、理论与概念、问题与进展、职责与规范等信息时常采用这种文体，其语义特征主要为客观性，体现在语义结构线性化、非人称化和名词化三个方面。

1 文体特征

在文体学上，专用科技论文被统称为科学散文。其文体结构具有如下特点：

1.1 词汇特点

科技英语在用词上最明显的特点是大量使用科技词汇。

（1）常用词汇的专业化

大量的科学技术语借之于常用词汇，但是用到某一专业领域时，就变成了专业技术用语，具有严格的科学含义。如：splash（水等"飞溅"），在英语中是一个常用词，但被空间科学借用，含义专业化，变为 to land in water, especially in the ocean, after a space flight（宇宙飞船等从太空归航时溅落于大洋水面）；message（信使），被遗传工程学借用，含义专业化，变为 a chemical substance which carries or transmits genetic information（一种携带或传递遗传信息的化学物质）。

（2）同一词语词义的多专业化

同一个英语常用词有时会被许多专业用来表达各自的专业概念，甚至在同一个专业中一个词又有许多不同词义。如：transmission，在无线电工程学中的词义是"发射""播送"，在机械学中是"传动""变速"，在物理学中的词义是"透射"，在医学中的含义是"遗传"，等等。power 的应用范围更广，在机械动力学的一个专业中，它的词义就有多种，如："力""电""电力""电源""动力""功率"等。

科技汉语与之不同，不存在同一词语词义的多专业化倾向。汉语的传统趋势是专词专用、跨专业科技汉语词汇多为基础科学常用或通用词汇。

1.2 语法特点

（1）动词名词化

名词化倾向主要是指科技英语中广泛使用能表示动作或状态的抽象名词。科技文章的任务是叙述事实和论证推断，因而要求言简意明，语言结构简化。

例1 the discovery of interferon 干扰素的发现（to discover interferon）

the standardization of the series 系列的标准化（to standardize the series）

the generation of heat by friction 摩擦生热（to generate heat by friction）

这种现象就是动词名词化。科技英语充分利用动词名词化这一手段，从而有效地简化了叙事层次和结构，即减少了使用句子或从句的频率，使行文更加直接、紧凑、简洁。

（2）行为动词代替 be 动词

由于科技英语在大多数情况下都是描述行为、过程、现象及发展，等等，因此多用表示行为的动词。表示行为的动词具有较鲜明的动态感，比较生动；表示存在的动词（be）给人以静态感，比较凝滞。

例2 Harries was the first to *utilize* of the double bond in order to *gain* an insight into the nature of the rubber molecule, and the evidence for the general skeletal structure and for the position of the double bond is *based* almost entirely on his ozonolysis experiments (1905–1912). By *passing* oxygen containing 6% of ozone into a solution of rubber in chloroform or ethyl acetate, Harries *obtained* a glassy explosive mass of the composition ($C_5H_8O_3$). Decomposition of the ozonide with water *afforded* levulinic aldehyde, its peroxide, its further oxidation product levulinic acid, and only minute traces of carbon dioxide, formic acid, and succinic acid. These experiments were later *verified* and *extended* by Pummerer (1931), who was able to *account* for about 95% of the carbon skeleton in the form of decomposition products, almost 90% of which consisted of levulinic compounds. This means that the isoprene units must be *linked* head to trail.

上例使用了 10 个不同形态的行为动词，使整段叙述的行动过程给人以强烈动感，比使用静态动词生动得多。

（3）谓语形态特点

① 多用现在时。尤其多用一般现在时，来表述"无时间性"的一般叙述，即通常发生的自然现象、过程、常规，等等。一般现在时在科技英语中用于表述科学定义、定力、方程式或公式的解说以及图表的说明，目的在于以精确无误的"无时间性"排除任何与时间牵连的误解，使行文更严谨。

② 多用被动语态。科技英语叙述的往往是客观的事物、现象或过程，而主体往往是从事某项工作（试验、研究、分析、观测等）的人或装置。这时使用被动语态不仅比较客观，而且可以使读者的注意力集中在叙述中的事物、现实或过程，即客体上。

③ 广泛使用动词的非限定式。科技英语倾向于广泛使用动词的非限定式，即分词、不定式和动名词，特别是分词。

以上三点，构成了现代科技英语文体中语法形态的主要特征和趋势。

1.3 文体特点概览

科技英语的显著特点是重叙事逻辑上的连贯及表达上的明晰与畅达；避免行文晦涩，避免表露个人感情，避免论证上的主观随意性。因此，科技英语总是力求少用或不用描述性形容词以及具有抒情作用的副词、感叹词及疑问词。科技英语力求平易和精确，因此尽力避免使用旨在加强语言感染力和宣传效果的各种修辞格，忌用夸张、借喻、讥讽、反诘、双关及押韵等修辞手段，以免使读者产生行文浮华、内容虚饰之感。

2 翻译原则

2.1 准确翻译科技词义

- 密切注意一个词在某一特定的专业领域中的专门词义。
- 掌握现代英语构词法。
- 仔细辨别词义，遵循专业技术领域的用语习惯，以约定俗成的译名翻译某一概念。
- 研究各种译词的手段，因为词是科技英语有别于其他语类的一个重要方面。

2.2 熟练掌握常用结构

科技英语虽然不像公文文体那样程式化，但它在语法结构上有较强的倾向性，许多句式出现的频率很大，熟练掌握这些句式的翻译规律，就既能保证译文的准确性和可读性，又可以提高翻译的效率。如：assuming that（假设，假定），provided that（倘若，只要），seeing that（由于，鉴于），等等。熟悉这类常用结构的翻译，是科技英语翻译的基本功。

2.3 透彻分析深层结构

准确翻译科技英语的关键，在于透彻理解原文，仅掌握单个词的词义和结构是不够的。实际使用中的科技英语句式结构复杂而多变。译者要能够辨别出词项与词项之间的语法关系，若仅凭感觉主观臆断、拼凑、串联词汇意义，则会错误百出。

第 9 章 摘要

摘要文体与翻译

国家标准 GB6447-86 对"摘要"的定义为:"以提供文献内容梗概为目的,不加评论和补充解释,简明、确切地记叙文献重要内容的短文。"

摘要,又称为概要,内容提要,美国称为 abstract,英国多用 summary,是论文内容的概括和浓缩,是现代学术论文的重要组成部分。一篇完整的摘要主要包括标题、摘要正文和关键词(主题词)三个部分。有的摘要除了正标题以外,还有副标题,用来说明论文的内容、范围,或者对正标题进行补充、说明或限制。

摘要作为科技论文的重要组成部分,有其特殊的意义和作用。它是国际间知识传播、学术交流与合作的桥梁和媒介,目前国际上几个主要检索机构的数据库对英文摘要的依赖性很强,因此,好的英文摘要对于增加期刊和论文的被检索引用机会、吸引读者、扩大影响起着不可忽视的作用。

本章学习如何正确、得体和流畅地翻译摘要的正文,了解摘要翻译中变译的应用前提和方法,学会和掌握规范的摘要翻译方法。

9.1 课前实践

9.1.1 摘要(1)

The Analysis of the Curriculum Implementation about the VTTE Program in TUDias

Abstract: This Paper examines the curriculum of the new VTTE program implemented in TUDias. The main objective was to examine

对德国德累斯顿理工大学职业学院职业与技术教师教育课程设置结构的分析

摘要:本文主旨在于评析德国德累斯顿理工大学职业学院职业与技术教师教育课程的实施情

whether the new curriculum complied with the needs in practice. It was planned by the year 2000, 75 percent of the students will be enrolled to study in the VTTE program in TUDias. It will emerge into a single focus teacher education institution with the four year Bachelor degree in VTTE as the flagship of the Institute. As such, the success of the VTTE program influences, to a large extent, the reputation and the future development of the Institute and the vocational technical teacher profession at large. The investigation will take into account the views expressed by teachers and students during the interviews.

Key words: curriculum; teaching method; ability of practice

况。该计划始于2000年，75%的学生将被招收进该项目。作为德国第一所能够授予职业技术教师教育学士学位的职业学院，德累斯顿理工大学职业学院的办学模式的成功与否决定了其学院未来的声誉及发展空间。调查将充分考虑教师和学生在访谈期间提出的意见。

关键词：课程论；教学方法；实践能力

9.1.2 摘要（2）

人际冲突下隐含修正用意的语用分析

摘要：隐含修正用意是言谈交际中说话人间接表达的非显性意图，表现为说话人通过一定的隐含方式，试图改变听话人的某一认识、观点、行为等，这利于在出现认识分歧、期待差异等情况下实现人际关系的缓和，因此隐含修正具有"和谐取向"的人际语用功能，如人际冲突缓解功能和人际关系的利他功能等。

Pragmatic Account of Implicit Repairs in Interpersonal Conflicts

Abstract: Aiming at exploring implicit repairs and their pragmatic functions in interpersonal conflicts, the present study has found differences between implicit repairs and explicit ones, the former are called pragmatic repairs in this study since they are used with implicit intentions to change or reformulate the addressee's opinions, viewpoints of forthcoming acts, thus with rapport orientation, such pragmatic functions can be realized for managing interpersonal relationships, such as mitigating disagreements in opinions and expectation differences, benefiting the other, etc.

关键词：隐含修正；语用修正；人际冲突；和谐取向

Key words: implicit repairs; pragmatic repairs; interpersonal conflicts; rapport orientation

9.1.3 摘要（3）

构建商务英语学科教学知识的研究框架

摘要：本文运用学科教学知识（PCK）理论，根据商务英语的跨学科属性考察商务英语学科中PCK要素的表现形式之后，构建了商务英语PCK研究框架。文章阐释了商务英语PCK研究框架的四个要素：商务英语教学目的和取向、学生对商务英语学科的理解和需求、商务英语学科的教学策略知识、商务英语课程知识，并揭示了各要素之间的双向互动关系。商务英语PCK研究框架有助于商务英语教师理解和增加教师必需的商务英语知识，使相关商务英语实证研究成为可能。

关键词：学科教学知识；商务英语学科；研究框架；学科教学知识要素

Construction of the Research Framework of PCK in Business English

Abstract: By employing the theory of pedagogical content knowledge (PCK) and examining PCK in business English, this paper proposes a study model of PCK for business English based on its cross-disciplinary nature. The paper dwells on the four PCK components of business English, namely knowledge of business English teaching purposes, knowledge of students' understanding of business English, knowledge of business English teaching strategies and knowledge of business English curriculum. Meanwhile, it illustrates the interrelationship among the four PCK components. The study model of PCK for business English enables business English teachers to understand and increase the essential teacher knowledge of business English, and provides possibility for empirical studies on business English.

Key words: pedagogical content knowledge; business English; study model; PCK components

9.2 文体特点

9.2.1 文体正式　用词规范

学术论文应使用书面化和正式化的语言，摘要是论文的一部分，用词也应正式。英文摘要有以下特点：

① 多使用拉丁语、希腊语的英语词汇；

② 多用单词，少用短语，以使文体正式、紧凑、简洁；

③ 忌用缩略语、俚语。

汉语摘要同样也要求用词正式。

9.2.2 句式严谨　避免含糊

摘要作为学术语体，要求语义明确，表述清楚、简洁、准确，因而句子的语法关系必须严谨，语义明确，避免含糊。英文摘要使用长句多于短句，句型多样化，适当运用并列句、复合句和并列复合句来表达复杂的思想；用适当的短语代替从句，大量使用非谓语动词形式及前置短语等，把从句信息浓缩在简单句的状语和定语中来表达复杂的思想。

9.2.3 结构固定　层次清楚

摘要的构成部分中英有别。中文摘要通常只有方法和结果两部分，而英文摘要通常包括4个部分：目的、方法、结果、讨论。摘要大体上遵循"三段式"章法，结构比较固定。开头为主题句，指出论文的主要内容；展开句阐明论文具体怎样做；结尾句得出结论及所得结果、结论的意义。句与句之间分别体现扩展、论证、层次等逻辑关系，有效地建立句与句之间的意义联系。由此，摘要的逻辑关系得以突出，说理的层次性得以体现，论证的要点得以显化。

9.3 翻译要领

9.3.1 标题简洁　多用省略

翻译中文论文标题时，应简洁、练达，尽量省略次要的单词或不必要的细节，用少量的单词表达相同的意思。常用省略法和缩写语。

（1）省略法

英译中文标题时，可省略冠词、系动词、介词、代词、连词等不影响达意的词汇。冠词的省略，常见的有：论……的艺术特色 (The) Artistic Features of...；关于……的

思考 (A) Thinking of...；人口学研究对象和方法，可简化为 Population Study: Objects and Methods 或者 Population Study: Objects & Methods。

有些专有名词、特殊名称、约定俗成的固定译文，其冠词不应省略，如：《三国演义》The Romance of the Three Kingdoms；《孔子与〈诗经〉》Confucius & The Book of Songs；《文心雕龙》Carving a Dragon at the Core of Literature 或 Carved Dragon at Literary Creation。

有些系动词，可以冒号代之，如："理论联系实际是繁荣社会科学的根本方针"，可简约地译为 Combining Theory with Practice: (the) Basic Principle for Mirroring Social Science，或者 Combining Theory with Practice: Basic Principle for Flourishing Social Science。

将介词短语结构变成单词，如：《浅论高校文科学报的功能》可译为 An Elementary Study on the Functions of University Periodicals of Humanities，也可简化译为 Elementary Study on University Periodical's Function，或者 Functions of University Periodicals: Preliminary Study。

对中文标题中"论""试论""刍议""浅谈""初探"等的翻译，大多数翻译成 on，但是根据英文简洁的需要，完全可以不译出来，直接翻译标题的中心内容即可。

（2）缩略语

英译标题可多用缩写词汇，但是只有已得到本行业人员公认的缩略语才可在标题中使用；对于可有多个解释的缩略语，应严加限制。缩略语主要限于国名、组织机构和专业术语，如：美国（美利坚合众国），可用 U.S.、U.S.A. 或 USA；专业术语，如：提单（Bill of Lading），可以缩写为 B/L；削减战略武器条约（Strategic Arms Reduction Treaty），可缩写为 START。

9.3.2 表达准确　句式得体

学术论文摘要的英译，除了要求准确达意（尤其是专业性术语），还要采用正式（书面）文体，避免使用 isn't、don't、hasn't、needn't、lots of、no problem、one hundred percent correct 等口语体形式。还要注意：

① 多用被动语态。被动语态能较好地表现客观性，主语部分可集中较多的信息，起到信息前置、鲜明突出的作用，所以在介绍研究对象、研究所用的设备、手段时都习惯用被动语态。

原文 A new set of color features robust to a large change in viewpoint, object geometry and illumination is proposed.

译文 提出了一套对视点、目标形状和光照鲁棒的新颜色特征。

另外，主动语态可以较好地突出作者的努力，所以一般介绍研究目的和结论时多用主动语态。到底采用主动还是被动，要根据意思、上下文和语句的连贯等来确定。

② 正确选用时态。英文摘要所使用的时态主要有三种：一般现在时、现在完成时和一般过去时。一般现在时使用得最为广泛，主要用于陈述性、资料性文摘中，介绍的是研究目的、内容、结果、结论等客观事实，如：The result shows/presents...；It is found that...。现在完成时用来说明论题的发展背景，表示已取得的成果、已完成的工作或已结束的研究项目。一般过去时主要用于说明某一具体项目的发展情况，介绍已进行的研究、实验、观察、调查、医疗等过程。

③ 尽量使用合成名词、词组和名词化结构。合成名词是指由两个及两个以上的名词共同构成一个具有完整概念的合成词，有时也会加上必要的修饰形容词，如：纤维改性 fiber modification；电子废弃物回收产业 E-waste recycling industry。名词化结构用词简洁、结构紧凑、表意具体、词句负载的信息容量大。

原文 对城市电子废弃物回收产业的创新性进行试验，将对我们进行循环经济研究赋予启发。

译文 The trying of the innovation for the city's e-waste recycling industry will inspire us to research the Circular Economy.

9.3.3 摘译变译　增补改写

在翻译汉语摘要时，一般来说，原语和目的语的摘要应该一致。但是，如果汉语摘要在内容上未必客观、完整，未能恰如其分地反映原文内容，在格式或结构上不符合目的语摘要的要求，存在类别、语言、语法等错误的情况下，译者可以对汉语摘要采取变译的方式：摘/删译、增/补译和改译（写）。此外，由于英语句子属于"树状结构"，汉语句式属于"流水句"。翻译时应注意汉语流水式的短句要转换成英语长句，按照英语句式的规范来改译。

原文 从焊丝钢用户反馈情况入手，从金相组织、化学成分、机械性能等几方面分析焊丝钢 ER70S-6 断丝偏高原因，并针对断丝原因采取应对措施，降低断丝率。

原译 In this paper, the user of NISCO such as Changzhou Yatai Welding steel users, Zhangjiagang Heng Chang feedback manufacturers starting in the microstructure, chemical composition analysis, mechanical property, such as steel welding wire ER70S-6 off the high wire causes, and the reasons for broken wires in the active response measures.

改译 The causes of broken wires of ER70S-6 welding-wire steel from feedback of clients are analyzed from several aspects such as microstructure, chemical composition and mechanical property. Some measures have been take to reduce wire breaking rate.

要特别注意的是，改译是有条件的，不是对原文随心所欲地胡乱改写。

9.4 译文赏评

9.4.1 摘要（1）

原文

This survey is conducted to find out what the effectiveness of GDUFS MTI interpreting curriculum and what the market expects of quality interpreting education, with the hope to provide suggestions to interpreting educators, especially in GDUFS, and to the MTI graduates of this major. Three questionnaires are designed and distributed both through paper and the Internet. To get more insightful comments, interviews are done as complements. Subjects are interpreting companies in Guangdong Province, teachers of the MTI program as well as students majored in MTI Interpreting, graduating in 2013 and 2014. Responses are elicited from 3 aspects, i.e. MTI graduates', teachers' and the interpreting company employers' perspectives. Based on the analysis of the results, the following suggestions are put forward:

(1) In terms of the GDUFS interpreting curriculum, more courses in regard to interpreting practice and language skills should be set up, and great importance should be placed on the cultivation of MTI graduates' attitude, learning and communication skills;

(2) As for the MTI graduates themselves, they should be more hard-working and self-dependent, so as to improve their comprehensive quality;

(3) Concerning the teaching methods, apart from class practice, case study, market practice and real time tasks should be involved in.

译文

笔者进行此次调查，旨在探寻广外MTI口译课程设置的效果和口译市场对专业人才的需求，希望就人才培养对口译教学者，尤其是广外的口译教学者有所启示，并对此专业的硕士研究生提出建议。此次调查问卷采用纸质问卷调查和网络问卷调查的形式。为能获得更多深见，将辅之以采访的形式。调查对象选取了广东省内的部分翻译服务单位、广外口译课程授课教师以及2011级与2012级MTI口译专业学生。主要从课程设置以及市场对口译人才需求方面进行调查。调查结果将从翻译服务单位人员、教师以及学生三方面进行分析与总结。此次调查结果可能得出的结论表明：

（1）在广外MTI课程设置上，应多设立有关口译实践及专业能力培养的课程，更注重培养该专业硕士研究生的职业态度、学习与沟通的能力；

（2）对于硕士研究生，他们应当更加努力、独立自主，不断提升自我综合素质；

（3）在教学方法上，除课堂练习外，应融入实践教学，包括案例分析、市场实践以及实时任务实践等。

赏评

这篇摘要格式清晰，层次分明。从研究问题提出、采用的研究方法、数据收集分析，到最后给出建议，是一篇规范的科技论文摘要。全文的四个步骤全部由被动句构成，译文采用句式转换的方法，将被动句结构译成以"笔者""此次调查结果"等为主语的主动句式，使译文更加符合汉语行文习惯。

9.4.2 摘要（2）

原文

行业特色高校产学研结合本科人才培养模式的探索与研究
——基于河南科技大学应用型人才培养的目标

摘要： 随着高校规模的迅速扩张，原行业特色高校开始向"多科化""多元化"方向发展，行业特色被淡化，再加上自身存在的各种弊端，严重影响了行业特色高校在社会上的影响力。如何使行业特色高校适应新形势下行业发展的需要，是摆在我们教育工作者面前的一个重要课题。河南科技大学作为一所典型的地方行业特色高校，通过加强与企事业单位的合作，凝练专业方向，构建了产学研相结合的人才培养模式，为我国粮食行业的发展，培养了大批专门人才。

关键词： 产学研结合；实验实习平台；校企合作

译文

Explore and research on the combination of the mold of generation, studying and research, and the mold of cultivating talents
—On the basis of the goal to cultivate practication-orientated talents of Henan University of the Technology

Abstract: As university scales expand rapidly, universities that originally bear features in certain arenas have taken on the developmental trend towards multi-subjectionization and multi-diversification, hence the encroachingly dissipating of such features. In addition, their natural defections have obviously diminished their competition in society. Thus it is a crucial issue that we, as educators, have to face and find ways to settle, of how to put universities of features in the track of new situations. And Henan University of Technology, typical of regional features, has established the mold of generation, studying and research, and fostered numerals of specialized talents for the development of national food industry, by strengthening the cooperation with enterprises and institutions, and refining major directions.

Key words: the mold of generation, studying and research; researches and factory practices; lab and training centers; cooperation with enterprise and institutions

赏评

此译文错误很多。很多单词拼写错误，如 talent、subjectionization、cooperation 等（此译文已改）；"河南科技大学"应译为 Henan University of Technology；很多措辞不够准确达意；有语法错误。

标题中英文字母的大小写有 3 种格式：全部字母都大写；每个词的首字母大写，但 4 个字母以下的冠词、连词、介词等虚词全部小写；第一个词的首字母大写，其余字母均小写。其中第二种用得最多。译文标题未按惯例区分大小写。

英文标题，宜采用名词化形式；"产学研"是字面对应的翻译，脱离了大学教育的语境，意为"通过课堂教学、生产实践、参与科研培养学生"；汉语标题较长，英译文不够简洁精练，可省去"探索与研究"以符合英语行文习惯，可改译为：Integrating Classroom Teaching, Research and Factory Practice to Cultivate Qualified Undergraduates in Industry-oriented University—Based on the Practical Talents Training Program in Henan University of Technology

"随着高校规模的迅速扩张"，原译文是字字对应的翻译，未考虑到中国大学升格以及扩招这一语境；"行业特色"只翻译出了字面意思，让人无法理解，可采取补充法译为 research advantages in certain industries。英美人士的思维习惯与中国人是有差异的。他们叙述因果关系时，往往先摆出结果，再追溯原因。所以第二句译文的句子排列过于依赖汉语句子，有些拘谨。

此译文可作如下改译：

改译

Integrating Classroom Teaching, Research and Factory Practice to Cultivate Qualified Undergraduates in Industry-oriented University
—Based on the Practical Talents Training Program in
Henan University of Technology

Abstract: Many colleges expanded rapidly and have been turned to be universities. They lost their important social status and great influence because of their born defects, in particular loss of research advantages in certain industries in their efforts to become multidisciplinary, diversified universities. It is a crucial topic for the Chinese educators to consider how universities nowadays adjust themselves to the development of the industries they involve and regain their reputation. Here is some experience drawn by the researchers through many years of practical attempts in Henan University of Technology, originally a typical college engaged in grain research and having cultivated a large quantities of professionals for the grain industry. The practical talents training program in Henan University of Technology is introduced, which is featured by integration of classroom teaching, research and factory practice.

Key words: integrating classroom teaching, research and factory practice; lab and training centers; cooperation between universities and enterprises

9.5 课后练习

（1）摘要标题翻译

① 一则汉英摘要翻译的话语分析理论研究 ＿＿＿＿＿＿＿＿＿＿＿＿＿＿＿

② 词类转译在科技论文摘要英译中的应用 ＿＿＿＿＿＿＿＿＿＿＿＿＿＿＿

③ 典籍英译中的"东方情调化翻译倾向"研究 ＿＿＿＿＿＿＿＿＿＿＿＿＿＿＿

④ "中国英语"语言特征及其社会历史成因研究 ＿＿＿＿＿＿＿＿＿＿＿＿＿＿＿

⑤ 关于中国金融监管制度转型的思考——从政府到市场 ＿＿＿＿＿＿＿＿＿＿＿＿＿＿＿

⑥ Post-process Method for Business Card Recognition Based on Fuzzy Reasoning ＿＿＿＿＿＿＿＿＿＿＿＿＿＿＿

⑦ Guaranteed Cost Reliable Control with Actuator Failures ＿＿＿＿＿＿＿＿＿＿＿＿＿＿＿

⑧ Raising Taxes to Reduce Smoking Prevalence in the US: A Simulation of the Anticipated Health and Economic Impacts ＿＿＿＿＿＿＿＿＿＿＿＿＿＿＿

⑨ Brand Management and the Challenge of Authenticity ＿＿＿＿＿＿＿＿＿＿＿＿＿＿＿

⑩ A Contrastive Analysis on Hero Narration ＿＿＿＿＿＿＿＿＿＿＿＿＿＿＿

Strategy in American and Chinese Disaster Report

（2）摘要正文翻译

运用基于Agent模拟的建模方法构建研究差别电价影响效果的多Agent模型，设计由政府Agent、电力Agent及行业Agent组成的多Agent框架，分Agent的目标及行为策略，设计系统的仿真流程。以高耗能行业实施差别电价为例，模拟对化学工业、建筑材料业、金属冶炼业实施差别电价对我国物价水平及电力消费所造成的影响。

第 10 章 科技论文

科技论文文体与翻译

"科技论文",又称"学术论文"或"科学论文",是对自然科学、社会科学、工程技术等领域进行探索研究、分析论证的文章。科技论文类型涵盖已经发表的科技论文和报告、非正式发表的实验报告和方案、各类科技情报和文字资料,科技使用手册,以及大学本科生、研究生的学期论文和毕业论文。论题包括基础理论、应用技术、实证考察等。这是一种在科技活动中广泛应用的文体,以传递科技信息和承载科技思想为目的,具有专业性、实用性、科学性等特征,主要功能是报道科学研究的创新成果。科技论文可分为自然科学科技论文和社会科学科技论文。

科技论文的语言有其自身的特点,其表达准确、客观、严谨、清楚。因此,在科技论文翻译中要根据其语言的文体特点,在准确理解原文的基础上,充分考虑科技翻译的目的和用途以及译语读者的认知习惯,采用恰当的翻译策略、方法和技巧。

本章学习了解科技论文的文体特点和常用的词汇以及句式;掌握不同种类科技论文的风格特征;了解科技论文翻译的特点、标准和要求;针对不同风格的科技论文,学会采用不同的翻译策略和方法,翻译出适用性强的论文来。

10.1 课前实践

10.1.1 医学论文

Identification and Functional Prediction of Cardiac Troponin I Interacting Protein in Newborn Mice

The study aims to isolate and identify the proteins that interact with cardiac troponin I (cTnI) in primary mouse cardiomyocyte, and to analyze their biological processes and signaling pathways by use of high throughput proteomics and bioinformatics techniques. The hearts of C57 neonatal mice were used to prepare the primary cardiomyocyte. The cTnI binding proteins were extracted from the whole cell protein by co-immunoprecipitation, and the proteins were analyzed and identified by mass spectrometry. Furthermore, the physicochemical properties, biological processes and signaling pathways of cTnI interacting proteins were predicted by bioinformatics tools. A total of 262 proteins were identified by mass spectrometry, cTnI binding proteins were involved in 14 biological processes and 33 KEGG biological pathways ($P<0.05$). In mouse cardiomyocyte, 262 kinds of proteins may interact with cTnI, and participate in regulation of calcium ion influx and PI3K-AKT signaling pathways.

新生小鼠心肌肌钙蛋白 I 相互作用蛋白的鉴定与功能预测

本研究旨在采用高通量蛋白质组学筛选鉴定小鼠心肌原代细胞中可能与心肌肌钙蛋白 I（cTnI）存在相互作用的蛋白质，并通过生物信息学软件分析其可能参与的生物过程及信号通路。取 C57 新生小鼠的心脏制备心肌原代细胞，提取细胞全蛋白进行免疫共沉淀实验筛选出 cTnI 的相互作用蛋白，通过质谱分析技术对其进行鉴定；将鉴定所得蛋白质信息输入生物信息学软件分析其理化性质，预测其可能参与的生物过程及信号通路。共鉴定出 262 种可能与 cTnI 存在相互作用的蛋白质，预测其可能参与的生物进程 14 条，KEGG 生物学通路 33 条（$P<0.05$）。在小鼠心肌细胞中，有 262 种蛋白可能与 cTnI 存在相互作用，其中部分蛋白可能参与心肌细胞钙离子内流及 PI3K-AKT 信号通路的调节。

10.1.2 管理学论文

动态系统影响优化分析

管理者通常需要确定系统参数及决策变量，以达成预期目标。但优化参数较多时，往往导致求解精度较低，甚至无法求解。为提高优化效果，在定义影响度的基础上提出了影响优化分析方法。依据影响度结果，从众多系统参数中选取那些对系统目标影响较大的参数。将原优化问题转化为非线性规划问题，引入遗传算法优化控制序列和所选参数。以库存系统为例进行数值仿真计算，得到了不同预期、需求条件下的订单处理时间和订货规律。该方法有效减少了优化变量个数，可更准确地为管理者制定运作计划。

Influence-optimization Analysis for Dynamic Systems

Managers often need to determine the system parameters and decision variables to achieve their desired goals. However, excessive parameters may reduce the accuracy and lead to no solutions. An influence-optimization analysis was developed based on the influence degree to identify parameters that have significant impact on the system goals. The original optimization problem is then converted into a nonlinear programming problem, with the control sequences and selected parameters obtained using a genetic algorithm. Simulations of an inventory system accurately predict order-processing time and ordering rules for different expectations and demand conditions. The number of optimization variables can be reduced using this method to improve the accuracy of operational plans.

10.1.3 空间科学论文

抗辐射加固"龙芯"处理器的空间辐射环境适应性研究及航天计算机设计评估

计算机在现代航天领域中起着关键的作用，但由于航天计算机所处的特殊运行环境，其抗辐射性及可靠性是重要的指标之

Research on Space Irradiation Environment Adaptability of Rad-Hard Godson Processor and an Design of Aerospace Computer Based on It

The computer plays a key role in modern aerospace applications. But the aerospace computer is working in the space environment, so the irradiation-tolerance and reliability are

一。由于航天发达国家对航天技术和对高性能宇航级器件的出口限制，致使我国的航天计算机发展受到种种制约。研究和开发国产高性能宇航CPU不仅可以满足日益增长的航天任务的需求，而且对于保障航天计算机的安全、提高航天计算机的可靠性、打破国外对于高性能宇航级器件的封锁，发展我国自主航天计算机技术有极为重要的意义。

"龙芯"CPU是采用正向设计，拥有完全自主知识产权的国产高性能CPU。为了适应"龙芯"CPU在航天任务中的应用，在中国科学院等单位的支持下，中国科学院计算技术研究所对此芯片进行了航天适应性改造，设计出了一款抗辐射加固"龙芯"SOC（System On Chip）——RH-GS 1-SOC。

本课题为RH-GS 1-SOC芯片设计了一个抗辐射实验单板机和一个基于Compact PCI总线的原理样机，对RH-GS 1-SOC进行了抗辐射效应地面模拟试验、温度稳定性试验。本文先介绍了国内外航天应用CPU的发展情况，然后对抗辐射实验单板机和原理样机的设计原理、各项实验方案做了完整描述，最后对RH-GS 1-SOC芯片是否满足航天计算机的应用要求做出了评价。

great respects. Because the countries advanced in aerospace research put some restrictions on the export of aerospace-grade or high-performance devices, China is constrained in developing aerospace computers. Researching and developing of China-made high-performance aerospace CPU can not only meet the growing demand of aerospace missions, but also have some great significance.

Based on top-down design, processor "Godson" achieves outstanding characteristics with full independent intellectual property of China. With the contribution and support of General Armament Department and Chinese Academy of Sciences, Godson was modified and upgraded in both of system architecture and silicon structure by CAS-ICT (Institute of Computing Technology, Chinese Academy of Science), which gives birth to the rad-hard "Godson" CPU: RH-GS 1-SOC.

In this project I designed an SBC (Single Board Computer) and a Compact-PCI-based prototype computer for RH-GS 1-SOC, performing a simulation experiment of tolerance of irradiation and an experiment of temperature stability. This article has put a review of the developing on aerospace CPU domestic and abroad, and then following the full description of the SBC, the prototype computer, and the detail of all experiences. At last, the evaluation of RH-GS 1-SOC in aerospace applications is given.

📖 10.2 文体特点

科技论文倡导简洁、平易的文体风格，反对故弄玄虚、故作高深的写作方法，一般具有专业性、学术性、原创性、真实性和科学性的文体特点。这些特点具体通过写作中的遣词造句、文法表达等语言手段得以体现，形成了独具特色的词汇和句法。

10.2.1 语言正式 用词端庄

科技论文一般都采用正式的书面语体，具有客观性强、知识性强、语言严谨、表意清晰等特点。科技论文具有极强的专业性。科技文体大都在语体格式、遣词造句上比较规范，经常使用固定的格式、套语，力求精确易懂，简洁明晰，结构紧凑，很少带有感情色彩，以冷静客观的风格陈述事实和揭示真理，避免论证上的主观随意性。

在词汇表达上，科技论文用词端重、典雅、规范、严谨，多倾向于使用正式语体的词语，除非出于修辞效果上的考虑，一般不用俚、俗语，忌讳"插科打诨"的语气，力求给人以庄重感，避免流于谐谑、轻诮，常常使用一些"大词"，即含义比较抽象、概括的词。为摆脱句子冗长、结构盘结之弊，科技论文重简明、畅达，重条理性、纪实性和充分的论据，它强调论理的客观性，不主张作者表露个人的感情，倡导在论证中排除感情因素，尽其"解释"而非"感召"之功能，因而多使用中性词、非人格化的词。

（1）用词规范、庄重、确切，避免口语化的词

科技论文是对某一专业领域的某一问题进行说明的文章，要求语言庄重，用词规范。作者必须清楚、明白、客观一致地表达自己的观点。因此，常常要避免使用俚语、俗语、方言、口语化的表达以及非正规的省略词语等。

（2）常用词汇专业化

英语科技论文的用词具有高度专业性，其专业术语多来源于拉丁语和希腊语。他们的意义比较稳定，利于精确地表达概念。

（3）用词简明客观

科技论文重简明、畅达和条理性，讲究论理的客观性和纪实性，在写作中往往使用中性词和非人格化的词汇，以表明作者的公正态度，不带个人情感色彩，它的突出特点是重"理"而不是重"情"。

（4）动词名词化

名词化倾向主要是指英语科技论文中广泛使用能表示动作或状态的抽象名词或

起名词功用的非限定动词。学术写作中的名词化倾向是与学术文体的基本要求密切相关的。科技论文的任务是叙述事实和论证推断,因而要求言简意明,语言结构的简化是达到这一目的的主要方法。

动词名词化使动词本身固有的动作过程冻结成静态的过程,这样可使论证分析变得容易。因而,动词名词化被认为是学术论文的一个重要语言特色,它有助于对事件的阐述从动态过程变成存在状态。

10.2.2　句子复杂　变化多样

英语科技论文的句法特点表现为句子结构较复杂,句型变化及扩展样式多。由于科技论文旨在解析思想,开发论点,辩明事理,展开论证,作者在阐发自己的观点时总是力求周密、深入,避免疏漏。因此,文章的逻辑性较强,文句结构一般比较讲究,重发展层次和谋篇布局。具体体现在:动词一般现在时和被动态的出现频率较高,多使用陈述句和复杂句,少用或不使用疑问句和感叹句;完全句多,省略句少;长句多,短句少;较多地使用形式主语 it 引导的句式和用 that 引导的主语从句;较多使用非谓语动词形式。另外,主从复合句、同位语、插入语的使用频率也较高。

10.2.3　结构紧凑　层次分明

科技论文描述的是较为复杂的事物、深奥的原理,要求准确、严密,所以必然要扩展句子的许多修饰、限定和附加成分,呈现"立体结构"。在篇章结构方面,科技论文组织严密,逻辑性强,文章的层次清楚,没有插叙、倒叙等情况,且在描述一项实验、论证问题时,常常采用比较固定的格式,如先是实验设计,再是实验过程、结果,最后是实验结论。行文模式化,框架结构固定。英语科技论文在文章的衔接与连贯方面,不仅大量使用指示词(如 it、this),也较多地使用衔接和连贯手段,还常常利用意义相同或相近的词组形式、词项复现等方式组织语篇,使论文的逻辑关系层次分明,篇章结构紧凑。

10.3　翻译要领

10.3.1　准确翻译专业术语

科技论文在内容、学科领域和功能上专业性很强,经常出现专业术语,因学科专业领域的不同而不同。在英语科技论文中,这些专业词汇的词根、前缀和后缀多来自于希腊语、拉丁语和法语,长度较长,如 semisomnus "半昏迷"、autoradiography "自动射线照相术"等;随着科技的发展,复合词不断出现,如 radiophotography "无线电传真"、oil film "油膜"等;缩略词使用较为频繁,如

FM "调频"、telesat "通信卫星"等。还有一些英语通用语中的词汇被应用于科技文体之中,具有了专业词汇的功能和特征,如 frame 在通用语中意为"框架",在机械领域指"机架",在通信领域指"帧"。

在汉译英语科技术语时,要结合传统的音译、意译、音义结合、形译、象译、增词等翻译方法,恰当地将英语科技术语翻译为主谓式、动宾式或偏正式等结构。如:

power supply 电力供应(主谓式)

flyover 立体交叉(偏正式)

pile driving 打桩(动宾式)

zinc-lead battery 铅锌电池(词序调整)

hormone 荷尔蒙(音译),激素(意译)

10.3.2 明确分析逻辑关系

翻译是以逻辑思维为基础的。在两种语言的相互转换中,基于逻辑规律的翻译就能准确通顺地表达原文的思想内容,就能为操这两种语言的人所普遍接受。科技文体讲究事实的可靠性和论证的逻辑性,所以对科技文章的翻译更应该注意从内容的逻辑关系上来理解原文的意义。如:"Shortly before the uninhabited space station reached orbit in May, 1973, aerodynamic pressure ripped off a meteoroid and heat shield." 这句的前半部分理解起来没有问题,主要的难点在于后半句。如果将其理解为"空气动力压力扯破了一个流星体和挡热板",就不符合事实和逻辑,因为无人空间站在运行过程中的空气动力产生的压力根本不可能与一颗流星体发生任何关系,否则后果将不堪设想。细看之下,meteoroid 和 heat 应该都是 shield 的定语,这个 shield 应该是被用来防护空间站受到流星体的撞击和穿越大气层时的高温的,因此可以译为"空气的压力扯破了一个防止流星体撞击和隔热的护罩"。

总之,在科技语篇中,一个词,一个短语,一个句子,都可能有几种不同的意思,因此要仔细分析,认真领会,根据语境把握彼此之间的逻辑关系,做到最为确切地理解和翻译。

10.3.3 准确简洁 整齐严密

① 准确性(Accuracy)。科技文章要求用词准确,在翻译时应尽量避免语义含糊不清和一词多义,表现出科技论文的权威性和专业性。如:离合器 clutch;明挖法 cut and cover method;送货上门 door-to-door transportation;dead air 静空气;cooling tower 冷却塔;condenser 冷凝器。

② 整齐性（Parallelism）。科技论文具有客观性、准确性和严密性，翻译时应采用合理的句子结构表现出这些特性。当一个句子有两个意义对等且语法功能相同的并列成分时，就应采用并列结构。

原文 制造方法可分为单件生产和批量生产，单件生产指小批量的生产，批量生产指大量相同零件的生产。

译文 Manufacturing processes may be classified as unit production with small quantities being made and mass production with large numbers of identical parts being produced.

原句中的"单件生产"和"批量生产"是两个并列成分，译文不但将两个概念并列，而且在每个概念后加上了with引导的短语进行修饰界定，在形式和内容上显得极为规整严密。

③ 简洁性（Conciseness）。科技英语往往将句子变成名词性短语，较少使用人称短语，体现了科技概念的客观性，并使行文流畅简洁。

原文 由于光学纤维频带较宽，损耗较低，光源更为可靠，因此在这一领域会更具竞争力。

译文 Larger fiber bandwidth, lower loss and more reliable optical sources would make optical fibers more competitive in this section.

译文将原文中的第一句话翻译成三个平行的名词性短语来做译文的主语，既体现了英语的行文特点，又显示出译文的简洁性。

④ 整体性（Wholeness）。科技论文的每个段落有一个主题，在形式和内容上形成了一个逻辑严密、衔接自然的有机整体，翻译时应该译出这种整体性。英语具有明显的"形合"特征，衔接词的使用必不可少。即使是一个小小语段的翻译，也应体现整体性原则。

原文 到2050年左右，土壤中细菌的碳释放量有可能大于林木的吸收量，地球会加速变暖。

译文 Around 2050, the amount of carbon released from the soil by bacteria would be greater than the amount soaked up by trees, and global warming would be accelerated.

译文中and具有很强的衔接性，不但使语法结构完整正确，而且使语义流畅，逻辑关系清楚。

10.4 常用词汇句型

① 有关状态、特性的句子：be +（形容词）+ 介词短语，或者 have/has + 名词。

② 句子中含有关涉意义的词（如"对于，关于"）：as for；as to；as far as... is concerned；so far as 等。

③ "这"字句：可译为由 which 引导的非限定性定语从句，或使用 it is... that/to do 结构。

④ "不是……而是……"：instead of being... be...；not that... but that...；not so much... as...；none other than 等。

⑤ 在主次并列句中，把主要动词译为谓语，次要动词译为非谓语动词、名词、介词短语或者从句。

⑥ 递进复句的翻译：not only... but (also)...；not only... but... too/not 等。

⑦ 选择复句的翻译：either... or...；whether... or...；otherwise；if not 等。

⑧ 解说复句中常用连词有"如，例如，即，就是说，总之"，可分别译为 for example/instance, such as, take... for example/instance; that is, that is to say, namely, in other words; in brief, in short, in conclusion, in a word, to sum up, 等等。

⑨ 目的复句中"要使，为了，以便，以免，以防"可译为：in order to；so as to；for；so that；in order that；lest；in case；for fear that，等等。

⑩ 英语条件句中常用 if，也可以用 provided/providing that；on condition that；suppose/supposing；granting/granted that；given that；with 等。

10.5 译文赏评

10.5.1 物理学论文

原文

The low-end challenge stems from molten salt's high freezing point. The mixture of molten potassium and sodium nitrate used in heat storage systems and in Enel's demo plant freezes when it cools below 220℃. Freezing is easy to prevent in centralized energy storage tanks, but presents a serious risk in kilometer-long stretches of collector tube. To counter the freezing threat, Enel's plant maintains the salt in its tubes above 290℃, using considerable heat that could otherwise be used to generate power. Mürau says Siemens is looking for a salt formulation with a 150℃ or lower freezing point, which would mean they'd have to use much less heat to prevent the tubes from freezing.

译文

　　低温方面的挑战缘自熔融盐的凝固温度很高。热量存储系统中以及意大利国家电力公司示范电厂所使用的熔融硝酸钾和硝酸钠混合液在温度低于220℃摄氏度时便会凝固。在集中式热量存储罐中凝固现象很容易预防，但在长达千米的太阳能集热管中却会形成严峻的威胁。为了防止凝固现象带来的威胁，意大利国家电力公司示范电厂为了维持集热管中的熔融盐温度高于290℃，需用到相当多的热量，而这些本可以用来发电。Mürau说西门子公司正在研发一种具有150℃或更低凝固度的盐配方，这意味着防止集热管凝固所需的热量将大大减少。

赏评

（1）在词汇层面上

　　① 专业术语。原文使用了大量专业术语，如potassium and sodium nitrate（熔融硝酸钾和硝酸钠），collector tube（太阳能集热管），salt（熔融盐），tube（集热管），译文译出了这些专业术语。

　　② 普通词汇专业化。tube本意为"管子"，此处专指"集热管"；salt本意为"盐，食盐"，此处指"熔融盐"。

　　③ 复合名词。原文在用词上的另一个特点是复合名词的使用，如：energy storage，而不是the storage of energy。复合名词的使用可以使文字紧凑利落，结构简洁。译文也相应地保留了原文紧凑的表达方式，将其译为"热量存储""盐配方"。

（2）在语法层面上

　　译文的表达欠缺明晰的逻辑，如"需用到相当多的热量，而这些本可以用来发电"，对长句的切分不明晰，语句也欠通顺。

（3）在篇章结构上

　　原文文章组织严谨，层次清楚，逻辑性强。第一句话"The low-end challenge stems from molten salt's high freezing point."概括了这段文字的中心意思，译文"低温方面的挑战缘自熔融盐的凝固温度很高。"也比较准确，之后进一步分析阐述了造成这个问题的原因和规避的办法。

10.5.2 生物医学论文

原文

面向生物医学仿真的表面重建和四面体化技术研究

随着生物医学和计算机应用技术的不断发展与相互结合,生物医学仿真系统的研究与开发已经逐渐渗透到现代医学的各个方面。其中比较典型的例子是以虚拟手术系统为代表的相关课题研究。虚拟手术系统从医学图像数据出发,在计算机中构造出生物组织空间模型,创造虚拟医学环境,并仿真各种交互式手术过程,让用户产生一种身临其境的体验和感觉。虚拟手术系统在培训、导航以及术前预测等方面优于传统手术,具备无污染、可重复利用和低消耗等特点,已成为学术及应用领域的研究热点之一。

以虚拟手术系统为代表的生物医学仿真涉及医学图像处理、计算机图形学、计算几何以及生物力学等诸多学科,是一个综合性较强的研究领域。针对不同的生物组织和仿真内容,需要重点研究的方面也存在差异,本文试图从较为通用的角度提出实现该系统的整体架构和关键技术。重点研究生物组织的几何建模技术,包括表面重建技术、通用并行计算架构(CUDA)下的交互式建模技术以及 Delaunay 三角化/四面化技术。

以虚拟内窥镜手术为背景,面向培训学员、专家以及研究人员,提出了生物医学仿真系统的整体架构并探讨了其中的关键技术。从仿真任务对实时性和真实性的不同要求出发,设计了通用的几何建模方案,同时满足系统对表面模型和四面体实体模型的双重需求。

对于生物组织表面重建技术,从拓扑和质量两个方面对 Marching Cubes(MC)算法进行了研究与改进。首先以 33 种扩展剖分模式和双曲线渐近线判别法为基础,通过构建二义性检测索引表,以简单统一的方式同时解决 MC 算法的面二义性和体二义性问题,得到了拓扑正确的表面模型;然后引入单体素和基于边组的质量分析方法,从根本上解释 MC 算法生成劣质单元的原因,在此基础上结合二义性检测索引表,提出扩展模式下的点偏移策略改进网格质量,得到了高质量且拓扑正确的表面模型。

在实时性建模方面,以交互式表面重建为目的,在保证网格质量的基础上,引入图形处理器中的 CUDA 架构,提出了两种 MC 改进算法。首先改进点偏移策略,使其适应 CUDA 并行模式,通过活跃体素和活跃边的并行提取、交点的并行计算等方式快速生成高质量表面模型;然后以边组概念为理论依据,采用改变三角剖分索引表的方式代替点偏移进行并行计算,将 MC 算法完全移植到图形处理器中执行,达到了高质量交互式建模的目的。

在四面体实体建模方面,从理论和实验出发,对 Delaunay refinement 算法进行研究与改进。首先以真实性为主要目的,以 MC 算法得到的三角表面为边界限定条件,提出了基于非弱相关点的改进算法,适度放松输入域的角度限制,并从理论上保证算法的收敛性。然后,从实时性和执行能力出发,设计面向四面体网格生成的 Delaunay 表面重建方法,针对等值面数据量庞大的问题,引入网格简化技术,提出了基于重心射线法的冗余网格去除方法对初始表面进行预处理,得到了单元数目适中的多面体表面,以四面体实体建模为目的,提出了基于限定点保护球的 Delaunay refinement 改进算法,对预处理后的模型进行重构,使其满足 Delaunay 准则,并从理论和实验两方面证实该方法的收敛性和有效性。

译文

Research on Surface Reconstruction and Tetrahedral Technology for Biomedical Simulation

With the fast development of biomedical engineering and computer application technology, the research and development of biomedical simulation system has gradually penetrated into the various aspects of modern medicine. The study of virtual surgery system is a typical illustration. Virtual surgery is an application of virtual reality in modern medicine. It can present real reappearance of the operation for user by vision and force feed back. Compared with conventional surgery, virtual surgery system has many advantages such as pollution-free, reusable, low consumption and so on that is why it has become a hot topic in the academic and application fields.

Biomedical simulation is a field in which multi-subject cooperate with each other, including medical image processing, computational geometry, biomechanics, and so on. For different biological tissues and simulation tasks, we need to focus on different research contents. In this thesis, the general architecture and key technologies are proposed for biomedical simulation system. Then, we make an intensive study of geometric modeling techniques for deformation and cutting simulation of biological tissues. The specific contents are surface reconstruction techniques, interactive modeling techniques under CUDA and Delaunay tetrahedral techniques.

Under the background of virtual endoscopic surgery, a full suite of development architecture is designed for trainees, experts and researchers. Key technologies are also discussed such as geometric modeling, deformation simulation, cutting simulation, collision detection, suture knot simulation and so on. In particular, for the balance between the realism and real-time, a general geometric modeling program is developed to meet the surface triangle modeling and tetrahedral modeling.

In the terms of surface reconstruction techniques, two improved Marching Cubes (MC) algorithm are presented to solve the problems about the ambiguity and generate mesh with high quality. Firstly, ambiguity-detection index tables are constructed based on 33 cases. Asymptotic decider based on face state is then proposed to solve the two classes of the ambiguity and generate surface model with correct topologies. Secondly, according to the analysis of degenerate triangle generated in a single voxel, a novel improved strategy called data offset is proposed to improve the mesh quality. Combined with ambiguity-detection index tables and face state based asymptotic decider, this improved method generates surface with correct topologies and high quality which can be used for further numerical analysis as well as visualization.

In the terms of real-time modeling, the CUDA architecture is introduced to meet the purpose of interactive surface modeling with high quality. Firstly, an improved data offset MC is proposed to adapt to the CUDA parallel programming model. In this method, the computations of active voxels, active edges and intersections are all designed in parallel modes. Then, another improved MC based on edge group is proposed to change the triangulation lookup table. Compared with the previous algorithm, this method transplants the MC to CUDA perfectly and meets the requirements for interactive surface modeling.

In the terms of tetrahedral mesh generation, two kinds of improved Delaunay refinement algorithms are proposed based on theories and experiments. Firstly, an improved method based on non-weak correlation points is proposed to meet the realism. This method takes the surface generated by MC as boundary constraints and relaxes the limitation of the input angle. Importantly, we present a strict proof for the convergence of this algorithm. Secondly, taking into account the real-time and feasibility, a novel Delaunay refinement remeshing method is presented based on simplified organ surface to meet the Delaunay surface triangle modeling and Delaunay tetrahedral modeling. In this method, the initial surface is preprocessed to create polyhedron representation of the domain including mesh simplification and internal redundant mesh deletion. Then a vertex protected sphere based Delaunay refinement algorithm is proposed to remesh the polyhedron and make it meet the Delaunay criteria. The convergence and effectiveness can be guaranteed by theoretical proof and some experiments.

赏评

本文选自一篇信息科学与工程学方面的博士论文，是典型的科技文体，具有很强的专业性。

原文主题明确，结构层次十分清晰，既使用了描述性语言对研究方法和过程进行说明，又大量地运用信息性语言对研究的主要内容，尤其是研究的结果进行了列举。句式虽然较为单一，但信息量极大，使用了大量的专业术语和客观数据，翻译起来难度较大。总体来说，译文基本做到了完整的信息处理；采用了变译或增减法等手段，句式结构基本符合英语科技文体的特点。

但是，译文中也存在一些问题。如：原文第二段"本文试图从较为通用的角度提出实现该系统的整体架构和关键技术"，译文中采用了被动句式"In this thesis, the general architecture and key technologies are proposed for biomedical simulation system."，符合科技论文注重客观性的特点。但是接下来的一句"重点研究生物组织的几何建模技术，包括表面重建技术、通用并行计算架构（CUDA）下的交互式建模技术以及 Delaunay 三角化/四面化技术"，译者将其译为"Then, we make an intensive study of geometric modeling techniques for deformation and cutting simulation of biological tissues..."，没有延续上一句的被动句式，而是转而使用了主动句式，没有遵循科技论文客观、科学的本质要求，在语法上也破坏了逻辑连续性，使得上下两句出现了被动、主动句式的混用，读者在理解上产生了跳跃。两个句式的混用，显示了文体的不一致并导致了意义上的模糊。

原文第一段第四句"虚拟手术系统在培训、导航以及术前预测等方面……的研究热点之一"未译出；译文第三段第二句"Key technologies are also discussed such as geometric modeling, deformation simulation, cutting simulation, collision detection, suture knot simulation and so on." 是原文中没有提及的内容；译文第四段第一句"... two improved Marching Cubes (MC) algorithm are presented to solve the problems about the ambiguity and generate mesh with high quality." 与原文不一致。

10.6 课后练习

（1）

A case study of teachers' implementation of curriculum innovation in English language teaching in Turkish primary education

This article reports a 2-year case study (2003–2005) on teachers' instructional practices, and the impact of teacher understandings and training upon the teachers' implementation of the Communicative Oriented Curriculum (COC) initiative in the context of a major curriculum innovation in teaching English to young learners in Turkish state schools. Using multidimensional qualitative research procedures, comprising classroom observations, teacher interviews and lesson transcripts, a picture is developed of how 32 teachers implemented COC. Results showed that teachers' instructional practices ranged along the transmission and interpretation teaching continuum, and teachers' understandings and their prior training had an impact on the extent of their implementation of the curriculum initiative. The study highlights the need to provide continuous teacher training and teacher development opportunities, particularly during the critical first few years of the innovation process to promote the implementation of curriculum innovation in Turkish primary education.

（2）

《中国名园》英译策略探讨

　　本文通过聚焦《中国名园》英译本的术语翻译诠释了翻译宏观定位与微观策略的关系。作者主张翻译策略的制定应以文本翻译的宏观定位为前提，并通过该书案例分析进一步诠释了这一观点。该书的翻译定位为看得懂、品得出、找得到，据此衍生出准确性、写意性和识别性的术语翻译策略。文中以"廊""静观"和"动观"以及专有园林名词的英译为案例，演绎了该书如何践行以上翻译策略，以期对专业术语翻译的实践和理论研究有所启发。

第 11 章 报告

报告文体与翻译

报告是对某一课题进行分析研究、调查评估所形成的正式书面文字材料，它广泛应用于商务、科研等领域。报告分为信息类报告和分析类报告，内容一般包括摘要、引言、讨论和结论四个部分。

报告应用广泛，种类繁多。主要包括调查报告、评估报告、可行性报告、论文的开题报告等。报告专业性强，含有大量专业术语，形式多变，结构复杂，多长句，给翻译造成了一定困难。因此，在翻译报告时，要正确判断报告的语域取向，把握好报告的结构特点，厘清长句逻辑，并掌握专业术语的含义。

本章学习了解报告的文体特点、翻译策略和常用句型结构，经过翻译实践练习，能够对报告进行恰当得体的翻译。

11.1 课前实践

11.1.1 实验报告

Laboratory Report on Vitamin C

[1] Purpose: In this laboratory you will learn to use the back titration procedure to analyze an unknown juice sample for the concentration of Vitamin C.

[2] Introduction: Vitamin C (or ascorbic acid), is a vitamin commonly found in fruits and vegetable which serves a wide variety

维生素 C 实验报告

[1] 目的：本次实验将学习用返滴定过程来分析一份未知果汁样品中的维生素 C 的浓度。

[2] 引言：维生素 C（亦称抗坏血酸），是一种广泛存在于水果和蔬菜中、含有多种多样生物化学作用的维生素。维生素 C

of biochemical functions. Vitamin C is a compound that is easily oxidized, and is therefore a good reducing agent. Because it is preferentially oxidized in the body, it serves as an antioxidant, protecting other substances in the body from oxidation. Recent studies suggest that antioxidant properties of Vitamin C are important part of its cancer fighting ability. Its formula is $C_6H_8O_6$. [3] Procedure: In this lab, you will be working individually. (1) Preparation and standardization of sodium thiosulfate (2) Analysis of an unknown sample (3) Analysis of Vitamin C in juice (4) Analysis and report	是一种容易被氧化的复合物，因此它是一种很好的还原剂。由于它在身体里优先被氧化，作为一种抗氧化剂，它保护身体里的其他物质不被氧化。近期研究表明抗氧化剂维生素C的性质是抗癌的一个重要部分。它的分子式是 $C_6H_8O_6$。 [3] 步骤：本次实验，由一个人操作。 （1）准备和标定 $Na_2S_2O_3$ （2）未知样品的分析 （3）果汁中维生素C的分析 （4）分析和报告

11.1.2 研究报告

中国高端人群消费行为研究报告（节选）	The Research Report on China's High-end Consumption Behavior (Excerpt)
[1] 为更好地理解中国高端人群的消费特征及其奢侈品消费行为，2009年5—7月期间，我们专门进行了高端人群的调查。采取网络预约的调查方式，调查对象选取一线城市北京、上海、广州作为初次调查的试点，最终采集有效样本648份。 [2] 一、高端消费人群的总体特征	[1] In order to better understand the consumption characteristics of China's high-end consumers and the consumer behavior, during May to July 2009, Market Research specifically carried out a survey on the high-end consumers. Through invited online survey, 648 valid samples were finally collected from the initially selected pilots first-tier cities, Beijing, Shanghai and Guangzhou. [2] I. General characteristics of high-end consumers

调查数据显示，中国高端消费人群呈以下特征：
1. 年轻化特征凸显
2. 女性消费者为主
3. 受到了良好教育
4. 企业的管理层居多

[3] 二、汽车产品

汽车作为一类重要的奢侈品，必将是高端消费人群不可或缺的，也是汽车厂家进行激烈竞争的重要领域。

The survey data showed that the high-end consumers in China have the following characteristics:
1. Remarkably young
2. Mainly women
3. Well educated
4. Mostly belong to the corporate management

[3] II. Auto products

As a type of important luxury products, automobile is indispensable for the high-end consumers and it is also a key area of intensive competition for the auto-makers.

11.1.3 总结报告

参加1996年秋季广交会的总结报告

Report and Recommendations based on Experiences at the 1996 Autumn Fair in Guangzhou

[1] 今年是我公司第六次参加秋季广交会。我们一向认为参展极有好处，既可以展示我们的特色产品，同时，也可以观察国内外其他生产厂家的动向。

[2] 根据我在今年展销会上的观察，塑料生产工艺出现两个重大变化：第一，竞争明显激烈，尤其是来自日本公司的竞争。很多摊位比我们公司的摊位

[1] This year was the sixth successive time that we have been represented at the annual Guangzhou Fair. We have always felt that it is useful in a general way to attend, to display a representative sample of our products and—not least—to have a look at what other manufacturers, both at home and abroad, are producing.

[2] According to my observation at this year's exhibition, there are two important developments in plastic manufacturing industry. First is that the competition, especially from Japanese companies, has

大，而且人员配备阵容强大。第二，很多客户及可望成为我们的客户，都要求了解有关产品的技术参数与指标。在此次展销会上，好几次出现这种情况，而我们的工作人员却无法提供确切的资料。

[3] 鉴于此，我想提两点建议供考虑，以使将来的参展收效更大。首先，应扩大我公司的摊位，增强阵容，以便与其他公司竞争。第二，参展工作人员应该至少包括一名技术专家，以便现场回答顾客的咨询。

[4] 欢迎对以上建议提出意见。

销售经理 高宇
1996 年 10 月 30 日

grown considerably, and several foreign stands were larger and better staffed than ours. Second, our customers and potential customers are increasingly demanding—as happened on several occasions during this exhibition—technical details and specifications which the people on our stand were unable to supply.

[3] I would therefore like to make two suggestions, which should be considered with a view to making our presence more effective at future exhibitions. First, the stand should be larger so as to make a greater impact and to keep up with our competitions. Second, the staffing should always include at least one of our technical experts, preferably a senior one, so that we can give on-the-spot advice to our potential customers.

[4] I would be pleased to hear reactions to these suggestions.

Gao Yu
Sales Manager

11.2 文体特点

11.2.1 词义丰富 句式灵活

由于报告具有鲜明的行业属性，属于书面语体，因此往往赋予普通词汇以专业意义，英语报告多使用长句、被动句、形式主语等，既能使报告内容通俗易懂，又能体现报告严谨客观求实的特点。

11.2.2 大量使用缩略语、数字 句式结构逻辑严密

报告的读者一般都是专业人士、专家或某公司、机构、组织中的关键人物，报告的具体内容涉及专业内容较多，报告双方都已熟悉和了解相关语境，所以报告中缩略语的出现频率很高。由于报告涉及的数据、事实、问题、说明、论证和建议

等都是通过多方面的调研和考察所得出的，因而具有准确、明白、科学、严谨的特点。如：LREC doesn't mean Language Resources and Evaluation Committee or Conference（语言资源与测评委员会 / 会议）as in the dictionary, but means Language Skills, Regional Expertise and Cultural Awareness（外语能力、区域知识和文化意识）。F14 starts the "calibration function"（F14 开启校准功能）；F16 opens the window "sampling cleaning"（F16 打开取样清洁窗口），F14、F16 这些数列表示按钮顺序。

11.2.3　行业特色显化　术语使用频率高

报告内容涉及各类专业，具有明显的语域特征，所涉及的专业知识繁多，大量使用专业性很强的词语和术语，比如教育调研报告中就涉及一定的教育学术语，如"课程设置""市场需求""MTI（翻译专业硕士）口译""实践教学"等。其他如机械、医学、生物、化工等报告都会涉及该行业的术语。

11.3　翻译要领

11.3.1　准确明晰　简洁客观

报告属于专用科技类文体，有准确、明晰、简洁的特点。客观是报告类文体翻译的首要原则。准确是指用词准确无误，科技文体要求用词恰当、准确，避免使用歧义、模糊词。明晰是指译文语言表述的质量。中文属"意合型"语言，不善使用表示句子逻辑关系的连接词和衔接手段，而英语属"形合型"语言，句子结构紧凑，往往依赖连接词显示句与句之间的逻辑关系，因而使得句子关系清晰、明确。报告篇幅一般较学术论文短，简洁是其基本特色之一。无论是调研报告、可行性报告，还是实践报告、项目报告等，都会大量使用事实、数据、图表等说明内容，因而具有客观性和科学性。如：ultrasonic hot-melt technology（超声波热熔技术）；color developing agent（显色剂）；thermal expansion coefficient（热膨胀系数）。

原文 模温过高会导致硫化，从而引起流动受阻。

译文 If the mold temperature is too high, it will lead to the vulcanization of silicone rubber, which will cause interruption to the circulation.

该句译文加入了连词 if 和 which，使得该句的逻辑关系非常清楚。

由于报告描述的内容具有客观性和科学性，相应地，译文语言也要符合其客观事实和物质属性。在报告翻译中，常常通过使用被动语态、长句等来达到这一目的。

原文 采用研究所开发的水质净化技术，即两级沙滤和一级高分子膜过滤。

译文 The water purification technology developed by the institute is adopted, including two levels of the sand filter and level of polymer membrane filtration.

译文采用了被动句式，使得对原句内容的表述客观，不带主观性。

11.3.2　长句复杂　调整句式

英汉报告的文体比较正式，所以较多用结构复杂的句子，以使句式规范。由于中英文在表达方式上的差异，在翻译复杂句子时，可以采用句式调整法，使译文更符合译入语的语言特点。

原文 公司在转换经营机制的同时，紧紧围绕主业，开拓相关业务，深化内部改革，实行单车承包，坚持从严管理，实行规范服务，使公司的各项经营指标得以全面完成。

译文 Effective measures have been taken while our company is undergoing a change of its management system: we have expanded our business to other areas related to our main business-taxi service; we have also carried out a new employment system in which a taxi is contracted to the individual driver and his income is related to his turnover; in addition, we have insisted on strict management and quality service. As a result, we have reached all our business targets.

原文中，6个动词性短语把句子的意思紧密地联系在一起，按照汉语的句式直译，会出现很多 and，使译文显得极其不自然，译文通过句式的变换使表达更流畅。

原文 With the development of regional economy and group economy, however, it is inevitable that the developing countries including China will have more frictions and conflicts with the developed countries or the regional economic groups.

译文 然而随着区域经济和集团经济的发展，包括中国在内的发展中国家不可避免地会与发达国家及区域经济集团产生更多摩擦和冲突。

原文句子结构复杂，句式规范，语言正式，而且运用了英语表达中常用的"it is + adj. + that"的句型，在翻译的时候，要充分考虑到中英文在表达方式上的差异。

11.3.3　语域明显　风格对等

翻译就是要在目标语言中重构原语言信息的自然对等，这种自然对等首先是在意义方面，其次是在风格方面。（Nida，1982）但是，要在译语中重构原作的风格，我们必须首先识别原作的风格。"就语际转换而言，对原语的风格分析工作至关重要，它是理解阶段的基本任务之一。忽视对原语风格的分析，就谈不上对原作全部意义的把握。"（刘宓庆，2012：23）

语域是情景的具体体现（Halliday，1978）。报告涉及的行业领域广泛，其文本语言随着使用场合环境不同而产生不同的语言变体，带有明显的专业特征。根据题材或话语范围，报告的语域可以细分为政府工作报告、实验报告、法律（或各类调查报告、研究报告等。这些报告涉及的语域都有各自的不同专业特征，如政治题材的文章语言庄重规范，结构严谨，长句多，句子的扩展大，逻辑性强，语言冗赘现象少，采用正规或极正规的文体；科技类英文报告准确凝练、客观冷静、逻辑严密、术语丰富、从句叠套、有名词化倾向、广泛使用被动语态和一般现在时；法律类英文报告力求内容准确、文字简洁和文章结构清晰。

因此，在翻译的过程中，为了使报告的内容通达、易懂，符合行业规范，要明确各行业领域背景，了解各行业的专业内涵和专门用语，把握不同语域的语场、语旨、语式，准确翻译术语，保持文本与专业术语翻译的一致性。

（1）语场对等

语场涉及话语的主题，不同的主题选词有所不同。因此，语场信息主要显现在词汇层面上，而在不同领域主题和情境中选择合适的词汇对实现语场对等来说尤为关键。在不同语域文本的翻译中，首先要仔细分析原文的选词特点并在译文中恰当选词，使译文充分再现原文的语场特征。

（2）语旨对等

语旨体现讲话者间的人际关系、社会角色及地位。在报告翻译中译者也应充分分析原文的语旨信息，使其在译文中得到再现。讲话者间的人际关系可以通过不同称谓及语气词汇的使用恰当表现出来。如：

原文 6.0.1 The CONTRACTOR shall ensure all performance parameters are understood, engineered, executed, commissioned and handed over to the OWNER complete in all respects. The scope of supply and services, technical and other requirements, design philosophies, material and equipment qualities, construction, inspection, testing, packing and transport, standards and codes and the like as defined by the following, are to be understood as minimum requirements. In case of discrepancies between different chapters or sections of the RFP, the BIDDER shall ask for OWNER's advice or the more demanding option shall prevail.

译文 6.0.1 承包商应确保所有的性能参数具有可读性、可设计性、可建造性、可执行性和可调试性，并将各方面完整地交付给业主。供应和服务的范围、技术及其他要求、设计原理、材料及设备质量、施工、检查、测试、包装运输、标准及规范及类似如下界定的内容应为理解的最低要求。如标书的不同章节有不一致之处，投标者应征询业主意见，或采用要求更高的选择。

contractor、owner 和 bidder 的运用反映出承标者与投标者间的密切关系，这是原文的语旨。译文选用了"承包商""业主"和"投标者"三个词，体现出报告对各方关系的清晰界定及报告逻辑的严谨性和明确性。译文表现出来的这种明确的人际关系不仅是原文语旨的再现,也有利于激发双方的情感,最终实现报告被接受的目的。

（3）语式对等

语式主要指话语交际的渠道,口头的还是书面的,同时也包括修辞手段的运用,而这些特征主要体现在语篇层面上。因此,在报告翻译中译者也应从语篇的角度充分分析原文的语式特征,使其在译文中得到再现。如：

原文 万众一心

译文 Million people united as one man

这个四字成语的翻译采用的是异化翻译法。其语式信息主要体现在修辞手段的运用上。作者将"万"与"一"对照,用来比喻"人心齐,泰山移"的意思,在译文中译者运用了比喻的修辞手段,重现了原文的语式信息。修辞手段的再现不仅实现了译文和原文的语式对等,还保留了原文语言的艺术美感。

11.4 常用词汇句型

① 表示报告的背景和报告要讨论的问题 The aim/purpose/objective of this report is to...

② 表示报告所显示的调查结果 According to the recent market research/investigation/survey/chart above/table above

③ 表示报告得出的结论 It was decided/agreed/felt that...

也可以直接陈述结果：Based on/according to the findings above, it can be concluded that...

④ 表示在报告中,收集信息或资料的方法和步骤 The information is mainly achieved by...

⑤ 表示报告提供图表统计数据来描述行情走势 The table/chart/grape/diagram/figure/statistics shows/describes/illustrates that...

⑥ 抽样调查 do a sample investigation on...

⑦ 对某一种现象的描述 In the past few decades, there is a marketed increase/decrease in...

⑧ 提出建议 It is suggested/proposed/recommended that...

11.5 译文赏评

11.5.1 政府报告

原文

2017 年荆州市人民政府工作报告

——2017 年 1 月 7 日在荆州市第五届人民代表大会第一次会议上的发言

市长 杨智

各位代表：

  现在，我代表市人民政府向大会做工作报告，请予审议，并请各位政协委员和列席人员提出意见。

  一、2016 年和过去六年工作回顾

  2016 年，是"十三五"的开局之年，也是壮腰工程"五年大跨越"的见效之年。面对经济下行压力和特大洪涝灾害双重考验，在省委、省政府和市委领导下，在市人大和市政协的监督支持下，我们团结全市人民，深入贯彻落实习近平总书记系列重要讲话精神，主动适应经济发展新常态，负重奋进、砥砺前行，经济社会发展呈现"稳中有进"的良好态势。初步核算，实现地区生产总值 1726.8 亿元、增长 7.3%。完成固定资产投资 2001 亿元、增长 18%；规模以上工业增加值增长 6.8%；社会消费品零售总额 1056 亿元、增长 11.6%；地方公共财政预算收入 115.45 亿元、增长 11.6%；城乡居民人均可支配收入分别达到 2.75 万元、1.59 万元，增长 8.5% 和 8%。

  ……

  各项改革稳步推进。建立"四单一网"。清理规范"红顶中介"215 家。推进荆州开发区"一区多园"管理体制改革。深化投融资体制改革和国企改革，南湖机械与中国航天科工实现重组联合。"营改增"全面完成，国地税征管合作机制改革领跑全省。党政群机关公车改革基本完成。机关事业单位养老保险制度改革顺利推进。不动产登记发证实现全覆盖。

  ……

  农业固本提质。全力抗灾复产，粮食提质稳产的基础进一步巩固。淡水产品、油菜籽产量保持全国市州第一。农产品加工业总产值 1550 亿元，规模以上企业净增 30 家、达到 542 家。新型农业经营主体 4.2 万个，总量全省第一。"荆楚味道"走俏湖北、迈向全国。有效使用的"三品一标"产品达到 429 个。省水产产业技术研究院落户荆州。华中农高区争创国家级农高区取得进展。洪湖市获评"中国名蟹第一市"。松滋市荣获国家农产品质量安全示范市。

译文

Report on the Work of Jingzhou Municipal Government
—Delivered at the First Session of the 5th Jingzhou Municipal People's Congress January 7, 2017

Mayor Yang Zhi

Fellow Deputies,

On behalf of the Municipal People's Government, I now report to you on the work of the government and ask for your deliberation and approval, and I also wish to have comments on my report from the members of Jingzhou Municipal Committee of Chinese People's Political Consultative Conference (CPPCC).

Let me begin with a review of our work in 2016.

The last year 2016, a great start of the 13th Five-Year Plan (2016–2020), witnessed our city's achievements in Strong Waist Project. In the past year, we faced interwoven challenges of mounting downward pressure on the economy and grave flooding disaster, however, under the firm leadership of the CPC (Communist Party of China) Provincial Committee, the Provincial Government and the CPC Municipal Committee, relying on the supervision and support of the Municipal People's Congress and the CPPCC Municipal Committee, with the joint efforts of all the people in our city, the Municipal Government comprehensively implemented the guiding principles of General Secretary Xi Jinping's major speeches; adapted to the new normal in economic development, we the Jingzhou people have risen to the challenge and worked hard to press ahead, driving forward a stable performance with good momentum for growth. In 2016, the gross domestic product (GDP) reached 172.68 billion yuan, rose by 7.3% over the previous year, the input in fixed assets exceeded 200.1 billion yuan, an increase of 18% and the added value of industries above a designated scale saw a 6.8% year-on-year rise, the total retail sales of consumer goods reached 105.6 billion yuan, representing 11.6% growth, the public finance budgeted revenue reached 11.545 billion yuan with an 11.6% increase. Urban per capita disposable income and rural per capita net income reached 27,500 yuan and 15,900 yuan, increased by 8.5% and 8% respectively.

...

Continued advances were made in all reforms. We established a system of "four lists and a network", the four lists refers to the power lists, the negative list of enterprise investment projects, the management list of financial special funds, the lists of responsibilities, the network means the government service network. 215 items of intermediary services Red Top Meditation were overhauled and standardized. We pushed ahead with the reform of "Multi-garden Park" management system in Jingzhou development zone. We stepped up work to investment and financing system reform and SOEs reform. The reorganization and restructuring of Aerospace Nanhu Electronic Information Technology Corporation and China Aerospace Science&Industry Corporation was achieved. The replacement of business tax with value added tax was extended to cover all sectors, the reform of office cars in parties, government, institutions was almost accomplished. We advanced reform of the old-age insurance system in office and institution. We formulated unified measures to register and certificate immovable property in all sectors.

...

In agriculture, we consolidated the foundation while raised quality. We do our all to provide effective rescue and relief to recover production and we had stable production with high quality. The production of fresh water products and rapeseed ranked first among cities around the country. The total value of agricultural products processing reached 155 billion yuan, the number of enterprises above a designated scale reached 542, including 30 new ones, and the number of new agricultural operating entities developed into 42,000, ranked first in Hubei Province. The flavor of Jingchu became famous in Hubei Province, setting pace towards the country. The number of in-force "three products and one brand", the pollution-free agricultural products, green products, organic agricultural products, special Chinese regional brand products passed 429 marks. Fisheries Research Institute of Hubei settled in Jingzhou. The Central China Agriculture High-tech Industry Development Zone made progress in developing national-class high-tech agriculture zone. Honghu city was regarded as the famous crab city in China. Songzi city won the title of national agricultural products quality demonstration city.

赏评

本例文选自一篇地方政府年度工作总结报告——《2017年荆州市人民政府工作报告》，是有关政府工作问题的题材。地方政府工作报告是地方政府向当地群众报告其工作状态的正式文本，内容涉及各类行业，专业知识繁多，大量使用数据、术语。语场正规，语旨严肃，语式复杂。原文语场是政府工作背景，语式涉及各级政府工作人员。

① 数据频现。本篇报告中有大量的专业数据。如："完成固定资产投资2001亿元、增长18%；规模以上工业增加值增长6.8%；社会消费品零售总额1056亿元、增长11.6%；地方公共财政预算收入115.45亿元、增长11.6%；城乡居民人均可支

配收入分别达到 2.75 万元、1.59 万元,增长 8.5% 和 8%",包含大量经济类数据和术语,句式采用并列陈述的方式,给人一气呵成、翔实、客观的感觉,译文沿用了原文的句式表述方法,把各项数据以并列句的方式,客观、准确地呈现在了读者面前。

② 一义多词,句式灵活。报告中对于各项工作的数据汇报使用了大量的动词,如:原文第三段中"增长"一词出现了 6 次。译文为了表达生动准确,选择了 6 种不同的英文表达:rose by, an increase of, saw a... rise, representing... growth, with an... increase。

③ 语态转换。原文"各项改革稳步推进"一句隐去了主语"政府",但句子逻辑关系依然清晰。译文则通过将其转换成被动语态,保留了原文主语的地位,译为"Continued advances were made in all reforms.",逻辑清晰,读者一看便懂。

11.5.2 调查报告

原文

2018 China Business Climate Survey Report

(Section One) Closing the Books on 2017

2017 was a good year financially to many AmCham China members. Some 64% member companies reported revenue growth in 2017, up from 58% last year and 55% in 2015. Only a record-low 7% reported a revenue decline. The Industrial&Resources and Consumer sectors enjoyed especially strong results. Profitability is climbing too, with nearly three-quarters of respondents reporting that they are profitable—the highest proportion in the last three years—and 51% reporting expanding EBIT margins. Such results reflect the relatively strong performance of the Chinese economy in 2017.

Revenue Growth hit its best level since 2014, with 64% reporting a rise in revenue and a record-low 7% recording a revenue decline. Employers wish at least 250 employees were more likely than smaller companies to see revenue growth.

Profitability rose for the second year in a row, with 73% respondents describing 2017 as a profitable year for them in China. Like revenue growth, profitability was strongest among large employers (>250), with 83% reporting a net profit for the year, compared with 57% of small employers.

第 11 章 报告

译文

2018 年度中国商务环境调查报告

第一部分 2017 年业绩盘点

2017 年企业财务状况不错，许多商会会员企业表示业绩有所回升。2017 年约有 64% 的会员企业收入有所增长，2016 年为 58%，2015 年为 55%。2017 年，只有 7% 的会员企业收入有所下滑，创历史新低。在工业、资源行业和消费行业的企业，盈利增长尤为迅猛。企业盈利能力也在攀升，近 75% 的受访企业表示实现盈利——这是过去三年比例最高的一次，有 51% 的受访企业表示息税前利润率持续长。上述结果也与中国经济 2017 年的优异表现相吻合。

收入增长达到 2014 年以来的最高值，64% 的会员企业表示收入上升，仅 7% 表示收入下滑，创历史新低。相比更小的企业而言，员工规模在 250 人以上的企业更可能实现收入增长。

盈利能力连续两年上升，73% 的受访企业表示，2017 年在华经营实现盈利。与收入增长相似，大型企业（员工人数在 250 人以上）的盈利能力最强，83% 的大型企业报告实现净利润，小型企业仅有 57% 实现净利润。

赏评

该调查报告属于商务专业领域，其语场为在华中美商务环境状况，语旨为中美商会及企业公司与中国市场的关系，语式是书面语，以大量数据说明目前中国商务环境状况，是对获取的情况和事实进行分析论证而写出的书面报告，具有内容翔实、逻辑性强和写实性特点。译文在很大程度上忠实地再现了原文的信息，意思表达较为正确，语体正式。

① 第一段呈现出了很多数据对比，以说明调查的准确性和专业性，译文把这些数据对比清晰地再现给了读者。

② 本例充分体现了汉英两种语言在表达方式上的不同：汉语靠意合，英语靠形合，因此在进行翻译的时候，为了达到功能对等，译者适当地对句式进行了调整，是一篇不错的译文。

11.6 课后练习

（1）调查报告

杭州市农村劳动力资源调查报告
杭州市农村劳动力调查报告课题组

一、我市农村劳动力资源总体状况

本报告所称农村劳动力，是指农村劳动年龄段内（男性 16—60 岁，女性 16—60 岁）常住人口。鉴于农村在校学生今后就业去向的不确定性，未将其列入本次统计分析范围。

调查显示，截止调查标准时点（2005 年 10 月 31 日），杭州市农村劳动力共计 1 978 517 人，其中男性 1 133 695 人，占 57.3%；女性 844 822 人，占 42.7%。我市农村劳动力中，98.9% 身体健康，具备完全劳动能力；72.8% 为 45 岁以下的青壮年劳动力；95.2% 已实现就业，参与各类社会经济活动。其中共产党员 3.58 万人，占总数的 1.8%；共青团员 2.24 万人，占总数的 1.1%；民主党派 8105 人，占总数的 0.4%。

调查统计，全市农村劳动力共有 1 587 710 人参加了一项或多项社会保险，占农村劳动力总数的 80.2%，其中参加城镇基本养老保险的 211 893 人，参加农村养老保险的 29 816 人，参加农村合作医疗 1 230 297 人。另有 193 481 人参加了其他保险。

调查显示，杭州市农村劳动力年收入为 1550 元（农村低保）以下的有 52 215 人，占农村劳动力总数的 2.64%；年收入为 1560—2520 元（城镇低保为 2520 元/年）的有 75 620 人，占 3.87%；年收入为 2520—7440 元（2005 年市最低工资为 7440 元/年）的有 462 729 人，占 23.39%；年收入为 7440—22 235 元（2005

年市平均工资为 22 235 元/年）的有 872 787 人，占 44.11%；年收入在 22 236 元及以上的有 64 736 人，占 3.27%。

调查发现，我市农村劳动力收入构成趋于多元化，农村劳动力的经济来源中，28.6% 来自务工，21.8% 来自务农，0.5% 来自房屋出租，6.9% 来自经商，42.2% 来自其他。也就是说，有 78.2% 的收入来自非农收入。由于调查对象的"藏富"心理，农村劳动力收入的调查结果趋于保守。

（2）分析报告

世界经济形势分析报告

一、全球经济分析与展望

世界经济在经历了 2010 年的复苏后，2011 年出现了很多新情况和新问题。预计 2012 年世界经济形势仍非常严峻，对其整体走势我们要高度关注，以做出分析和判断，制定有效的应对措施。

（一）世界经济总体上仍十分严峻复杂，国际经济形势难以明显好转。受主要发达国家主权债务风险、金融系统的脆弱性、低增长和高失业率交织以及政策空间受到政治和经济制约等因素的综合影响，2011 年世界各国经济出现集体减速的征兆，世界经济下行风险增加，2012 年总体形势十分严峻。但只要有关国家能够积极携手、有效应对，世界经济还是能够避免"二次探底"，仍有望维持低速增长态势。尽管各国际组织也相继降低了对 2012 年全球经济增速的预测值，结果也不尽相同，但预测方向还是基本一致的，即 2012 年将基本维持 2011 年的低速增长态势。2011 年 9 月份国际货币基金组织（IMF）预测 2012 年全球经济增速维持在 4.0% 的水平，世界银行对 2012 年全球经济增速的预测值为 3.6%，联合国 12 月发布的报告预测世界经济 2012 年将增长 2.6%，亚洲最大的信息咨询公司野村证券预测，尽管 2011 年全球经济屡次受到打击，仍将实现 3.8% 左右的增长，尽管全球经济增长明显面临下行风险，但 2012 年全球经济增速仍有望达到 3.2%。主要发达国家经济复苏步伐放缓，都不同程度面临债务负担沉重、失业率高企、经济增长乏力等困境的挑战。

（3）开题报告

Function and Application of Descriptive Translation Studies

[1] Introduction

The intention of this study is to explore possible advantages of Descriptive Translation Studies as in its application in translation practice and translation analysis. Since the early 20th century, translation studies gradually broke away from the marginal status within other related disciplines and established itself as an empirical science. From then on, schools of thought have kept coming out and each claims its legitimacy for existence. Among these schools is Descriptive Translation Studies (DTS). DTS approaches translation from an empirical perspective. Translation is viewed to be a social activity having significant importance in the receiving culture and for the target community. Therefore, translation is dealt with beyond the linguistic realization and language comparison, and is incorporated in social and cultural context. My attention was first directed to DTS by its peculiar characteristic of observation, description and explanation. The subject is whatever happens in translation practice, from the determination of prospective function of translation to the process of translator's choice of strategies, brainstorming and the revision, to the final product making appearance in the target community. The method of DTS is basically descriptive. The prescriptive tendency and the problem-solution pattern are abandoned. Translation phenomena are noted down. With accumulated data, some underlying truths about translation will come out which will prove to be instructive not only for theoretical probe but also for applied translation practice. I will apply this descriptive method in the case study of this thesis. A convenient tool has been set up to conduct DTS. "Norm" is operative at every stage of description and explanation. Function, process and product and their relationship as well are skeletal structure of what constitute descriptive studies. Translation phenomena are accounted for with the help of norm. The case taken in this thesis is the Chinese classic *A Dream of Red Mansions*. Two English versions translated respectively by Yang Hsien-yi and David Hawks are compared and observations are made in regard to their translation approaches. In this regard, my observations are limited to several aspects, I hope in-depth observation and explanation will done in light of DTS.

[2] Outline

2.1 Development and major concepts of DTS: In this part I will describe Holms' basic map of DTS and the relationship between function, process and product. I will also discuss some important concepts such as pseudo-translation, multiple translation, translationese, norm, etc.

2.2 Methodology: I will in this part discuss the methodology of DTS before I apply the same to the case study in this thesis with emphasis to be placed on semiotic approach and the concept norm.

2.3 DTS in contrast to other theories: A contrast study will be conducted here with the objective to find the difference of DTS from other theories such as equivalence theory and the Chinese Xin Da Ya criteria. Some advantages will possibly be shown in this study.

2.4 Case study: In this part, translation of *A Dream of Red Mansions* (also translated as *The Story of the Stone*) will be under investigation in light of DTS. Translation samples to be quoted here will be selected at random.

2.5 Conclusion: Based on the above elaboration of DTS and the case study, possible conclusion will be on the advantage of DTS in specific study of translation. Suggestions on further research efforts will be made also. (Note: While the topic will remain the same, the above arrangement of contents is subject to change in the process of writing.)

第四编　文学文体与翻译

导论

第12章　小说

第13章　戏剧

第14章　散文

第15章　诗歌

导 论

　　文学文体不同于实用文体、商贸文书文体和专用科技文体，后三者作为应用型文体，具有明确的目的和具体的用途，而文学作品不拘一格，很难局限于某一特殊的目的和用途。文学文体学，特指以阐释文学文本的主题意义和美学价值为目的的文体学派。

　　从体裁、语体两个方面来看，应用型文体一般不讲个性，无所谓风格。文学文体表达方式多样，风格丰富。体裁和语体，可以还原为语言的组合方式。应用类文章归结为语言符号的系统，而文学作品却是一种艺术样式，有其自身的艺术结构和功能，它不仅是语言符号，更是艺术符号。换句话说，文学作品不像一般文本那样用语言直接表达意思，而是先要将语言符号转换为艺术符号，再通过艺术符号的组合来传达其内在的意蕴。这样，文学作品就有了双重符号系统，外层是语言符号，里层是艺术符号，从而建立起区别于一般文本的结构模式，即文学作品是由"言""象""意"三个层面组合而成的大系统，"言以尽象、象以尽意"，从语言经由意象达到意蕴，形成文学文本由外而内的通道，来实现它自身的基本建构。所以文学文本的结构是"言—象—意"式的三层结构，而应用类文章的文本结构则是"言—意"式的两层结构。文学作品这种特殊的结构方式对读者的解读既是一种制约，又留下"空白"，使读者可以做出种种积极的想象。应用类文章由于其简单的组合方式，使作者的写作和读者的解读都很直接，人们无须追求"言外之意"和"象下之义"。

　　从语域层面来看，应用文是处理公私事务、解决实际问题的工具，因此语体以社会化的书面语体为主，避免使用个性化色彩强烈的语言、方言俚语、过于通俗的口头语以及超常规的句式和生僻词汇，关键部分常用规范化、模式化语言。如英语应用类文章的开头用语及段落起首语常用表示目的、原因、依据的介词结构，承起衔接语、称谓用语、表态用语都为模式化语言。行文中主要使用陈述句和祈使句，大量使用介宾词组作状语、定语成分。在修辞手段的选择运用上也很慎重，一般只用比喻、对比、排比、对偶等少量的修辞格，而不用夸张、比拟、反语、双关、象征等修辞格，以避虚浮失实。而文学语体追求艺术的审美价值，它要求读者思而得之，有充分想象与回味的余地，所以可以选用任何词语、句式句型和修辞方式，讲究音韵美、和谐美、自由美。为尽情达意，可以反复形容，细致描绘。句法上，常使用意合法，少用介词、助词、连词，而且允许打乱词语之间的正常排列顺序和组合关系，往往不能用一般的语法规则去解释，即可以追求语言的"反常化"或"陌生化"。此外，还要"文如其人"，文学语言要表现作者个人的语言风格，表现个性。

在思维方式上，应用文是人们交际的重要工具，是为了解决实际问题而作，因此应用文以抽象思维（即理性思维）为主。应用文作者要抛开事物的感性形式，寻求其内在的联系，找到事物的内在规律，要善于运用逻辑思维、模式思维等思维方式。文学文体的思维方式主要是想象。

从社会功用来看，功利性与非功利性的审美性，是区分应用文体和文学文体最主要的尺度。应用文体与文学文体都会对社会产生影响，但影响的方式、程度等有所不同。应用文体对社会产生直接效应，因为应用文体的根本特征就是实用性，其写作目的是现实的，其目标是明确的，其效果也是直接的。文学文体的作者不求通过文学写作解决现实生活中的具体问题，主要是为了抒写个人对社会的感受、认识，体现个人的个性、情趣等，即文学创作没有明显的实用目的和功利目的，所追求的是情感的愉悦和精神的享受，且这种情感或精神也没有具体的现实要求。文学文体对社会产生的效应是通过读者的审美而渐渐体现的，而且针对不同的读者会产生不同的效应。因此，文学文体的社会功用是间接的，是附着在文学作品的审美价值之上的。一般而言，文学文体具有认识作用、教育作用和审美作用三大社会功能，而应用文体可能具有认识、教育功能，但不必有审美功能。

在写作主体与接受主体上，文学文体的创作主体可以是社会中的任何一个人，只要有表达、表现的欲望，都可用文学文体中的各种形式来表现。而应用文体的写作主体却相对固定，可以是私人文书的创作者，或者是当事人自己，或者请相关人代书。如公务文书的创作者，往往具有受命性，即领导指定或单位任命的。因为个人对于公务文书一般不会产生创作冲动，即使有，创作出的成品也没有任何意义，比如行政公文，没有生效标识，文章即等于一张废纸。因此应用文体的创作主体也与其写作目的、文章受体等因素有密切关系。

因此，文学文体与应用文体的写作目的不同，受体也有所不同。应用文是为了实现其功利目的或现实效应，必然有相对特定的读者对象，如个人书信、单据、请假条、写给领导个人的报告、送阅材料等只能是特定的个人读者；大部分党政公文只能供部分机关领导和相关人员阅读；而一些专用文种的读者限定性更强，如法律文书中的起诉状，只供审判团成员及相关法律工作者阅读。文学文体没有固定的读者对象，作者在创作时并没有刻意要给什么人看，只能根据可能的读者群将读者大致分为几类：专业读者（在专业知识领域里有一定造诣的或懂行的读者，如文学创作者、文学评论者等）；文学爱好者（具有中等以上文化水平、比较关心写作活动、阅读兴趣广泛、有一定求知欲望的读者）；一般读者。

在主旨内涵上，文学文体的写作主体从社会生活中获得了体验，有了一定的认识和见解，产生了要将这些信息传递给别人的愿望的时候，便通过语言载体，将内在的思想意向、感情外在化、固定化，创造出自己的作品，并希望自己的作品能够得到读者的认可。但当阅读主体接触到文学客体之后，却有一个不断创造与不断生成的解读过程。由于文学文本本身所具有的开放性、文学语言的复义性、文学形象的不确定性和所反映现实生活的广阔性、作家思想情感的暗合性，等等，也由于读者对生活有自己的体验与理解，有自己的爱好和志趣，对文本可能会做出这样或那样的反应，即读者对文章主题内涵的感悟不是被动的，而是积极主动地探索，努力发现隐藏在艺术形象深处的内涵，甚至是连作者自己也未曾认识到的东西。这样就导致文学文体的主旨出现了效果与动机的同一性与差异性两种可能，即文学文体允许双主题、多主题，甚至"无主题"。这就是所谓"仁者见仁，智者见智""一千个读者就有一千个哈姆雷特"。而应用文体由于写作主体写作目的的单一性和功利性，决定了主题先行的写作思路与写作方式，即从实际出发，先确立主题，然后找材料说明，主题居主导地位，主题要求写什么就写什么，非有感而发，而是为事物而作，不以个人意志为转移，这必然导致文本意义的单一性和确定性，所以读者在解读过程中毋须作创造性地发挥，也导致了文章主旨动机与效果的统一性，即文章主旨内涵是单一的、直接的、明确的。（谢延秀，2006）

文学是中外交流，促进人与人之间相互理解和社会发展的主要方式，文学文体的特征十分明显，按照分类，文学文体大体包括小说、戏剧、散文和诗歌四大类，而每一类别里都涵盖了更多更具体的次分类。如小说又分为人物传记和古今小说，散文又有游记札记和艺术散文，戏剧包括电影电视及各种戏剧脚本，诗歌也可分为古典诗歌与现代诗歌。文学翻译要真实地再现原作中的生活映像或心理映像，在翻译时就必须揭示出原作品的风格，揭示出原作者在作品中所反映出的自身对世界的独特见解和深刻感受。而文学作品的风格不只反映在文学作品所表达的思想上，还反映在作品的语言上。所以在进行文学翻译时，与翻译应用文体不同，不是把内容传达正确就可以，还要尽力传达原作的语言形式、语言的味道、语言的活力，等等。文学翻译的关键是要做到"神""形"统一。

文学作品的翻译对人们了解不同文化、不同社会风情有着重要的作用。因为文学文体的种类较多，在翻译时，要根据文体类型的不同，采取不同的翻译技巧和策略，诗歌和小说的翻译技巧和策略显然不可完全一致，而散文翻译和戏剧翻译的措辞又有明显的不同。因此，文学文体的翻译需要了解不同的文学文体类型的呈现方式，以及针对不同文体的翻译技巧和策略，才能更好地提升对文学翻译作品的鉴赏能力。

1 文体特征

文学文体学是作者为表达或加强文本的主题意义或美学效果而有意识选择的语言特征。（谢谦，2005）文学作品可以说是语言的艺术。科学语言是直指的，它要求语言符号与其所指的对象完全吻合，因此科学语言趋于使用类似数学或符号逻辑学那种标志系统。文学语言则更偏向于形象性。它不仅仅用来指称或说明什么，它还有表意传情的一面，说明作者或人物的态度和语气，甚至强调文字符号本身的意义，强调词语的声音象征，如格律、音韵等。

在文学作品中，语言被用来写景，渲染气氛；写人，塑造形象；写心，分析心理；写情，呼唤人性；写物，树立象征；写事，制造悬念。文学语言具有形象、抒情、含蓄、幽默、讽刺性、象征性和韵律感等特征。

1.1 行文结构多变 内容情意结合

文学文体与科技类、报告类和其他应用类文体不同，后者更注重内容的准确性和科学性，而前者则更注重将原文作者的情感表达出来。因为文学作品自身的魅力就体现在作者字里行间所传达出来的美，以及通过不同的情节设定所碰撞出的火花，使得文学作品自身也带有作者所特有的表达方式和人格魅力。因此，文学作品本身是充满"情怀"和"情调"的。

文学文本承载着作者对于其所描述对象和现实的个人观点及情感。作者在其作品中抒写自己的感受体验。换句话说，文学作品中传达的观点和感受往往局限于作者所处的社会和文学环境，所以具有很强的主观性和独特性。此外，文学作品还具有很强的美感功能，能够感染读者情绪。具有丰富想象力和原创性的作品会震撼读者。文学语言不仅仅用以传递信息，更重要的是进行一种美感和意境的创造与传达。再者，文学作品中很多信息都是隐含的而并非明确表达的。其往往通过与表达信息相关且极为丰富的词汇、句式和修辞手段来激起读者的共鸣。因此，语言形式及行文风格是文学作品最重要的特点。文学语言的独特风格也就使得作品成为自身个性的反射。

1.2 语言表述丰富 描述特征明显

文学作品最明显的特征之一就是描述性，文学类文本的描述对象源于生活却高于生活，在一定程度上可以被虚构、夸大或处理，以满足一定的艺术需要。具体表现为语法现象的灵活运用、修辞手法的切换、词汇运用的范围广阔。

① 形象性。文学作品善于用生动的语言描绘出各种栩栩如生的形象，给读者

以具体而深刻的印象。尤其是在写景时，一幅幅真实的图画呈现在读者眼前，创造出一种着意渲染的气氛。

②抒情性。将客观环境与主观心理结合、将抒情与景象结合的描写手法是抒情的典型手段。

③含蓄性。好的文学作品往往具有启示性作用，一般要求读者有更大的参与性。作者往往不把意思明白地说出，而是尽量留有余地，让读者自己去思索、去寻找结论，这种意犹未尽、回味无穷的含蓄性手法，是文学作品吸引读者兴趣的特有方式。

④幽默感。文学作品以揭发事物矛盾、通过对不合理的社会现象加以嘲讽来达到引人入胜的效果。这种以短小精悍的形式、诙谐风趣的语言、辛辣尖锐的讽刺，通过善意的讥笑，使读者有所领悟的幽默手法，增强了文学作品的表达魅力。

⑤讽刺性。即反语法（irony），说的是一回事，其含义却是另一回事，字面的意思和深层的含义正好相反。这是文学作品中常用的一种修辞手段。它可以使文字分外生动，深化要表达的思想，给读者以强烈印象，同时也是创造幽默的一种方式。

⑥象征性。它可以包括明喻、暗喻、转喻等修辞手段。象征是用某一具体事物来表示某种抽象的意义。例如，人们常用玫瑰来象征爱情，白雪来象征纯洁等。在文学作品中除了这些通常为大家所接受的象征外，在不同的上下文中，某些具体的事物具有作者赋予它的特殊意义。

⑦韵律感。文学语言不同于一般的实用性语言，不仅有内容美，还有形式美，即语言形式本身的美。这种美主要表现在语言的韵律和节奏上。诗歌是最能表现这种美的文学形式。同样，散文作品强烈的节奏感也会使人对语言表达的意义留下深刻印象。

2 翻译原则

文学语言丰富的描述性特征给文学作品的翻译带来了很大的困难。要想将描述性的语言成功译出，需从几个层面着手。首先，译者要有对文章宏观把握的能力，从而了解作者的创作意图和方向；其次，译者要有深厚的语言功底，能够了解段与段之间的逻辑关系、段内的逻辑关系甚至句内的逻辑关系。在此基础上，译者还需要能够敏锐地察觉到不同时态、语态及句子结构所带来的不同效果，在翻译中处理好时态、语态及句子结构等不同语法习惯带来的问题。

文学翻译中对描述性语言的处理尤为重要，而其中尤以对情态的翻译最为突出。因为情态可以通过微妙的方式体现作者的倾向或观点，而译者又可能因为缺乏经验而忽略情态的表达，因此如何正确地体现出情态的各种功能是文学翻译中描述性语言运用的一大难点。

2.1 文化先于翻译 创造基于事实

在文学翻译中，文化概念的主导地位不可忽视，而正是因为文化因素的出现，才使得文学翻译难度非常大，甚至会出现一些不可译的文化概念。比如"毛笔"，无论翻译成 Chinese pen 还是 writing brush，都无法令外国读者产生一个与我们的概念中的毛笔所对等的物体，这就是所谓的文化差异。正因为如此，译者在翻译过程中，必须要尊重文化，尽可能地将文化的差异性体现出来，而不要为了迁就目的语读者而放弃对文化概念的解释。

与此同时，翻译又是一个再创造的过程，也是一个审美的过程，一个优秀的作品如何在翻译过后依旧优秀，靠的就是译者的深厚功底，对美的把握，对词汇运用的把握，以及还原作者思想的能力。只有这样的译作才能像原作一样，让人欣赏，反之，则会令人失望。一直以来，翻译就被称为是文学作品的再创造，但是这种创造必须是基于事实的创造，是译者文字功底的体现，而非天马行空的想象，不能肆意改变原文意义。

2.2 音、形、意统一 情义结合审美

在翻译过程中，译者往往强调对原文内容的忠实，而原文的形式却往往被忽略。例如，人们通常认为小说的情节发展才是引人入胜的关键，而语言形式只不过是渲染气氛的辅助工具。殊不知，这些有外在美的语言形式正是文学翻译的文学性的重要体现。与非文学翻译不同，文学翻译不仅要传达原文的信息内涵，还要体现原作的思想内涵和作者的审美追求。文学翻译的文体意义是能够体现文学中的美学意义、主题思想和作者叙事风格的语言形式特点。作者遣词造句的特点不仅是其创作风格的显现，也是作品的主题意义和美学功能的反映。"风格即出自于美学和主题考虑的语言形式选择"（申丹，1995：26）。"对读者而言，文学作品具有一种特殊的审美或诗学效果"（Christiane Nord，2001：37）。要传达原作的艺术性，就要保证译文的内容与形式有机统一，使译入语读者获得与原语读者相同的审美体验。

在文学翻译中，不仅要将作者的写作意图或者写作内容翻译出来，译者还必须能够对原文作品有深刻的了解，从文学的层面去体会和感悟作者的写作目的、写作动机，去理解作者在遣词造句上的深刻用意，方能将文学作品中的"情"翻译出来，无"情"则不足以称为文学翻译。

在文学作品的翻译中，译者需要运用多种技巧来体现原文的"情"，保留原文

的"意",既不能出现偏离原文内容的美,也不能完全丢弃美感去直译。钱锺书先生提出的"化境"理论,就是要让译文不着痕迹地体现原文的风韵。这就是翻译中情意结合的最高境界。

2.3 再现原文语言方式 再现原文整体审美

散文的形式一般较为灵活随意,是作者内心世界的抒发和感想,每个作者在散文创作过程中带入自己的语言特色和行文方式,因此,译者在翻译过程中必须熟悉了解每一位作者在写作散文时的个性化语言特点,从而做到高度还原文章的艺术特色和语言特性。

除此以外,要做到再现原文整体性的审美。中文对于散文的评判标准是"形散而神不散",即散文虽然语言方式各异,写作方法不同,但是都有自己的中心主旨和核心概念。译者在翻译过程中,要宏观把握这种核心概念或者主旨,在翻译过程中用与原文相吻合的方式来翻译,来谋篇布局,切记不要一句一句地照字面意思直译,以免损失原文的韵味和特色。

2.4 再现人物特征 重塑人物形象

在小说翻译中,人物的塑造是必不可少的。人物是小说的灵魂,是小说剧情发展的线索,因此,如何重现原作品中的人物,是译者的主要任务。通常情况下,再现人物分为再现人物性格特征和再现人物形象两个方面。性格特征可以由文中所提及的社会地位、职业、修养和性别年龄等几方面的因素来决定。人物形象相对于性格特征要更加微观,人物形象应该是一系列人物个性特征的话语、动作、内心活动等细节信息所缔造出来的,理解人物的形象本身就需要一个过程,稍有不慎就会产生认识上的偏差,所以译者在试图再现人物形象之前,一定要对故事中的人物形象有深刻的认知,才能在选词用句上达到一致。

2.5 音韵结构现形美 节奏意象现意境

诗歌是凝练的艺术,是含蓄的艺术,诗歌的翻译可以从音美、形美、意美等几个层面来探讨。首先,诗歌是有音乐性的,诗歌的音乐性是通过音韵体现出来的。在英诗中,主要的音韵包括头韵(alliteration)、谐元韵(assonance)、行内韵(internal rhyme)、尾韵(end rhyme)等。汉诗中,诗人一般喜欢押尾韵,又叫韵脚,这也是中国诗歌的一个最主要特征。在音韵的翻译过程中,有的译者倾向于将韵脚或者头韵等翻译出来供读者欣赏,而有的译者则认为,强行翻译音韵有的时候会丢失关键的意象,因此在音韵的翻译中我们需注意的是,要结合全文的内容来看,是否适合翻译出与原文相似的结构和韵律。

其次，诗歌要有形美。诗歌的外在形式是其最为显著的特征，也是诗歌区别于其他文学文体的一个主要特征。诗歌形式有定型形式与非定型形式之分，前者对于字数、平仄、音步、音韵等都有较为严格的要求，因此，译者在处理定型形式的时候，应尽量做到还原诗歌的形式美，因为形式上的美感是原诗的主要审美之一，只有翻译出原诗的形式才能体现。

诗歌还要有意境。诗歌是充满艺术魅力的一种文学形式，诗人在有限的空间内，运用各种修辞手法，给予诗歌无限的艺术魅力。这都是意境的组成部分。要想成功地翻译一首诗歌，就必须将原诗中的意境美再创造出来，而意境美的再创造需要译者理解诗歌中的每一个小词、每一处结构、每一个意象和修辞，并将其正确表达出来。

2.6 再现生活故事 放大人物性格

戏剧在文学中占据重要的地位，而戏剧的翻译也因其形式的特殊而较难掌握。一般来说，戏剧的翻译需要注意三点。第一，根据其口语化的特点，要注意在翻译时呈现出口语所特有的活力和爆发力，要能够将人物的性格特征、情感情趣等多种特征体现出来。第二，戏剧的动作性。无论是莎士比亚的《哈姆雷特》，还是曹禺的《雷雨》，戏剧的主要目的就是为了最终搬上舞台，展现给大家看。所以，戏剧的表现形式决定了戏剧的动作性。因为肢体动作和语言决定了一部戏剧的走向和完整与否。因此，在戏剧的翻译过程中，我们要将动作描述的部分着重翻译出来，一旦忽略了动作，就会导致戏剧表演缺乏张力，无法体现人物的饱满性格。第三，语言的含蓄性。虽然是口语化的艺术，但是戏剧的表现形式却是典型的源于生活却高于生活的艺术，在戏剧的表现过程中，口语化的语言都是经过一定的提炼的，不会是不假思索地随口说出的，这有别于我们所谓的真正的生活语言。尤其，戏剧是有节奏感的，是会有韵律之美出现的，表现得最为明显的便是《哈姆雷特》中最经典的台词：To be, or not to be: that is the question:/Whether 'tis nobler in the mind to suffer/The slings and arrows of outrageous fortune,/Or to take arms against a sea of troubles,/And by opposing end them? 很明显我们可以感觉出原文结构的韵律之美，而这一种美属于含蓄的表达，译者在翻译时是不可以忽略的。

总之，文学文体的翻译要注意文学作品丰富的语言特征，包括富于变化的句式和各种修辞手段。文学作品的译文也必须是文学作品，它必须将原作的文学特征忠实地、丝毫不差地传达给读者，不仅是思想感情，还包括语言形式，不但要达到信息上的等值，还应达到艺术上的等值。

第 12 章　小说

小说文体与翻译

小说是最为大众所熟知和接受的文学文体之一。

古往今来，小说一直扮演着传承人类文明、沟通古今、传递文化要义、体现时代价值取向的角色。小说不仅是文字工作者表达内心情感的方式，也是反映社会现实的手段之一。

小说，是一种通过完整故事情节的叙述和具体的环境描写反映社会生活形象的文学体裁，它是拥有完整布局、发展及主题的文学作品。小说的核心三要素是：人物形象、故事情节、环境描写。优秀的小说有着扣人心弦、排列紧凑的故事情节；还有丝丝入扣、惟妙惟肖的人物刻画；更有潜藏在字里行间的人生观、价值观和世界观。

小说体裁种类繁多。根据流派，可分为现实主义小说、浪漫主义小说、表现主义小说等；根据表现方法，可分为叙述体小说、散文体小说、诗体小说、生活意识流小说等；根据题材，有儿童小说、武侠小说、侦探小说、历史小说、神话小说、言情小说、科幻小说等。

小说文体特征明显，词汇表达灵活、多样，内涵意义丰富，大量使用各种修辞手法。小说文体的翻译，要注意句法结构表达的内涵意义，避免假象等值。

12.1 课前实践

12.1.1 现实主义小说

The Kite Runner

Khaled Hosseini

Chapter I

I became what I am today at the age of twelve, on a frigid overcast day in the winter of 1975. I remember the precise moment, crouching behind a crumbling mud wall, peeking into the alley near the frozen creek. That was a long time ago, but it's wrong what they say about the past, I've learned, about how you can bury it. Because the past claws its way out. Looking back now, I realize I have been peeking into that deserted alley for the last twenty-six years.

One day last summer, my friend Rahim Khan called from Pakistan. He asked me to come see him. Standing in the kitchen with the receiver to my ear, I knew it wasn't just Rahim Khan on the line. It was my past of unatoned sins. After I hung up, I went for a walk along Spreckels Lake on the northern edge of Golden Gate Park. The early afternoon sun sparkled on the water where dozens of miniature boats sailed, propelled by a crisp breeze. Then I glanced up and saw a pair of kites, red with long blue tails, soaring in the sky. They danced high above the trees on the west end of the park, over the windmills, floating side by side like a pair of eyes looking down on San Francisco, the city

追风筝的人

卡勒德·胡赛尼

第一章

我成为今天的我，是在1975年某个阴云密布的寒冷冬日，那年我十二岁。我清楚地记得当时自己趴在一堵坍塌的泥墙后面，窥视着那条小巷，旁边是结冰的小溪。许多年过去了，人们说陈年旧事可以被埋葬，然而我终于明白这是错的，因为往事会自行爬上来。回首前尘，我意识到在过去二十六年里，自己始终在窥视着那荒芜的小径。

去年夏季的某天，朋友拉辛汗从巴基斯坦打来电话，要我回去探望他。我站在厨房里，听筒贴在耳朵上，我知道电话线连着的，并不只是拉辛汗，还有我过去那些未曾赎还的罪行。挂了电话，我离开家门，到金门公园北边的斯普瑞柯湖边散步。晌午的骄阳照在波光粼粼的水面上，数十艘轻舟在和风的吹拂中漂行。我抬起头，望见两只红色的风筝，带着长长的蓝色尾巴，在天空中冉冉升起。它们舞动着，飞越公园西边的树林，飞越风车，并排飘浮着，如同一双眼睛俯视着旧

I now call home. And suddenly Hassan's voice whispered in my head: For you a thousand times over. Hassan the harelipped kite runner.

  I sat on a park bench near a willow tree. I thought about something Rahim Khan said just before he hung up, almost as an after thought. There is a way to be good again. I looked up at those twin kites. I thought about Hassan. Thought about Baba. Ali. Kabul. I thought of the life I had lived until the winter of 1975 came and changed everything. And made me what I am today.

金山,这个我现在当成家园的城市。突然间,哈桑的声音在我脑中响起:为你,千千万万遍。哈桑,那个兔唇的哈桑,那个追风筝的人。

  我在公园里柳树下的长凳坐下,想着拉辛汗在电话中说的那些事情,再三思量。那儿有再次成为好人的路。我抬眼看看那比翼齐飞的风筝。我忆起哈桑。我缅怀爸爸。我想到阿里。我思念喀布尔。我想起曾经的生活,想起1975年那个改变了一切的冬天。那造就了今天的我。

12.1.2 叙述体小说

The Great Gatsby
F. S. Fitzgerald

Chapter I

  In my younger and more vulnerable years, my father gave me some advice that I've been turning over in my mind ever since.

  "Whenever you feel like criticizing any one," he told me. "Just remember that all the people in this world haven't had the advantages that you've had." He didn't say any more, but we've always been unusually communicative in a reserved way, and I understood that he meant a great deal more than that. In consequence, I'm inclined to reserve all judgments, a habit that has opened up many curious natures to

了不起的盖茨比
弗朗西斯·司各特·菲茨杰拉德

第一章

  在我还很幼稚,经受不起波折的那些岁月里,我父亲就曾给过我一句忠告,那句忠告我至今都铭记在心,常常反复回味。

  "每当你想要批评什么人的时候,"他告诫我说,"千万要记住,这世上的人不一定各个都具备你所拥有的这些优点。"他没再多说,不过,我们向来都是用一种心照不宣的方式进行交流的。再说我也明白,他的言下之意远比这句话要深刻得多。久而

me and also made me the victim of not a few veteran bores. The abnormal mind is quick to detect and attach itself to this quality when it appears in a normal person, and so it came about that in college I was unjustly accused of being a politician, because I was privy to the secret griefs of wild, unknown men. Most of the confidences were unsought frequently I have feigned sleep, preoccupation, or a hostile levity when I realized by some unmistakable sign that an intimate revelation was quivering on the horizon; for the intimate revelations of young men, or at least the terms in which they express them, are usually plagiaristic and marred by obvious suppressions. Reserving judgments is a matter of infinite hope. I am still a little afraid of missing something if I forget that, as my father snobbishly suggested, and I snobbishly repeat, a sense of the fundamental decencies is parceled out unequally at birth.

久之，我便养成了对一切评判都有所保留的习惯，这种习惯既使许多性格乖僻的人愿意向我敞开心扉，也使我成了不少老爱不厌其烦地唠叨的人的受害者。倘若这一性格特点在一个心智正常的人身上表现出来时，心理不正常的人很快就会发现，并且会抓住不放，为此，在我还在念大学的时候，人家就很不公正地指责过我，说我就是个政客，因为我知道那些行为放荡却又无人知道的家伙的隐秘的伤心事。那些推心置腹的私房话绝大多数都不是我故意要他们说给我听的——每当我根据某个明白无误的迹象看出，一场亲密无间的倾诉衷肠已经跃跃欲试地出现端倪的时候，我往往都假装睡着了，或者假装出一副心事重重的样子，或者假装出不怀好意的轻浮态度——因为年轻人的那种亲密无间的倾诉衷肠，或者至少可以说，他们表述那些隐私时所用的语言，通常都是剽窃来的，而且由于明显想隐瞒实情而断章取义。对评判有所保留是一个关系到要不要对未来寄予无限希望的问题。我现在已然还有点儿担心会错过了什么，唯恐我万一忘了那句话，就是我父亲曾经非常势利地暗示过，而我现在又在非常势利地重复的那句话：人的基本礼仪廉耻观是分配不均的。

12.1.3 浪漫主义小说

The Moon and Sixpence
W. Somerset Maugham

Chapter I

I confess that when first I made acquaintance with Charles Strickland I never for a moment discerned that there was in him anything out of the ordinary. Yet now few will be found to deny his greatness. I do not speak of that greatness which is achieved by the fortunate politician or the successful soldier; that is a quality which belongs to the place he occupies rather than to the man; and a change of circumstance reduces it to very discreet proportions. The Prime Minister out of office is seen, too often, to have been but a pompous rhetorician, and the General without an army is but the tame hero of a market town. The greatness of Charles Strickland was authentic. It may be that you do not like his art, but at all events you can hardly refuse it the tribute of your interest. He disturbs and arrests. The time has passed when he was an object of ridicule, and it is no longer a mark of eccentricity to defend or of perversity to extol him. His faults are accepted as the necessary complement to his merits. It is still possible to discuss his place in art, and the adulation of his admirers is perhaps no less capricious than the disparagement of his detractors; but one thing can never be doubtful, and that is that he had genius. To my mind the most interesting thing in art is the personality of

月亮和六便士
威廉·萨默赛特·毛姆

第一章

老实说，我刚刚认识查理斯·思特里克兰德的时候，从来没注意到这个人有什么与众不同的地方，但是今天却很少有人不承认他的伟大了。我所谓的伟大不是走红运的政治家或是立战功的军人的伟大；这种人显赫一时，与其说是他们本身的特质倒不如说沾了他们地位的光，一旦事过境迁，他们的伟大也就黯然失色了。人们常常发现一位离了职的首相当年只不过是个大言不惭的演说家；一个解甲归田的将军无非是个平淡乏味的市井英雄。但是查理斯·思特里克兰德的伟大却是真正的伟大。你可能不喜欢他的艺术，但无论如何你不能不对它感到兴趣。他的作品使你不能平静，扣紧你的心弦。思特里克兰德受人揶揄讥嘲的时代已经过去了，为他辩护或甚至对他赞誉也不再被看作是某些人的奇行怪癖了。他的瑕疵在世人的眼中已经成为他的优点的必不可少的派生物。他在艺术史上的地位尽可以继续争论。崇拜者对他的赞颂同贬抑者对他的诋毁固然都可能出于偏颇和任性，但是有一点

the artist; and if that is singular, I am willing to excuse a thousand faults. I suppose Velasquez was a better painter than EL Greco, but custom stales one's admiration for him: the Cretan, sensual and tragic, proffers the mystery of his soul like a standing sacrifice. The artist, painter, poet, or musician, by his decoration, sublime or beautiful, satisfies the aesthetic sense; but that is akin to the sexual instinct, and shares its barbarity: he lays before you also the greater gift of himself.

是不容置疑的，那就是他具有天才。在我看来，艺术中最令人感兴趣的就是艺术家的个性；如果艺术家赋有独特的性格，尽管他有一千个缺点，我也可以原谅。我料想，委拉斯凯兹是个比埃尔·格列柯更高超的画家，可是由于所见过多，却使我们感到他的绘画有些乏味。而那位克里特岛画家的作品却有一种肉欲和悲剧性的美，仿佛作为永恒的牺牲似地把自己灵魂的秘密呈献出来。一个艺术家——画家也好，诗人也好，音乐家也好，用他的崇高的或者美丽的作品把世界装点起来，满足了人们的审美意识，但这也同人类的性本能不无相似的地方，都有其粗野狂暴的一面。在把作品奉献给世人的同时，艺术家也把他个人的伟大才能呈现到你眼前。

12.2 文体特点

12.2.1 词汇内涵丰富　句法形式多变

小说语言词汇内涵丰富，作者往往运用这一特点表达特定的意义：或是为了烘托主人公的某种性格特征，或是为了对接下来的情节进行铺垫；或是为了创造艺术冲突，产生矛盾，烘托戏剧化效果。作者巧妙运用词汇来体现文章的不同色彩和基调，有时用于强调，有时用于反讽或转折，以此来达到小说出神入化、引人入胜的效果。

小说的句法形式多变。小说常常通过各种语法现象的频繁变化来服务于情节的发展变化。英语小说中，语法现象更为丰富，特别是假设语气和绝对式分词结构等其他文体较少使用的语法手段，在小说中都会频繁出现。汉语语言重意合，文章内容的突出或转折常通过文章节奏的变化来体现;英语重形合,语言表达的主次关系一般通过句型的转变来达成。因此在英文小说中,不同形式的复杂句、简单句和省略句在小说中屡屡呈现。

12.2.2 语域变化频繁　风格形态迥异

在非文学文体中,语域一般较为稳定且前后统一,而文学文体的多变性,使得其语域也同样变幻莫测。文学文体会通过语域的转换或不同语域之间的交互作用来产生特定的美学效果或者特定的主题意义。例如,小说文体的语域,不可简单归结为一般的正式语言或非正式语言,它会随着情节的发展而变化,因此无法确保自始至终选择同一种语域。在小说中,作者常常通过语域的变化,直接生动地表达出人物所属的不同社会阶层,展示出不同人物的思维风格,或通过模仿人物的不同语域产生滑稽模仿的效果,并暗示作者的同情或者反讽立场。小说中语域上的变化也是巧妙实现视角转换的一种重要手段。(Fowler,1977)

根据题材、写作形式和流派的不同,产生了许多不同的小说类型。每一种小说都有其独特的魅力。鲁迅小说中的辛辣讽刺,钱锺书小说中的睿智幽默,海明威小说中的简洁表达与蕴含的深刻哲理,每一位作者的写作风格都会在其作品中表达得淋漓尽致,都反映出了不同体裁小说不同的文体风格。其用词的独特巧妙、句型的前后变化、语法的纵横交错和内容情节的柳暗花明,都是对小说作品的具体风格的体现。

12.2.3 美学价值突出　情感色彩丰富

美学价值是一部小说成功的必要因素。小说中美的传递超越了字里行间的信息,能够让读者体会到小说的厚重与底蕴。任何一部小说都要从不同的方面展现自身的美学价值。例如,托马斯·哈代的小说,悲剧是主体,也是主题,更是美的体现。哈代小说中的悲剧成分,包括社会悲剧、性格悲剧、命运悲剧等,都是美的延续。这些悲剧因素升华了小说的主题,更升华了小说中"苔丝"和"裘德"等主人公的灵魂和精神。悲剧,作为一种美学范畴,其特性尽管集中体现在作为文体的悲剧里,但同时也能通过营造的各种氛围,让人感受到文学中的庄严、肃穆、典雅、凝重甚至悲怆。(陈静,2003:38)再如,许多年来,中国的"红学"研究者从未停止过对《红楼梦》的研究,因为《红楼梦》是小说中美学价值突出的集大成之作。《红楼梦》中的一词一句,书中人物的一颦一笑,都极富传统韵味和古典美。关于"红学"之美的研究早已深入到书中各个微观领域,如诗学角度的美,服饰着装角度的美,饮食起居角度的美,空间设计角度的美,等等。综合起来,促成了《红楼梦》的独特的文学美,让美无处不在。(周中明,1982:65)

翻译美学的体现也服务于主题，凸显了小说故事的主题和情感，让情感在"美"的烘托下得以绽放。在悲剧的烘托中，"德伯家的苔丝"最后的死，悲壮却又美丽，黎明与黑暗交汇，读者的情绪也随之几经波澜。在大观园的热闹繁华中，读者慢慢感到将死的冷寂，感受到凋零。从大喜到大悲的转变，让人对故事中的人物不甚唏嘘，潸然泪下。在"葬花吟"的悲凉小调中，读者感受到了一个大家族的鼎盛与衰退，从有到无。这些情绪的渲染，最终都成为情绪的宣泄。因此，小说的美学与情感相辅相成，互为因果，互相衬托。

12.3 翻译要领

小说的表达形式多种多样，其语体特征会随主题、内容、价值的不同而各有侧重。因此，小说的翻译既要从宏观高度把握主旨，又要从细节处着眼，谨防语体传达失误，避免"假象等值"。小说作品的情感表达最持久、最丰富，不同的小说类型，不仅内容和主题有差异，其文章基调和情感色彩也有所不同。把握不同作家的个人风格，是把握好文体风格翻译的前提条件。小说的主题和情感鲜明、丰富，小说翻译也应体现其美学表达的特殊方式，凸显情感在"美"的烘托下对小说主题的表达作用。

12.3.1　正确解读　减少偏离

小说翻译中，对于词汇的准确把握直接决定了译文的准确性。在文体风格层面上，小说文体，尤其是叙述体小说存在大量的人物对话交流，涉及各种言语集团或群体，这些不同的言语集团在社会背景、文化背景、人物阶层等语域方面都不相同，他们使用的语言表明小说中的词汇、句法、修辞等表达方式也会受到不同语域的影响。为了忠实地再现原文的丰富内涵和语言表达色彩，翻译中要尽量注意词、句的语体作用。（刘宓庆，2012：146）在语言层面上，要正确理解词汇的表层含义和深层含义，准确把握词、句、修辞手段的作用，传达主题，破解原文的美学价值，从而实现译文的传神达意，再现原文的审美价值。翻译小说时要能够摆脱自身的情感影响，不过度添加个人色彩，不使译文偏离原文主题意义，要做到深入理解和把握词语丰富的内涵意义，言简意赅，避免译文的冗余。如：

原文 Well, well, what's done can't be undone. I'm sure I don't know why children o' my bringing forth should all be bigger simpletons than other people's—not to know better than to blab such that, when he couldn't ha' found it out till too late'... (Thomas Hardy, *Tess of the d'Urbervilles*)

译文 得，得；已经泼出去的水还有什么法儿收回？俺不明白，怎么俺养的儿女，比别人的都傻——连这样的事该不该说都不知道！你要是不说，他自己会知道吗？

等他发现了，那就生米做成熟饭了……（张若谷译）

原文作者在词汇上选用了 o'、my、ha' 来体现苔丝父亲的方言，原文的语域特征明显，目的在于体现苔丝父亲的阶层，从而推断出他的狭隘思想是如何得来的。而在中文译本中，张译将原文的方言语域转到 I 上，将其译成"俺"，而这个侧重点并不是原文用以体现语域特征的明显词汇，因此，这样的翻译导致了一定程度上的文本风格传译的失误，将读者从原文语境和语域中剥离出来。又如：

原文 古人所说的梧桐一叶而天下知秋的遥想，大约也就在这些深沉的地方。（郁达夫《故都的秋》）

译文 The same depth of implication is found in the ancient saying that a single fallen leaf from the wutong tree is more than enough to inform the world of autumn's presence.（张培基译）

此处原文运用夸张的手法，描写了故都的秋来临之美，"梧桐一叶天下知秋"是极富中国韵味的表达，含蓄内敛，却给人以足够的想象空间，有如泼墨画一般的留白之美。而这样一种夸张在译文中被保留下来，让译文读者也能透过这一夸张的修辞手法感受到故都秋天的美。

12.3.2　厘清句法　把握内容

小说的句法形式多变，语法特征突出，各种形式的句法结构和表达方式层出不穷，翻译时要准确把握原文的句法结构变化。首先，从句法层面上看，译者需熟悉两种不同语言之间的句法差异。中英文在体现节奏快慢、情节高低起伏、人物性格特征等方面，采用的方式不尽相同，因此译者必须能够充分认识到两种语言之间不同的句法结构、句际关系和句内关系及它们对文本内容所起的作用，译者也需将原语中的句法特征转换为相应的目标语句法结构，才能让读者有身临其境之感。其次，从语法层面上看，译者要熟悉不同的时态、语态、语气所产生的不同效果，须对时态和语态等语法构成所造成的微妙情感变化保持高度警惕，重视时态、语态、语气等对文章内容走向的微妙作用，恰当地将原文内容、故事情节传递给读者。如：

原文 刘姥姥不敢过去，且掸了掸衣服，又教了板儿几句话，然后溜到角门前。（曹雪芹等《红楼梦》）

译文 1 There, at each side of the stone lions which flanked the gates of the Rong Mansion, she saw a cluster of horses and palanquins. <u>Not daring to go straight up, she first dusted down her clothes and rehearsed Ban-er's little repertoire of phrases before sidling up to one of the side entrances.</u>（Hawkes 译）

译文 2 But Granny Liu was too overawed by the crowd of sedan chairs and horses there to venture near the stone lions which flanked the Rong Mansion's main gate. <u>Having dusted off her clothes and given Baner fresh instructions, she timidly approached the side entrance where some arrogant,</u> corpulent servants were sunning themselves on long benches, engaged in a lively discussion.（杨宪益、戴乃迭译）

从两个译本（画线部分）中我们可以清楚地体会到句法结构的改变对于原语内容意义体现的差别。原文中能体现刘姥姥性格和身份的动词词组为"掸了掸衣服""教了板儿""溜到角门"，如何体现这几组动词是翻译这段话的关键。首先，译文1将这几组动词译作并列的从句，从位置上突出了这几组动作的重要性，后接分词before doing，使整句话达到连贯，这样一来，三组动词的重要程度均衡，从而让读者能够注意到这一系列动作中所包含的心理因素，使读者得以回味。而译文2中，"溜到角门前"，译者直接翻译成了主句"she timidly approached the side entrance where..."，而将另外两个动词处理成了伴随状语前置，这样的句型结构必然导致目标语读者的重点落在主句 timidly approached 上，则会忽略另外两个在中文原语中同样重要的动词。因此，这个例子向大家传递了句法结构对于目标语读者对文本理解的影响。（申丹，1998：175）

12.3.3 熟悉语域切换　避免假象等值

语域的切换是小说文体不同于其他文体的主要特征，而是否能准确地把握语域变化所带来的戏剧效果也是小说翻译的前提。译者时常会对原文某些不合理的地方进行修改从而使其变得"合理"，然而却忽视了原文的不合理正是情节冲突的一种表现形式。因此，译者在理解原文时，要充分把握原文的表达意象，理解原文主旨，充分把握原文中语域变化与主题的关联。例如，在翻译时，要注意勿将人物的想法客观化或事实化；勿随意改变原文中的人称，不要将第一人称、第二人称随意改成第三人称，不要改变文章想要表达的主题意义。

语域的理解误差导致的翻译失误屡见不鲜。译者在翻译前，一定要仔细审阅理解原文的主旨意义和审美意义才能尽可能减少翻译失误所造成的"假象等值"。如：

原文 黛玉听了这话，不觉又喜又惊，又悲又叹。所喜者：果然自己眼力不错，素日认他是个知己，果然是个知己。所惊者：他在人前一片私心称扬于我，其亲热厚密竟不避嫌疑。所叹者：你既为我的知己，自然我也可为你的知己，既你我为知己，又何必有"金玉"之论呢？既有"金玉"之论，也该你我有之，又何必来一宝钗？（曹雪芹等《红楼梦》）

译文 This surprised and delighted Tai-yu but also distressed and grieved her. She was delighted to know she had not misjudged him, for he had now proved just as understanding as she has always thought. Surprised that he had been so indiscreet as to acknowledge his preference for her openly. Distressed because their mutual understanding ought to preclude all talk about gold matching jade, or she instead of Pao-chai should have the gold locket to match his jade amulet.（杨宪益、戴乃迭译）

这段话的翻译是非常典型的语域转换，其侧重点不在于词汇层面或者句法层面的对应，而在于语言形式本身的对应。如若忽略了语言形式的对应则会导致"假象等值"。原文是《红楼梦》第32章中的一段，原文中的"所喜者""所惊者""所叹者"为叙述者的评论，冒号后面出现的内容则是用直接引语表达黛玉的内心想法。即，由三个平行的叙述者的话语向人物内心想法的突然转换。这三个平行的突转在原文语境中看起来较为自然，但是直接译成英语则会显得不太协调。译文为了让读者更好地接受文本内容，直接用转述叙述语的方式进行翻译，但却只是一种假象等值。因为，这样的翻译，会给读者以错觉，将黛玉心中的想法客观化或者事实化；此外，在原文中有人称的变化，在黛玉的心理活动之初，黛玉使用的是第一人称，随后却改为了第二人称，这种人称的变化非常精妙地表达了黛玉和宝玉之间感情的微妙变化，而译文的间接引语无法体现这层情感的变化。（申丹，2002：11）

因此，文体中的等值是一个既宏观又微观的概念，翻译时既要从文体的整体特征中把握文章的特征，又要从细节处准确体现文本内容，不丢失原文精华。

12.4 译文赏评

12.4.1 现实主义小说

Gone with the Wind
Margaret Mitchell

Chapter I

Scarlett O'hara was not beautiful, but men seldom realized it when caught by her charm as the Tarleton twins were. In her face were too sharply blended the delicate features of her mother, a Coast aristocrat of French descent, and the heavy ones of her florid Irish father. But it was an arresting face, pointed of chin, square of jaw. Her eyes were pale green without a touch of hazel, starred with bristly black lashes and slightly tilted at the ends. Above them, her thick black brows slanted upward, cutting a startling oblique line in her magnolia-white skin—that skin so prized by Southern women and so carefully guarded with bonnets, veils, and mittens against hot Georgia suns.

第 12 章 小说

译文

飘
玛格丽特·米切尔

第一章

那郝思嘉小姐长得并不美，可是极富魅力，男人见了她，往往要着迷，就像汤家那一对双胞胎兄弟似的。原来这位小姐脸上混杂着两种特质：一种是母亲给她的娇柔，一种是父亲给她的豪爽。因为她母亲是个法兰西血统的海滨贵族，父亲是个皮色深浓的爱尔兰人，所以遗传给她的质地难免不调和。可是质地虽然不调和，她那一张脸蛋儿实在迷人得很，下巴颏儿尖尖的，牙床骨儿方方的。她的眼珠子是一味的淡绿色，不杂一丝儿的茶褐，周围竖着一圈儿粗黑的睫毛，眼角微微有点翘，上面斜竖着两撇墨墨的蛾眉，在她那木兰花一般白的皮肤上，划出两条异常惹眼的斜线。就是她那一身皮肤，也正是南方女人最最喜爱的，谁要长着这样的皮肤，就要拿帽子、面罩、手套之类当心保护着，舍不得让那大热的阳光晒黑。

赏评

《飘》是美国作家玛格丽特所写的以南北战争为题材的故事。书中的主要人物是 Scarlett O'hara，是个有着饱满性格的主人公。《飘》的翻译关键在于是否能再现原文女性角色 Scarlett O'hara 的性格特征。然而此篇译文中，有多处与 Scarlett O'hara 性格不甚符合的译文。例如，首先，主人公的姓名采用了归化的译法，将其译成"郝思嘉"，寓意着一个温婉尔雅、贤淑端庄的淑女形象，这与原文中主人公爱慕虚荣、贪婪执着、性格倔强的特征不符。此种译法常见于 20 世纪中期，当时，归化翻译是主流的翻译方法。但是，随着翻译的文化转向，人们对于外来事物的接受程度日益增高，外来语言的内在魅力更加受到重视和青睐。因此，后来的译本都倾向于把 Scarlett O'hara 音译为"斯嘉丽"，不仅保留了原文的发音特色，更通过"嘉丽"谐音"佳丽"，成功地暗示了斯嘉丽的风情万种和魅力之过人，读者接受度高。其次，该段翻译中多处用到了归化的翻译手法，例如"蛾眉""木兰花一般"都带有浓郁的中国风，这样的翻译会很有中式美，但难以让人感受到斯嘉丽作为一个美国南方姑娘的风情和韵味。再如："In her face were too sharply blended the delicate features of her mother, a Coast aristocrat of French descent, and the heavy ones of her florid Irish father."（原来这位小姐脸上混杂着两种特质：一种是母亲给她的娇柔，一种是父亲给她的豪爽。因为她母亲是个法兰西血统的海滨贵族，父亲是个皮色深浓的爱尔兰人，所以遗传给她的质地难免不调和）。此句话的翻译，明显采用了增词法，十分巧妙。如不采用增词法，直接的硬译则不能使原文内含的关于斯嘉丽出身的信息展现清楚，读者的理解会出现困难。

从整体语言风格上看，该段译文流畅通顺，描述生动，注重细节，符合中文用语习惯，可读性强。

12.4.2 古典章回体小说

原文

红 楼 梦
曹雪芹

第六回

次日天未明，刘姥姥便起来梳洗了，又将板儿教训了几句。那板儿才五六岁的孩子，一无所知，听见刘姥姥带他进城逛去，便喜的无不应承。于是刘姥姥带他进城，找至宁荣街。来至荣府大门石狮子前，只见簇簇轿马，刘姥姥便不敢过去，且掸了掸衣服，又教了板儿几句话，然后蹭到角门前。只见几个挺胸叠肚指手画脚的人，坐在大板凳上，说东谈西呢。刘姥姥只得蹭上来问："太爷们纳福。"众人打量了他一会儿便问："那里来的？"刘姥姥赔笑道："我找太太的陪房周大爷的，烦哪位太爷替我请他老出来。"那些人听了，都不瞅睬，半日方说道："你远远地在那墙角下等着，一会子他们家就有人出来的。"内中有一老年人道："不要误他的事，何苦唚他。"因向刘姥姥道："那周大爷已往南边去了。他在后一带住着，他娘子却在家。你要找时，从这边绕到后街上后门上去问就是了。"

译文

A Dream of Red Mansions
Cao Xueqin

Chapter 6

The next day Granny Liu got up before dawn to wash and comb her hair and to coach Baner. Being an ignorant child of five or six, he was so delighted at the prospect of a trip to the city that he agreed to everything he was told. In town they asked their way to Rong Ning Street. But Granny Liu was too overawed by the crowd of sedan chairs and horses there to venture near the stone lions which flanked the Rong Mansion's main gate. Having dusted off her clothes and given Baner fresh instructions, she timidly approached the side entrance where some arrogant, corpulent servants were sunning themselves on long benches, engaged in a lively discussion.

Granny Liu edged forward and said, "Greetings, gentlemen."

The men surveyed her from head to foot before condescending to ask where she had come from.

"I've come to see Mr. Zhou who came with Lady Wang when she was married," she told them with a smile. "May I trouble one of you gentlemen to fetch him out for me?"

The men ignored her for a while, but finally one of them said, "Wait over there by that corner. One of his family may come out by and by."

An older man interposed, "Why make a fool of her and waste her time?" He told Granny Liu, "Old Zhou has gone south but his wife is at home. His house is at the back. Go round to the back gate and ask for her there."

赏评

本段选自《红楼梦》小说的第六回"贾宝玉初试云雨情 刘姥姥一进荣国府"中的片段。本段描绘了刘姥姥一大早带着板儿到荣国府找王夫人求助。原文通过动作的刻画，生动地描述了刘姥姥对于进入荣国府的一种敬而生畏之心，也反应出刘姥姥的农妇身份，也从侧面描写了荣国府的奢华大气。

从词汇的层面看，体现刘姥姥情绪的最主要的几个动词，如"蹭到角门前""蹭上来问""赔笑"等，译者用了几个十分形象的动词，如 edge forward，这个短语有贴着墙根慢慢向前挪动的意思，活灵活现地展现了刘姥姥心中甚是惶恐的心态，读者不难想象刘姥姥谦卑的态度。此外，译文也很好地还原了原文的神态。例如，"Wait over there by that corner. One of his family may come out by and by." 这一句用了祈使句，读者可以从中感受到荣国府下人狐假虎威、作威作福的神态。

12.4.3 现代讽刺小说

原文

The Catcher in the Rye
J. David Salinger

Old Phoebe said something then, but I couldn't hear her. She had the side of her mouth right smack on the pillow, and I couldn't hear her.

"What?" I said. "Take your mouth away. I can't hear you with your mouth that way."

"You don't like anything that's happening."

It made me even more depressed when she said that.

"Yes, I do. Yes I do. Sure I do. Don't say that. Why the hell do you say that?"

"Because you don't. You don't like any schools. You don't like a million things. You don't."

"I do! That's where you're wrong—that's exactly where you're wrong! Why the hell do you have to say that?" I said. Boy, was she depressing me.

"Because you don't," she said. "Name one thing."

"One thing? One thing I like?" I said. "Okay."

The trouble was, I couldn't concentrate too hot. Sometimes it's hard to concentrate.

"One thing I like a lot you mean?" I asked her.

She didn't answer me, though. She was in a cock-eyed position way the hell over the other side of the bed. She was about a thousand miles away. "C'mon, answer me, " I said. "One thing I like a lot or one thing I just like?"

"You like a lot."

"Anyway, I like it now," I said. "I mean right now. Sitting here with you and just chewing the fat and horsing—"

"That isn't anything really!"

"It is so something really! Certainly it is! Why the hell isn't it? People never think anything is anything really. I'm getting goddam sick of it."

"Stop swearing. All right, name something else. Name something you'd like to be. Like a scientist. Or a lawyer or something."

"I couldn't be a scientist. I'm no good in science."

"Well, a lawyer—like Daddy and all."

"Lawyers are all right, I guess—but it doesn't appeal to me," I said. "I mean they're all right if they go around saving innocent guy's lives all the time, and like that, but you don't do that kind of stuff if you're a lawyer. All you do is make a lot of dough and play golf and play bridge and buy cars and drink Martinis and look like a hotshot. And besides. Even if you did go around saving guys' lives and all, how would you know if you did it because you really wanted to save guys' lives, or because you did it because what you really wanted to do was be a terrific lawyer, with everybody slapping you on the back and congratulating you in court when the goddam trial was over, the reporters and everybody, the way it is in the dirty movies? How would you know you weren't being a phony? The trouble is, you wouldn't."

第 12 章 小说

译文

麦田里的守望者
杰罗姆·大卫·塞林格

老菲碧这时说了句什么话,我没听清。她把一个嘴角整个儿压在枕头上,所以我听不清她说的话。

"什么?"我说,"把你的头拿开。你这样把嘴压着,我根本听不清你在说什么。"

"你不喜欢正在发生的事情,所有的。"

她这么一说,我心里不由得更烦了。

"我喜欢,我喜欢,我当然喜欢。别说这种话。你干吗要说这种见鬼的话呢?"

"因为你不喜欢。你讨厌上学。你讨厌好多东西。你不喜欢。"

"我喜欢!你错就错在这里——你完完全全错在这里!你为什么非要说这种见鬼的话呢?"我说。天哪,她真让我烦透了。

"因为你不喜欢,"她说。"说一样东西让我听听。"

"说一样东西?一样我喜欢的东西?"我说,"好吧。"

问题是,我没法集中思想。思想有时候是很难集中的。

"你是说,一样我非常喜欢的东西?"我问她。

她没作声。她躺在床的另一边,斜着眼看我。感觉好像离得很远。"喂,回答我,"我说。"是一样我非常喜欢的东西呢,还是我喜欢的东西就行?"

"你非常喜欢的。"

"不管怎样,我喜欢现在这样,"我说。"我是说就像现在这样,跟你一起坐着,聊聊天,逗逗乐……"

"这可不是什么真正的东西!"

"这是真正的东西!当然是的!他妈的为什么不是?人们就是不把真正的东西当东西看待。我他妈的都腻烦透这个了。"

"别骂啦。好吧,说些别的吧,说说你的理想吧。你是想当个科学家呢,还是想当个律师什么的。"

"我当不了科学家,我不懂科学。"

"那,当个律师,像爸爸一样。"

"律师倒是不错,我想——可是不适合我,"我说。"我是说他们要是老出去搭救受冤枉的人的性命,那倒是不错,可你一旦当了律师,就不干那样的事了。你只知道挣大钱，打高尔夫球，打桥牌，买汽车，喝马提尼酒，摆臭架子。再说，即便你真的出去救人了，你怎么知道这样做到底是因为你真的想要救人性命呢，还是因为你真正的动机是想当一个大律师，等审判一结束，那些记者什么的就会向你涌来，向你道贺，就像那些下流电影里演的那样？你怎么知道自己不是个伪君子？问题是，你根本就不知道。"

赏评

《麦田里的守望者》是二十世纪美国文学的经典作品之一，也是新型文体"口语体文学"的一种。口语体文学文体松散、自由、生动、自然，语气幽默，有时含有嘲讽，这种口语体文学以其鲜明的语言特色吸引了读者，也成为翻译中一个值得关注的新课题。《麦田里的守望者》基于其口语体文学特征，句式结构大多简单，多用短句，少用复杂句和长难句。如："Old Phoebe said something then, but I couldn't hear her. She had the side of her mouth right smack on the pillow, and I couldn't hear her." 这句话中，作者使用了许多连接词，且都是最简单的 and、but、then 等。此外，连接词衔接的句子都是简单句，这些简单句的使用，表明了一种口语化的倾向，而口语表达也体现了主人公"霍尔顿"的年少不谙世事和故事情节的生活化。文中大量出现的短句，加强了句子的节奏感。句末高频率地使用附着语，如小说主人公喜欢在每句话的句末加上无实际意义的 "and all" "or something" 等，成为霍尔顿独具风格的语言特色，成为刻画人物性格特征的一部分。这些词汇的使用并无任何语法和句法作用，却给人一种含混、松弛的印象，读者可以从这种附着语中感受到霍尔顿的思索过程，好似霍尔顿对于这一问题意犹未尽但又不愿意再多费口舌，因而总用 and all 一类词语来收尾（芮雪梅，2012：90），也体现了霍尔顿的人物性格特征中那不善于、不喜欢将情感完全表达出来的叛逆性格。另外，小说中充斥着大量诅咒语、脏话以及俚语，这些诅咒语和脏话是对主人公性格特征的真实反映，这些细微之处体现着霍尔顿的情绪变化。

在译文的处理上，译者也同样选取了短句呼应的方法，以体现文体效果。比如，为了体现老菲碧的年龄老了，原文对话中菲碧的表达总是简单明了，词句很短，无任何限定表达或从句。在译文中，译者将老菲碧的话也处理得简洁明了，如 "Because you don't. You don't like any schools. You don't like a million things. You don't." 一句，译者没有添加任何并列连词，直译为 "因为你不喜欢。你讨厌上学。你讨厌好多东西。你不喜欢。" 这样的短句，能够带来一种压迫感，也符合说话人的身份情况。此外，对于原文中高频率使用的句末附着语，译者也采取了简洁、含混、松弛的译法，如"and all" "or something" 等，相应地译为 "……什么的" "……一样"，顺应了原文中霍尔顿独具风格的语言特色，使译文读者领略到了原文刻画人物性格特征的风格手法。除此之外，原文中使用了大量的诅咒语和脏话以及俚语来展示主人公的性格特征，译文也采用了直译的方法，如"见鬼的""他妈的""我他妈的"等，把原文主人公情绪变化的细微之处体现在了译文中。

📖 12.5 课后练习

（1）Jane Eyre

The chamber looked such a bright little place to me as the sun shone in between the gay blue chintz window curtains, showing papered walls and a carpeted floor, so unlike the bare planks and stained plaster of Lowood, that my spirits rose at the view. Externals have a great effect on the young: I thought that fairer era of life was beginning for me, —one that was to have its flowers and pleasures, as well as its thorns and toils. My faculties, roused by the change of scene, the new field offered to hope, seemed all astir. I cannot precisely define what they expected, but it was something pleasant: not perhaps that day or that month, but at an indefinite future period.

I rose; I dressed myself with care: obliged to be plain—for I had no article of attire that was not made with extreme simplicity—I was still by nature solicitous to be neat. It was not my habit to be disregardful of appearance, or careless of the impression I made: on the contrary, I ever wished to look as well as I could, and to please as much as my want of beauty would permit. I sometimes regretted that I was not handsomer: I sometimes wished to have rosy cheeks, a straight nose, and small cherry mouth; I desired to be tall, stately, and finely developed in figure; I felt it a misfortune that I was so little, so pale, and had features so irregular and so marked. And why had

I these aspirations and these regrets? It would be difficult to say: I could not then distinctly say it to myself; yet I had a reason, and a logical, natural reason too. However. When I had brushed my hair wery smooth, and put on my black frock—which, Quakerlike as it was, at least had the merit of fitting to a nicety—and adjusted my clean white tucker, I thought I should do respectably enough to appear before Mrs. Fairfax; and that my new pupil would not at least recoil from me with antipathy. Having opened my chamber window, and seen that I left all things straight and neat on the toilet table, I ventured forth.

（2）一件小事

我从乡下跑进城里，一转眼已经六年了。其间耳闻目睹的所谓国家大事，算起来也很不少；但在我心里，都不留什么痕迹，倘要我寻出这些事的影响来说，便只是增长了我的坏脾气——老实说，便是教我一天比一天的看不起人。但有一件小事，却于我有意义，将我从坏脾气里拖开，使我至今忘记不得。这是民国六年的冬天，北风刮得正猛，我因为生计关系，不得不一早在路上走。一路几乎遇不见人，好不容易才雇定了一辆人力车，叫他拉到S门去。不一会，北风小了，路上浮尘早已刮净，剩下一条洁白的大道来，车夫也跑得更快。刚近S门，忽而车把上带着一个人，慢慢地倒了。跌倒的是一个老女人，花白头发，衣服都很破烂。伊从马路边上突然向车前横截过来；车夫已经让开道，但伊的破棉背心没有上扣，微风吹着，向外展开，所以终于兜着车把。幸而车夫早有点停步，否则伊定要栽一个大斤斗，跌到头破血出了。伊伏在地上；车夫便也立住脚。我料

第 12 章 小说

定这老女人并没有伤，又没有别人看见，便很怪他多事，要是自己惹出是非，也误了我的路。我便对他说，"没有什么的。走你的罢！"车夫毫不理会，或者并没有听到，却放下车子，扶那老女人慢慢起来，搀着臂膊立定，问伊说："您怎么啦？""我摔坏了。"我想，我眼见你慢慢倒地，怎么会摔坏呢，装腔作势罢了，这真可憎恶。车夫多事，也正是自讨苦吃，现在你自己想法去。车夫听了这老女人的话，却毫不踌躇，搀着伊的臂膊，便一步一步地向前走。我有些诧异，忙看前面，是一所巡警分驻所，大风之后，外面也不见人。这车夫扶着那老女人，便正是向那大门走去。我这时突然感到一种异样的感觉，觉得他满身灰尘的后影，刹时高大了，而且愈走愈大，须仰视才见。而且他对于我，渐渐地又几乎变成一种威压，甚而至于要榨出皮袍下面藏着的"小"来。我的活力这时大约有些凝滞了，坐着没有动，也没有想，直到看见分驻所里走出一个巡警，才下了车。巡警走近我说："你自己雇车罢，他不能拉你了。"我没有思索地从外套袋里抓出一大把铜元，交给巡警，说，"请你给他……"风全住了，路上还很静。我一路走着，几乎怕敢想到我自己。以前的事姑且搁起，这一大把铜元又是什么意思，奖他么？我还能裁判车夫么？我不能回答自己。这事到了现在，还是时时记起。我因此也时时煞了苦痛，努力地要想到我自己。几年来的文治武力，在我早如幼小时候所读过的"子曰诗云"一般，背不上半句了。独有这一件小事，却总是浮在我眼前，有时反更分明，教我惭愧，催我自新，并增长我的勇气和希望。

第 13 章　戏剧

戏剧文体与翻译

戏剧，是一种独特的文学体裁，有着悠久的历史，也有着丰富的表达形式。戏剧融合了小说、诗歌、散文等文体的特点，又从具体形态上区别于上述体裁。戏剧有着素体诗的结构，却又不局限于诗歌结构；戏剧的情节线索突出，起承转合紧凑，却又比小说情节的表达更加强烈。

戏剧是综合性的艺术表达方式，不仅可供阅读，还能通过舞台演出的形式体现其艺术价值。戏剧的表达涉及服装、道具、灯光、音响等多方位因素。

戏剧的种类繁多。根据故事情节可以分为：悲剧、喜剧；根据艺术表现形式可以分为：话剧、歌剧、舞剧、戏曲等；根据篇幅可以分为：独幕剧、多幕剧；根据时代特征可以分为：历史剧、现代剧。

戏剧通过独白、对白以及旁白的方式来呈现剧情内容，因此，文本中多用生活化、浅显易懂的语言，这样才符合戏剧最终的舞台目的。但是戏剧又有兼容性，其表达兼具了小说的故事性和诗歌的韵律感，每一个戏剧的表达都是一个故事的推进，有铺垫、有高潮、有结局。此外，因为戏剧是一种表现型的文体形式，语音语调与语言的格律在戏剧的表现中也占有重要地位。

戏剧文体是一种特殊的文学文体，它既是舞台演出的蓝本，又是可供独立阅读的文学作品。戏剧文本的翻译也是为了最终使戏剧被搬上舞台进行表演而发生的。因此戏剧文体的翻译是多种翻译手法的综合产物，可以通过文内增译，即补充原文缺失的内容让目标语读者了解剧情；也可以通过解释文化负载，即将文化内涵丰富的词汇运用相应的表达呈现给读者等方式来完成对戏剧作品的翻译。

第13章 戏剧

13.1 课前实践

13.1.1 喜剧

The Merchant of Venice	威尼斯商人
Shakespeare	莎士比亚
Act IV Scene 1	第四幕第一场

Scene 1. Venice. A Court of Justice
Enter the DUKE, the Magnificoes, ANTONIO, BASSANIO, GRATIANO, SOLANDI, SALARINO, and others.

DUKE: What, is Antonio here?

ANTONIO: Ready, so please your grace.

DUKE:
I am sorry for thee; thou art come to answer
A stony adversary, an inhuman wretch
Uncapable of pity, void and empty
From any dram of mercy.

ANTONIO:
I have heard
Your grace hath ta'en great pains to qualify
His rigorous course; but since he stands obdurate,
And that no lawful means can carry me
Out of his envy's reach, I do oppose
My patience to his fury, and am arm'd
To suffer, with a quietness of spirit,
The very tyranny and rage of his.

DUKE: Go one, and call the Jew into the court.

SALERIO:
He is ready at the door; he comes, my lord
Enter SHYLOCK

DUKE:
Make room, and let him stand before our face.
Shylock, the world thinks, and I think so too,

（第一场　威尼斯法庭）
（公爵、众绅士、安东尼奥、巴萨尼奥、葛莱西安诺、萨拉里诺、萨莱尼奥及余人等同上。）

公爵：安东尼奥有没有来

安东尼奥：有，殿下

公爵：我很为你不快乐；你是来跟一个心如铁石的对手当庭质对，一个不懂得怜悯，没有一丝慈悲心的不近人情的恶汉。

安东尼奥：听说殿下曾经用尽力量劝他不要过为已甚，可是他一味坚持，不肯略作让步。既然没有合法的手段可以使我脱离他的怨毒的掌握，我只有用默忍迎受他的愤怒，安心等待着他的残暴的处置。

公爵：来人，传那犹太人到庭。

萨拉里诺：他在门口等着；他来了，殿下

（夏洛克上。）

公爵：大家让开些，让他站在我面前。夏洛克，人家都以为——我也这么想——你不过故意装出来这一副凶恶的姿态，到了最后关头，就会显出你的仁慈恻隐来，比你现在这种表面上

That thou but lead'st this fashion of thy malice.
To the last hour of act, and then, 'tis thought.
Thou' lt show thy mercy and remorse more strange.
Than is thy strange apparent cruelty;
And where thou now exact'st the penalty,
Which is a pound of this poor merchant's flesh.
Thou wilt not only lose thy forfeiture,
But, touch'd with human gentleness and love,
Forgive a moiety of the principal,
Glancing an eye of pity on his losses,
That have of late so huddled on his back,
Enow to press a royal merchant down,
And pluck commiseration of his state
From brassy bosoms and rough hearts of flint,
From stubborn Turks and Tartars, never train'd
To offices of tender courtesy.
We all expect a gentle answer, Jew.

SHYLOCK:
I have possess'd your grace of what I purpose
And by our holy Sabbath have I sworn
To have the due and forfeit of my bond.
If you deny it, let the danger light
Upon your charter and your city's freedom
You'll ask me why I rather choose to have
A weight of carrion flesh than to receive
Three thousand ducats. I'll not answer that,
But say it is my humour. Is it answered?
What if my house be troubled with a rat,
And I be pleas'd to give ten thousand ducats
To have it ban'd? What, are you answer'd yet?
Some men there are love not a gaping pig,
Some that are mad if they behold a cat,
And others, when the bagpipe sings I' th'nose
Cannot contain their urine; for affection,

的残酷更加出人意料；现在你虽然坚持着照约处罚，一定要从这个不幸的商人身上割下一磅肉来，到了那时候，你不但愿意放弃这一种处罚，而且因为受到良心上的感动，说不定还会豁免他一部分的欠款。你看他最近接连遭受的巨大损失，足以使无论怎样富有的商人倾家荡产，即使铁石一样的心肠，从来不知道人类同情的野蛮人，也不能不对他的境遇发生怜悯。犹太人，我们都在等候你一句温和的回答。

夏洛克：我的意思已经向殿下告禀过了；我也已经指着我们的圣安息日起誓，一定要照约执行处罚；要是殿下不准许我的请求，那就是蔑视宪章，我要到京城里去上告，要求撤销贵帮的特权。您要是问我为什么不愿接收三千块钱，宁愿拿一块腐烂的臭肉，那我可没什么理由可以回答您，我只能说我欢喜这样，这是不是一个回答。要是我的屋子里有了耗子，我高兴出一万块钱叫人把它们赶掉，谁管得了我？这不是回答了您么？有的人不爱看张开嘴的猪，有的人瞧见一只猫就要发脾气，还有人听见人家吹风笛的声音，就忍不住要小便；因为一个人的感情完全受着喜恶支配，谁也做不了自己的

Mistress of passion, sways it to the mood Of what it likes or loathes. Now for your answer As there is no firm reason to be render'd Why he cannot abide a gaping pig, Why he, a harmless necessary cat, Why he, a woolen bagpipe, but of force Must yield to such inevitable shame As to offend, himself being offend'd; So can I give no reason, nor I will not, More than a lodg'd hate and a certain loathing I bear Antonio, that I follow thus A losing suit against him. Are you answered?	主。现在我就这样回答您：为什么有人受不住一头张开嘴的猪，有人受不住一只有益无害的猫，还有人受不住咿咿呜呜的风笛的声音，这些都是毫无充分的理由的，只是因为天生的癖性，使他们一受到刺激，就会情不自禁地现出丑相来；所以我不能举什么理由，也不愿举什么理由，除了因为我对于安东尼奥抱着久积的仇恨和深刻的反感，所以才会向他进行这一场对于我自己并没有好处的诉讼。现在您不是已经得到我的答案了吗？

13.1.2 悲剧

Death of a Salesman

Arthur Miller

Act II Excerpt

推销员之死

阿瑟·米勒

第二幕　节选

Willy: Wonderful coffee. Meal in itself.

Linda: Can I make you some eggs?

Willy: No. Take a breath.

Linda: You look so rested, dear.

Willy: I slept like a dead one. First time in months. Imagine, sleeping till ten on a Tuesday morning. Boys left nice and early, heh?

Linda: They were out of here by eight o'clock.

Willy: Good work!

Linda: It was so thrilling to see them leaving

威利：咖啡真棒。能顶一顿饭。

林达：我给你做点鸡蛋吧？

威利：不用，你歇会儿吧。

林达：看样子你歇得挺好，亲爱的。

威利：我睡得好香啊，好几个月没这么香了。想想看，礼拜二早上一觉睡到十点，俩孩子一早就高高兴兴地走了？

林达：不到八点就出门了。

威利：好样儿的！

林达：看着他们俩一道走，真叫人

together. I can't get over the shaving lotion in this house!

Willy: (smiling) Mmm...

Linda: Biff was very changed this morning. His whole attitude seemed to be hopeful. He couldn't wait to get downtime to see Oliver.

Willy: He's heading for a change. There's no question, there simply are certain men that longer to get—solidified. How did he dress?

Linda: His blue suit. He's so handsome in that suit. He could be a—anything in that suit!

(Willy gets up from the table. Linda holds his jacket for him.)

Willy: There's no question, no question at all. Gee, on the way home tonight I'd like to buy some seeds.

Linda: (laughing) That'd be wonderful. But not enough sun gets back there. Nothing'll grow any more.

Willy: You wait, kid, before it's all over we're gonna get a little place out in the country, and I'll raise some vegetables, a couple of chickens...

Linda: You'll do it yet, dear.

(Willy walks out of his jacket. Linda follows him.)

Willy: And they'll get married, and come for a weekend. I'd build a little guest house. 'Cause I got so many fine tools, all I'd need would be a little lumber and some peace of mind.

高兴。满屋子都是刮胡子膏的香味儿，我真闻不够！

威利：（笑着）哼……

林达：比夫今天早晨可变样了。他整个态度都好像有奔头了。他简直等不及地要去城里见奥利弗。

威利：他是要转运了。毫无问题，有些人就是这样——大器晚成。他穿的什么衣服？

林达：那身蓝西装。他穿上那套衣服可神气了，简直像是——说他是什么人都行！

（威利离开桌子站起来。林达拿起上衣准备给他穿上。）

威利：没有问题，毫无问题。哎哟，今天晚上回家的路上我想去买点种子。

林达：（笑）那敢情好。可是这边阳光进不来，种什么也不长。

威利：你别忙，要不了多久，咱们在乡下弄一块小地方，我种上点菜，养上几只鸡……

林达：你准能做到，亲爱的。

（威利往前走，把外套甩下了。林达跟随着他。）

威利：到那会儿孩子们都结婚了，可以来跟咱们过周末，我可以盖一间小客房，反正我用的是最好的工具，我只要点木料，再就是心里别老这么乱。

Linda: (joyfully) I sewed the lining...

Willy: I could build two guest houses, so they'd both come. Did he decide how much he's going to ask Oliver for?

Linda: (getting him into the jacket) He didn't mention it, but I imagine ten or fifteen thousand. You're going to talk to Howard today?

Willy: Yeah. I'll put it to him straight and simple. He'll just have to take me off the road.

Linda: And Willy, don't forget to ask for a little advance, because we've got the insurance premium. It's the grace period now.

Willy: That's a hundred...?

Linda: A hundred and eight, sixty-eight. Because we're little short again.

Willy: Why are we short?

Linda: Well, you had the motor job on the car...

Willy: That goddam Studebaker!

Linda: And you got one more payment on the refrigerator...

Willy: But it just broke again!

Linda: Well, it's old, dear.

Willy: I told you we should've bought a well-advertised machine. Charley bought a General Electric and it's twenty years old and it's still good, that son-of-a-bitch.

Linda: But, Willy...

Willy: Whoever heard of a Hastings refrigerator? Once in my life I would like to own something outright before it's broken! I'm always in a race with the junkyard!

林达：（高兴地）我把里子缝好了……

威利：我可以盖两间客房，他们俩都可以来。他打定主意问奥利弗借多少了吗？

林达：（帮他穿上外套）他没提，不过我想是一万或者一万五。你今天要跟霍华德谈吗？

威利：谈。我要跟他们开门见山。他不能叫我再跑码头了。

林达：还有，威利，别忘了跟他预支点工资，因为咱们得付保险费。已经是宽限期了。

威利：那得一百……

林达：一百零八块六毛八。咱们最近手头又紧了。

威利：为什么手头又紧了？

林达：那，汽车的马达修理费……

威利：这个该死的斯图贝克！

林达：电冰箱还得付一期款……

威利：可它最近又坏过一回！

林达：那，的确也够旧的了，亲爱的。

威利：我早说过咱们应该买一个登大广告的名牌货。查理买的是通用牌的，二十年了，还挺好用，那个兔崽子！

林达：可是，威利……

威利：谁听说过黑斯丁斯牌的冰箱？我真盼望，哪怕一辈子有一回呢，等我付清了分期付款之后，东西还能

I just finished paying for the car and it's on its last legs. The refrigerator consumes belts like a goddam maniac. They time those things. They time them so when you finally paid for them, they're used up.

不坏！我现在是一天到晚跟垃圾场竞赛呢！我这辆汽车款刚刚付清，这辆车也快要散架了。电冰箱就疯子似的一根接着一根吃传动皮带。他们生产这种东西的时候都计算好了。等你付清最后一笔款，东西也就该坏了。

13.1.3 戏曲

牡 丹 亭

汤显祖

第一出 标目

【蝶恋花】
（末上）忙处抛人闲处住。
百计思量，没个为欢处。
白日消磨肠断句，世间只有情难诉。
玉茗堂前朝后暮，红烛迎人，俊得江山助。
但是相思莫相负，牡丹亭上三生路。

【汉宫春】
杜宝黄堂，生丽娘小姐，爱踏春阳。
感梦书生折柳，竟为情伤。
写真留记，葬梅花道院凄凉。
三年上，有梦梅柳子，
于此赴高唐。
果尔回生定配。

The Peony Pavilion

Tang Xianzu

Scene One Prelude

[To the tune of Dielianhua]
Announcer 2:
All the men prefer remaining free;
Yet howe'er they try,
They are as worried as can be.
Among the sentimental tales I write
Love is as mysterious as the sea.
I write the tale from morning till night,
With candles burning bright,
Enlightening me in the brightest ray.
When a beauty falls in love with a man
The Peony Pavilion sees her ardent way.

[To the tune of Hangongchun]
"Du Bao, the magistrate,
Has a daughter by the name of Liniang,
Who strolls in a sunny springtime date.
When she dreams of a scholar breaking willows,

> She's thrown into a grievous state.
> She draws a self-portrait
> And pines away lamenting o'er her fate.
> When three years have passed by,
> Liu Mengmei comes along
> To meet her in the garden once again.
> Du Liniang gains her second life.

13.2 文体特点

13.2.1 文章兼容并蓄　修辞手法多样

　　戏剧文体最显著的特征就是兼容性。戏剧具有诗歌的特点，如《哈姆雷特》中的经典章节"To be or not to be..."就是由素体诗（blank verse）写成的，外在节奏表现为每行都是五音步抑扬格。戏剧中的诗歌性是体现戏剧美学价值的一个重要方面。戏剧也具有小说的特性。戏剧的最终目的就是将戏剧故事搬上舞台表演，因此戏剧本身必须是一个有起承转合的完整故事，包含完整的人物刻画和成熟的故事情节，这既是小说的特点，也是戏剧的主要特征。然而，戏剧的情节冲突比小说的情节冲突更加重要。根据类型的不同，小说可以选择不同的表达手法。部分小说，根据其写作目的，可以没有跌宕的情节。但是作为舞台表现形式的一种，戏剧必须有冲突和高潮，以达到戏剧效果。因此，戏剧文体是一种兼容并蓄、囊括各种文体特征却自成一派的文体形式。

　　戏剧语言通常十分生动形象，情感丰富而饱满，时而让人捧腹大笑，时而让人潸然泪下，戏剧中常常使用多种多样的修辞手法，例如矛盾修饰法、押韵、双关、比喻、夸张等，这些修辞手法的运用使得戏剧语言更加鲜活，更加充满生命力。

13.2.2 语域特征显著　动作揭示个性

　　在戏剧文体中，语言是推动戏剧情节发展的第一要素，戏剧语言语域特征显著，突出表现为具有强烈的口语化特征。口语化也是戏剧区别于其他文学文体的重要特征。戏剧文体的另一个显著特征是其语言的动作性。戏剧语言的动作性，主要涉及两个方面：第一是指对话发出时随之产生的动作，如相关的面部表情，配合的手势，语调的提升或者降低，内心活动的体现等；第二是指对话所导致的行为，如因对话中的争执而导致的相互的暴力冲突，或者经过商谈后所做出的一致性选择等，这些都是戏剧语言的动作性体现，而这些动作性对于戏剧内容的呈现至关重要。戏剧语言的动作性可以突出主题思想，也可以突出人物性格，还可以突出人物关系，甚至可以因此而引起观众丰富的想象。（焦菊隐，1979：21）因此，对于戏剧语言动作性的了解，是挖掘戏剧的内在隐藏信息和独特魅力的基础。

此外，戏剧的动作，与戏剧中人物的鲜明个性息息相关。每一个戏剧人物都有着自己独特的性格特征，而这些性格特征除了通过对话来体现以外，还必须通过人物的动作来表达。不同的性别、性格、职业、年龄都会导致说话人的语气、神态、动作差异巨大。因此，对于戏剧语言、动作的细腻传达是揭示戏剧人物所处的社会环境、身份地位、性格特征的最主要方式。戏剧的人物性格与戏剧动作不可分割。

13.2.3　语言浅显易懂　意境自成高格

戏剧是"源于生活却高于生活"的艺术表现形式，戏剧表演是对生活的高度理想化，是生活性和艺术性的融合。戏剧的语言是精练后的生活语言。一方面，戏剧语言有它日常的一面，剧中人物所说之话一定是和他在剧中的身份、角色、成长环境、性格特征相一致的，真实而自然，特别像现实生活中的对话，一般很少有加工痕迹。然而，从另一个角度看，戏剧语言是不会出现日常口语中的"口误"的，戏剧语言一般句子结构完整，符合语法规则，比较讲究修辞。（俞东明：1996）

此外，戏剧的表现，是对生活故事的提炼，是浓缩的生活，是缩小又放大了的语言，是经过精心挑选的语言。这些精练的生活化语言统一为戏剧的情节推动和发展服务。看似精简的对话实际则包含了戏剧情节和舞台人物的全部魅力，让戏剧意境悠扬，久久不息。

13.3　翻译要领

13.3.1　注重语言特点　解读语言动作

由于戏剧的瞬时性和视听性特点，戏剧的翻译是不能完全套用其他翻译原则和标准的，有其独特的指引原则。戏剧的主要目的就是表演，因此戏剧的翻译也必须注重表演艺术的语言特点。在戏剧翻译的过程中，一定要从受众的角度出发，考虑受众的接受度，使用生活化、简明达意的表达方式，词汇选择既言简意赅，又富有生活气息，表达准确又有力度，充满情趣又不失时代气息。（张保红，2011：183）如：

原文 Willy: Wonderful coffee. Meal in itself. (Authur Miller, *Death of a Salesman*)

译文 威利：咖啡真棒。能顶一顿饭。（英若诚译）

原文 Willy: Goddammit, now I'm gonna do it! (Authur Miller, *Death of a Salesman*)

译文 威利：他妈的，我这下要动真格了！（朱生豪译）

从上述两个句子可以看出，在戏剧的表达中，译者选取的词汇不以优美为首要原则，而要符合人物的性格特点，要有生活气息。此处的"真棒""能顶""动真格"都属于有生命力、有生活气息的鲜活的口头用语，为戏剧表演增色不少。

此外，在戏剧翻译中，要注意戏剧语言动作的解读。戏剧语言的动作性原则，要求戏剧首先是在剧本语言（主要指台词）上要能够显示出形体动作；其次是剧本语言要能够揭示人物发出某个形体动作时的环境、气氛、心情；再次，剧本语言中要能够透露出行为动机和目的。剧本语言（对话）要有刺激对方的功能，从而具有推动"动作与反动作"的力量，即推动冲突发展的力量；最后，剧本语言要能够表现内心动作和情感意志，即表现心理活动。（高壮丽，2016：108）如：

原文 Lear: Peace, Kent!

　　　　Come not between the dragon and his wrath.

　　　　I lov'd her most, and thought to set my rest

　　　　On her kind nursery.

　　　　Hence, and avoid my sight! (Shakespeare, *King Lear*)

译文 李尔：闭嘴，肯特！

　　　　不要来批怒龙的逆鳞。

　　　　她是我最爱的一个，我本来想要在她的殷勤看护之下，

　　　　终养我的天年。

　　　　去，不要让我看见你的脸！（朱生豪译）

此段译文中，peace 在译文中被翻译成了有非常明显动作形态的"闭嘴"，读者可以根据这个词想象到做出该动作的具体环境、气氛、和说话者的心情、情绪状态。我们从这个单词的翻译中可以感受到愤怒而强烈的情绪，如若将 peace 译为如"安静""缄默不言"等，那么说话人情绪的愤怒就无从体现，情感表达就不如"闭嘴"来的强烈。又如：

原文 Regan: Sister, you'll go with us?

　　　　Goneril: No.

　　　　Regan: 'Tis most convenient; pray you, go with us. (Shakespeare, *King Lear*)

译文1 里根：姊姊，您也该和我们一块儿去吗？

　　　　高瑞纳：不。

　　　　里根：您怎么可以不去？来，请吧。（朱生豪译）

译文2 瑞：您和我们一同吧，姊姊。

　　　　刚：不。

瑞：这样最好，你和我们来吧。（梁实秋译）

这里的对话语言形象地显示出了戏剧语言的心理斗争。这里 Regan 不愿意姐姐与 Edmund 单独待在一起，极力劝其同自己一起离开。上述两个译本中，译文 1 改变了原文的呈现方式，用了反问，这种手法经常出现在中国的话剧和电视表演中；且用了"来，请吧"，寥寥数字，就构造了一幅画面，通过反问和精简概括的表达，可以感受到两姐妹心中暗暗较量，剑拔弩张的紧张态势；译文 2 整体感觉更为柔和，因此，没能将两姐妹的心理状态完美呈现出来，但是却十分忠实于原文的结构，这也是动作体现心理的表现。

13.3.2　注重指示性语言　还原真实戏剧

指示性语言对于戏剧的翻译有着重要的指导作用。"戏剧的意义依靠其中的指示系统实现，因为指示语规范着各种语言行为的实施，甚至句法、语法和修辞都依赖于指示语将各种意义包含、组合在一起，不管这些意义来自哪个方面——形象、不同语体的语言、人物的多种语言模式、语调、节奏、代理关系或者动作，等等"。（Bassnett, 1990: 94）由此可以看出，指示语的翻译直接影响到观众或读者对戏剧的理解和接受。

指示语包括一般指示语和舞台提示语。一般指示语通常分为人称、地点、时间指示语，以及社交指示语和语篇指示语。一般指示语看似不重要，但是在戏剧的翻译中，指示语的翻译却起到了决定性作用。90% 以上的陈述句都包括说话人、听话人、时间、地点等的隐形指示信息（何自然、冉永平，2006：39）。正是因为如此，通过翻译一般指示语，能帮助读者获取完整信息，从而帮助理解话语的内在隐藏含义。如：

原文 **Linda:** He was crestfallen, Willy.

You know how he admires you. I think if he finds himself,

then you'll both be happier and not fight any more.

Willy: How can he find himself on a farm? Is that a life?

A farm hand? In the beginning, when he was young, I thought, well, a young man, it's good for him to tramp around, take a lot of different jobs.

But it's more than ten years now and he has yet to make thirty-five dollars a week! (Authur Miller, *Death of a Salesman*)

译文 1 林达：他可垂头丧气了，威利。你知道他多么崇拜你。

我看等到他真能够发挥他的长处的时候，你们两个就都高兴了，就不打架了。

威利：他待在个农场上怎么发挥长处？那也叫生活吗？

当个农业工人？一开头，他还年轻，我想嘛，年轻人，到处闯练闯练也好，各种行当都试试。

可是已经过去不止十年了，他一个礼拜还挣不了三十五块钱！（英若诚译）

译文2 **林妲：** 他垂头丧气，惟利。你知道他多崇拜你。

我想，他要是心里有了落儿，你们爷儿俩会快活得多，不会再闹别扭了。

惟利： 他怎么能到农场去呐？这也算一条出路吗？

做个长工？起初，他年纪小的时候，我觉得也能，小孩子家，让他多做些各种行业，闯练闯练也是好的。可是，现在过了十多年，他一星期还不过挣三十五块钱。（姚克译）

两个中文译本对内容的处理都很到位，都极富口语特色。但在语篇指示语 that 上，两者的处理却不同。原文中 that 指的是"Biff finds himself on the farm."这件事，英译直接翻译成了"那"；而姚译却翻译成了"这"，使整个指示系统发生混乱，影响戏剧效果。

其次，舞台提示语的翻译对于戏剧的表现也至关重要。所谓的"舞台提示"是指剧本中不要求在演出时说出的文字说明部分，一般包括对剧情发生的时间、地点的交代，对布景、灯光、音效等艺术处理的要求，以及对人物形体动作、心理活动和场景气氛的指示等，它是戏剧艺术从案头走上舞台的重要桥梁。（任晓霏、张吟，2014：86）早期的戏剧翻译中，译者并不看重对舞台提示语的翻译，但是，随着剧作家们开始逐渐通过变化舞台上灯光、位置、地点、布景等来体现对艺术的细致描绘后，译者们也开始重视对于舞台提示语的翻译。如：

原文 Linda, his wife, has stirred in her bed at the right. She gets out and puts on a robe, listening. Most often jovial, she has developed an iron repression of her exceptions to Willy's—she more than loves him, she admires him, as though his mercurial nature, his temper, his massive dreams and little cruelties, served her only as sharp reminders of the turbulent longings within him, longings which she shares but lacks the temperament to utter and follow to their end.

译文1 在右边的屋里，他的妻子林达在床上翻动了一下。她起床，披上一件睡袍，倾耳听着。她通常是个乐呵呵的人，但多年来已经形成克制自己的习惯，决不允许自己对威利的表现有任何不满，——她不仅仅是爱威利，她崇拜他，威利的反复无常的性格，他的脾气，他那些大而无当的梦想和小小的使她伤心的行为，似乎对她只是一个提醒，使她更痛心地感到威利心里那些折磨他的渴望，而这些渴望在她心中也同样存在，只不过她说不出来，也缺少把这

些渴望追求到底的气质。（英若诚译）

译文2 他的太太林妲在右边厢的床上，已经睡醒了。她下了床，穿上一件寝袍，耸耳倾听。她经常是有说有笑的；虽然对惟利的行径不以为然，她可养成了铁一般的逆来顺受之道。她不单只爱他，简直敬仰他。他从容不定的本性，他的脾气，他无涯际的梦想和些微的残忍，好像只会使她更敏锐地憬悟他内心激湍似的歆羡。她也有同样的歆羡，可是限於性格，她不会直说出来和贯彻到底。（姚克译）

这是戏剧即将开场前的一段舞台提示语，作者十分用心地剖析人物之间微妙的关系和复杂的心理，是整个剧情重要的铺垫。我们发现，译文1通过巧妙添加"自己""那些""这些"指示语，使人物关系、复杂心理豁然开朗，有利于导演和演员从一开始就进入剧情。而译文2只限于语言表层的处理，语言不够明白晓畅，没有有效地实现舞台提示语的功能。

综上所述，对于舞台提示语和指示性语言的翻译是确保读者和观众获取最原汁原味的戏剧故事的重要保障。

13.3.3 填补文内缺失 类比替换概念

根据戏剧的瞬时性、无注性和表演性特征，文后加注的形式对于戏剧文体而言显然是行不通的。因此，戏剧的翻译，在出现文化内涵意义丰富的词汇时，主要采用文内增译的方式。通过简单的词组的添加，让观众能够快速了解原剧本想要传递的核心概念。如：

原文 眉头一纵，计上心来。只把美人图点上些破绽，到京师必定发入冷宫，教他受苦一世。（马致远《汉宫秋》第一折）

译文 As soon as I knit my brow to think, a scheme comes up. I need only to disfigure the girl's portrait a little, so that when she arrives at the capital, she will be sent to the "cold palace" for neglected ladies to suffer a whole life long. （John Francis Davis 等译）

此处的文化负载词是"冷宫"，中国读者因为观看过清宫剧或古代小说，因此大部分人对"冷宫"这一词汇都耳熟能详，然而外国观众则因为文化差异而无法理解"冷宫"所表达的内在含义。因此，在译文中，译者通过增译 for neglected ladies 这一概念，显化了冷宫的内在含义，让外国读者能够一目了然。"如果一句台词所蕴含的文化内涵很深厚时，需要花很多的笔墨来解释，放入台词显然是不大妥当的。找到其他的戏剧表演符号来代替这一内容，这样一来，可以保留其应有的戏剧内容和效果，可以达到功能上的对等。"（熊婷婷，2006：6）

戏剧中常常出现一些有丰富的文化内涵和社会历史背景的词汇，翻译时难以在有限的字数内解释完整，如中国传统文化中带有宗教色彩的词汇："净土""西天""三生""化缘";其他中国传统文化词汇,如"生肖""古代时辰"等。部分词汇需结合原文上下文或社会大背景才能正确理解,这些词的翻译都可通过转化核心概念来完成。如:

原文 周秀花:你想得倒好,可哪那么容易!去吧,小花,在路上留神吉普车!(老舍《茶馆》)

译文 Zhou Xiuhua: That's a nice thought, but it's not as easy as that. Off to school now, Xiaohua, and watch out for those drunken American jeep drivers.
(John Howard-Gibbon 译)

原文出现的"吉普车"是有潜在内涵意义的词汇,体现了当时中国社会的下层人士对现状敢怒而不敢言的一种状态。如不结合上下文,观众无法将"吉普车"与所特指的对象进行关联,因此,译者直接替换了吉普车的概念,改为"开吉普车的美国大兵",并增译了 drunken 一词,让观众了然于心。

因此,在翻译涉及文化内涵或特定内容的戏剧时,要将数种翻译技巧结合使用,才能达到最理想的效果。

13.4 译文赏评

13.4.1 历史剧

原文

Henry IV Part I

Shakespeare

Act 1 Scene 2

London. An apartment of the Prince's

Enter Henry, Prince of Wales and Sir John Falstaff

...

Enter POINS

PRINCE HENRY: Good morrow, Ned.

POINS: Good morrow, sweet Hal. What says Monsieur Remorse? What says Sir John Sack and Sugar, Jack? How agrees the devil and thee about thy soul, that thou soldest him on Good Friday last for a cup of Madeira and a cold capon's leg?

PRINCE HENRY: Sir John stands to his word, the devil shall have his bargain; for he was never yet a breaker of proverbs: he will give the devil his due.

POINS: Then art thou damned for keeping thy word with the devil.

PRINCE HENRY: Else he had been damned for cozening the devil.

POINS: But, my lads, my lads, tomorrow morning, by four o'clock, early at Gad's Hill, there are pilgrims going to Canterbury with rich offerings, and traders riding to London with fat purses. I have vizards for you all; you have horses for yourselves. Gadshill lies tonight in Rochester. I have bespoke supper tomorrow night in Eastcheap; we may do it as secure as sleep. If you will go, I will stuff your purses full of crowns; if you will not, tarry at home and be hanged.

FALSTAFF: Hear ye, Yedward, if I tarry at home and go not, I'll hang you for going.

POINS: You will, chops?

FALSTAFF: Hal, wilt thou make one?

PRINCE HENRY: Who, I rob? I a thief? Not I.

FALSTAFF: There's neither honesty, manhood, nor good fellowship in thee, nor thou cam'st not of the blood royal, if thou dar'st not stand for ten shillings.

PRINCE HENRY: Well then, once in my days I'll be a madcap.

FALSTAFF: Why, that's well said.

PRINCE HENRY: Well, come what will, I'll tarry at home.

FALSTAFF: I'll be a traitor then, when thou art king.

PRINCE HENRY: I care not.

POINS: Sir John, I prithee leave the prince and me alone: I will lay him down such reasons for this adventure that he shall go.

FALSTAFF: Well, mayst thou have the spirit of persuasion and he the ears of profiting, that what thou speakest may move and what he hears may be believed, that the true prince may, for recreation sake, prove a false thief; for the poor abuses of the time want countenance. Farewell. You shall find me in Eastcheap.

PRINCE HENRY: Farewell, the latter spring! Farewell, All-hallown summer!

Exit FALSTAFF

POINS: Now, my good sweet honey lord, ride with us tomorrow. I have a jest to execute that I cannot manage alone. Falstaff, Peto, Bardolph and Gadshill shall rob those men that we have already waylaid: yourself and I will not be there. And when they have the booty, if you and I do not rob them, cut this head from my shoulders.

PRINCE HENRY: But how shall we part with them in setting forth?

POINS: Why, we will set forth before or after them, and appoint them a place of meeting, wherein it is at our pleasure to fail; and then will they adventure upon the exploit themselves, which they shall have no sooner achieved, but we'll set upon them.

PRINCE HENRY: Yea, but 'tis like that they will know us by our horses, by our habits and by every other appointment, to be ourselves.

POINS: Tut! Our horses they shall not see: I'll tie them in the wood. Our vizards we will change after we leave them. And, sirrah, I have cases of buckram for then once, to immask our noted outward garments.

PRINCE HENRY: But I doubt they will be too hard for us.

POINS: Well, for two of them, I know them to be as true-bred cowards as ever turned back. And for the third, if he fight longer than he sees reason, I'll forswear arms. The virtue of this jest will be the incomprehensible lies that this fat rogue will tell us when we meet at supper: how thirty at least he fought with, what wards, what blows, what extremities he endured; and in the reproof of this lies the jest.

PRINCE HENRY: Well, I'll go with thee. Provide us all things necessary and meet me tomorrow night in Eastcheap. There I'll sup. Farewell.

POINS: Farewell, my lord.

Exit POINS

PRINCE HENRY:

I know you all, and will awhile uphold

The unyoked humour of your idleness.

Yet herein will I imitate the sun,

Who doth permit the base contagious clouds

To smother up his beauty from the world,

That when he please again to be himself,

Being wanted, he may be more wondered at,

By breaking through the foul and ugly mists

Of vapours that did seem to strangle him.

If all the year were playing holidays,

To sport would be as tedious as to work;

But when they seldom come, they wished for come,

And nothing pleaseth but rare accidents.

So, when this loose behaviour I throw off

And pay the debt I never promisèd,

By how much better than my word I am,

By so much shall I falsify men's hopes,

And like bright metal on a sullen ground,

My reformation, glittering o'er my fault,

Shall show more goodly and attract more eyes

Than that which hath no foil to set it off.

I'll so offend to make offence a skill,

Redeeming time when men think least I will.

Exit

译文

亨利四世（上）

莎士比亚

第一幕　第二场

伦敦。具体地点不详，可能在王子的住所

（威尔士亲王亨利与约翰·福斯塔夫爵士上）

……

（波因斯上）

亨利王子：早安，奈德。

波因斯：早安，可爱的哈尔。悔恨先生说什么来着？甜酒约翰爵士说什么来着，杰克？在去年耶稣受难日那天，你为一杯马德拉酒和一只冷阉鸡腿答应把你的灵魂出卖给魔鬼，你同魔鬼如何达成协议的？

亨利王子：约翰爵士一诺千金，魔鬼一定会买个好价钱，因为他从来不违背古谚的训诫：该是魔鬼还得给他。

波因斯：同魔鬼讲守约履诺，你会下地狱。

亨利王子：如果他欺骗魔鬼，他早就下地狱了。

波因斯：伙计们，听着，伙计们，明晨一早四点钟，在盖兹山有一群香客带着大量的供品前往坎特伯雷，还有一些商人骑马去伦敦，也是囊中丰肥。我为你们准备好了面具，马匹各人自备。盖兹希尔今晚在罗切斯特过夜。明天的晚饭我已在依斯特溪泊给大家预订好了。这笔生意像睡觉一样十拿九稳。如果你们要去，我保证你们的口袋塞满金币而归；如果不去，就待在家里吊死吧。

福斯塔夫：听着，爱德华，如果我待在家里不去的话，我将告官，把你弄去吊死。

波因斯：你要去吗，肥佬？

福斯塔夫：哈尔，你去吗？

亨利王子：谁？我，去抢劫？我，当小偷？我不。

福斯塔夫：如果你连十先令的胆量也没有，那你这人既无诚信，又无男子汉气概，还不讲交情，枉为皇家子弟。

亨利王子：那么，一生一世我就荒唐这一次吧。

福斯塔夫：对啦，这才叫话。

亨利王子：算了，无论如何我还是待在家里。

福斯塔夫：等你当了国王，我也要当叛徒。

亨利王子：我不在乎。

波因斯：约翰爵士，请你让我同亲王单独谈谈，我要向他陈述此次冒险的充分理由以说服他参与。

福斯塔夫：那好，但愿你的嘴循循善诱，他的耳言听计从，你的话叫他心动，令他信服，如此这般，一位当朝的真王子为寻开心可暂做一个假贼；因为当今的作奸犯科之事都需冠冕堂皇的荫庇。再见吧，到时候你们到依斯特溪泊酒店来找我。

亨利王子：再见，暮春先生！再见，残夏之人！

（福斯塔夫下）

波因斯：听我说，我的亲爱的亲密的好殿下，明天同我们一起去吧。我要开一个大玩笑，但我孤掌难鸣。福斯塔夫、皮多、巴道夫和盖兹希尔要去拦劫那群客商，我们已经设好了埋伏；而你和我不跟他们一块，等他们把赃物抢到手，我俩再从他们手中抢过来，假如办不到，我输我肩头上这颗脑袋给你。

亨利王子：可是如果同他们一起动身，我们如何同他们分手呢？

波因斯：嗨，我们先同他们约定一个会合的地点，然后比他们早些或晚些动身，到时候我们故意不去同他们见面，他们自己就会去抢，而他们一得手，我们立即抢他们。

亨利王子：但是他们可能从我们骑的马、穿的衣和其他行头上认出我们。

波因斯：得啦，我们的马匹不会让他们看见：我要把马拴在树林里。至于我们的面具，同他们一分手我就把它们换了。老兄，我还准备了两套粗布衣服，到时候往身上一套，就什么都遮盖了。

亨利王子：可是我担心我俩不是他们的对手。

波因斯：嘿，他们中有两个，就我所知，是天生的懦夫，逃命跑得最快。另一个更明白恋战于他不利的道理，假如他会拼命来斗，我愿从此解甲挂刀剑。这场玩笑的精彩之处在于，我们晚饭聚在一起时，这个无赖的胖子会给大家撒弥天大谎：吹他如何同至少三十个人交手，如何攻防，如何奋勇当先，如何身陷险境而孤身坚持。然后，我们一一揭穿他的谎言，狠狠羞辱他一顿，教训他一番，这个玩笑就大功告成了。

亨利王子：好吧，我与你们前往。把一切都准备妥当，明天晚上到依斯特溪泊酒店来见我，我在此晚餐。再见。

波因斯：再见，殿下。

（波因斯下）

亨利王子：

我深知众卿所作所为，

暂与你们的懒散德性

相呼相应，放浪无行。

为此我要效仿太阳，

让恶云暂蔽其威光，

一旦云垒破雾障散，

他重现真身，因为久仰，

世人倍加礼赞他的辉煌。

倘若天天皆佳节喜庆，

游乐就会乏味如劳作；

为其稀有，众人渴求；

事物罕见，兴味盎然；

一旦我收敛放荡行状，

还清我从未承诺要还的欠账，

我之所为必远胜我之所言，

一举破除世人于我的成见。

如金银衬于暗底而耀眼，

我一旦幡然改进，

则愈显今之上进，

更赢天下人之羡钦；

此道助我，相反相成：

犯过实为日后补过矫正，

在人们最难料时弃旧图新。

（下）

赏评

　　素体诗在莎士比亚戏剧，尤其是历史剧中占有重要的地位。莎士比亚历史剧由于其描述背景（王朝历史更迭）的特殊性，出场人物多为公爵、亲王等皇室成员，因此，用无韵素体诗文体，符合剧中出现的正式场合，符合剧中人物的受教育程度和尊贵身份。然而，在《亨利四世（上、下）》中，亨利王子因其放荡的个性，混迹于市井民间，因此一反常态地使用了散文体与市民交流，这一散文体在戏剧最初是为了体现亨利王子表面上的自甘堕落。而本节最后，亨利王子的内心活动却一改常态，用素体诗表达，表明了亨利王子放荡不羁的外表下，依旧拥有着一颗属于上流社会的心，与看似打成一片的波因斯之间，其实仍有着不可逾越的鸿沟，为后文故事的逆转埋下了伏笔。

　　从词汇层面看，原文中运用了大量生活化的词汇，如 lads、chops 和 madcap 等，这些市井词汇有着强烈的生活气息，能够与枯燥的、一板一眼的王室生活形成对比，形象生动，能够激发读者的兴趣。译者在翻译过程中，也选择了能体现人物形象的对应的生活化词语，如将 chops 翻译成"肥佬"更能体现福斯塔夫和波因斯之间的关系，既低俗又亲密。此外，该版译文保留了多处原文语境的文化概念，如将 All-hallown summer 翻译成"残夏之人"，此处想表达的实际意义是福斯塔夫言行不一致的行为可以追溯到其年轻时代，但是如果不阅读注释，读者无法快速理解，这样的翻译虽然忠实于原文，但是容易造成读者的阅读障碍。

　　从句子结构看，原文采用了大量的散文体，表示接近生活的对话，有粗俗，有戏谑，最后幕尾亨利王子的内心独白重回诗体，揭示王子内心的雄伟抱负。寥寥数行诗句，与之前的散文体相比，显得更加庄重严肃。译者在译文的处理上，体现了音韵美，使用了"效仿""威光"、"久仰""辉煌"等押韵的词汇，使得诗歌在此处读起来荡气回肠。此外，双元音、长元音的使用使得表达的力度得以增强。从画面感受上来看，原文色彩对比强烈，bright metal on sullen ground 突出了明暗对比，也体现了王子的内心，认为自己依旧是这篇混沌土地上的闪耀之星，因此，译文通过"如金银衬于暗底而耀眼"这一句，尽可能地体现了色彩对比之强烈，但"金银衬于暗底"已经足够体现这种强烈的反差,然而译者还是通过增添"而耀眼"来进一步阐释这样一种烘托的作用,虽能够帮助读者流畅地理解原文,却使读者丧失了自己思考的机会,缩减了原剧中对于空间美的留存。

13.4.2 话剧

原文

茶 馆

老舍

第二幕

宋恩子:后面住着的都是什么人?

王利发:多半是大学生,还有几位熟人。我有登记簿子,随时报告给"巡警阁子"。我拿来,二位看看?

吴祥子:我们不看簿子,看人!

王利发:您甭看,准保都是靠得住的人!

宋恩子:你为什么爱租学生们呢?学生不是什么老实家伙呀!

王利发:这年月,作官的今天上任,明天撤职,作买卖的今天开市,明天关门,都不可靠!只有学生有钱,能够按月交房租,没钱的就上不了大学啊!您看,是这么一笔账不是?

宋恩子:都叫你咂摸透了!你想的对!现在,连我们也欠饷啊!

吴祥子:是呀,所以非天天拿人不可,好得点津贴!

宋恩子:就仗着有错拿,没错放的,拿住人就有津贴!走吧,到后边看看去!

吴祥子:走!

王利发:二位,二位!您放心,准保没错儿!

宋恩子:不看,拿不到人,谁给我们津贴呢?

吴祥子:王掌柜不愿意咱们看,王掌柜必会给咱们想办法!咱们得给王掌柜留个面子!对吧?王掌柜!

王利发:我……

宋恩子:我出个不很高明的主意:干脆来个包月,每月一号,按阳历算,你把那点……

吴祥子:那点意思!

宋恩子:对,那点意思送到,你省事,我们也省事!

王利发:那点意思得多少呢?

吴祥子:多年的交情,你看着办!你聪明,还能把那点意思闹成不好意思吗?

译文

Teahouse
Lao She
Act Two

Song Enzi: Who do you have lodging back there?

Wang Lifa: Mostly university students, and a few friends as well. I keep a register and report to police Headquarters from time to time. Shall I get it for you?

Wu Xiangzi: We don't watch registers, we watch people.

Wang Lifa: You don't need to watch anyone here, I guarantee they're all solid citizens.

Song Enzi: Just why do you like renting to students, eh? Students aren't such a reliable lot.

Wang Lifa: Nowadays officials are appointed one day and dismissed the next. Merchants open shop today and tomorrow they're broke. You can't depend on them. It's only the students who have money to pay rent each month; if they didn't have money they wouldn't be in university. Think about it. Makes sense, doesn't it?

Song Enzi: To the last detail. You're dead right. We haven't been paid lately ourselves.

Wu Xiangzi: That's right. So we have to nab somebody everyday just to keep in pocket money.

Song Enzi: We're not too fussy about who we nab, but we are about who we let go. Making arrests is what keeps us in pocket money. Come on, let's take a look out back.

Wu Xiangzi: After you.

Wang Lifa: Gentlemen, gentlemen, don't trouble yourselves. I assure you, nobody here's broken the law.

Song Enzi: But if we don't look, we can't nab anybody. And if we don't what do we do for cash?

Wu Xiangzi: If Proprietor Wang doesn't want us to look, he'll surely be able to think of something else for us. We've got to give Proprietor Wang a chance to save face. Right, Proprietor Wang?

Wang Lifa: I...

Song Enzi: It's not too bright, but I've got an idea: how about a simple monthly reckoning? On the first of every month—by the Western calendar—you can send us this little...

Wu Xiangzi: Little expression of gratitude.

Song Enzi: Right. Just a little expression of gratitude. Save you time, and save us time.

Wang Lifa: This little expression of gratitude—how much will it come to?

Wu Xiangzi: We're old friends; do as you see fit. You understand these things—you wouldn't want to turn an expression of gratitude into ingratitude, would you?

赏评

原文选自《茶馆》第二幕的一处对话。由于戏剧是显性的文学，是对人物形象、故事线索的再次呈现，具有表演性，因此，词汇和语言的选择都有简洁、通俗易懂的特性，能够让人们感受到文化的冲击和故事情节的推进。本段虽只有几句话的对白，但戏剧冲突已经非常明显。王利发的聪明和善良，宋恩子和吴祥子的丑恶嘴脸，在这几句对白中已经一览无余。因此，翻译时需要考虑的是：①如何保留原文简洁的结构；②如何顺利地翻译出原文中具有文化特征的词汇，如"都叫你唖摸透了""准保没错儿""那点意思"等。本译文选自霍华德的版本。在词汇层面上，译文还原了原文的简洁结构，而且选词也符合目标读者的阅读习惯。如："您甭看，准保都是靠得住的人！"一句中，将"靠得住"译成 solid citizens，英国人在口语中经常用这个词组表示"靠得住的人"。但是，"您看，是这么一笔账不是？"霍华德译成"Think about it. Makes sense, doesn't it?" 译文虽简洁且符合口语习惯，但是，却没有能够体现出原文的态度，原文中的王利发为了极力避免与宋恩子两人发生矛盾，用语极其谨慎，处处都非常尊重二人，问询也是小心翼翼，而译成"Think about it."这种祈使句，则有点生硬，不像王利发的作风。另外，译者注意到了宋恩子和吴祥子两人市侩、趋炎附势的嘴脸，在用词上体现了二人的粗俗、粗鄙，如"you are dead right""so we have to nab somebody"等。原文最经典的就是最后一句，吴祥子的这一句话饱含了中国文字的艺术，又体现出了他巧取豪夺、威逼利诱的嘴脸。如何将字面意思和内涵艺术两者恰如其分地表现出来，是戏剧翻译中的一个难题。霍华德的译本将"意思"理解为 expression of gratitude，把"不好意思"译成 ingratitude，这里确实让人可以感受到原文所要表达的意思，但是 gratitude 本身却体现不出原文的讽刺意味。若译成"I'm sure you wouldn't want this token of friendship to seem unfriendly, would you?"（英若诚译），把"那点意思"译成 a token of friendship，就极具讽刺意味，让人能够真切地感受到这些人虚伪卑劣的态度。

13.4.3 戏剧

原文

邯 郸 记
汤显祖

第六出　赠试

【绕地游】

（旦上）偶然心上。做尽风流样，懒妆成又偎人半晌。

（老贴笑上）营勾了腰肢通笼绣帐，听得来愁人夜长。

【丑奴儿】

（旦）红围粉簇清幽路，那得人游？

（老）天与风流，有客窥帘动玉钩。

（贴）探香觅翠芙蓉架，官了私休。

（合）此处人留，蝶梦迷花正起头。

（老）姐姐，天上吊下一个卢郎

（贴）不是吊下卢郎，是个驴郎。

（旦）蠢丫头，说出本相。思想起我家七辈无白衣女婿，要打发他应举，你道如何？

（老）好哩，姐夫得官回，你做夫人了。

【卜算子】

（生上）长宵清话长，广被风情广。似笑如颦在画堂。费劲佳人想

（见介）

（旦）卢郎，（集唐）你不羡名公乐此身，

（生）这风光别似武陵春。

（旦）百花仙酿能留客，

（生）一面红妆恼煞人。

（旦）卢郎，自招你在此，成了夫妇。和你朝欢暮乐，百纵千随，真人间得意之事也。但我家七辈无白衣女婿，你功名之兴，却是何如？

（生）不欺娘子说：小生书史虽然得读，儒冠误了多年。今日天缘，现成受用，功名二字，再也休提。

（旦）咳，秀才家好说这话。且问你会过几场来。

【朱奴儿】

（生）我也忘记起春秋几场

则翰林苑不看文章。

没气力头白功名纸半张，

直那等豪门贵党。

（合）高名望，时来运当，平白地为卿相。

（旦）说豪门贵党，也怪不的他。则你交游不多，才名未广，以致淹迟。奴家四门亲戚，多在要津，你去长安，都须拜在门下。

（生）领教了。

（旦）还一件来，公门要路，能勾容易近他？奴家再着一家兄相帮引进，取状元如反掌耳。

（生）令兄有这样行止？

（旦）从来如此了。

译文

The Handan Dream

Tang Xianzu

Scene Six Funding for the Imperial Examination

[To the tune of Raodiyou]

(Enter Miss Cui)

Miss Cui: To please my sweetheart

I've done my best to give and take

And stay by his side when I wake

(Enter Maidservant and Meixiang in smiles)

Maidservant, Meixiang: The man and wife embrace each other

In bed in the dim light

What and enticing night!

[To the tune of Chounu'er]

Miss Cui: Within scarlet walls with red blooms and quiet paths,

Visitors seldom arrive.

Maidservant: With heavenly bliss,

A stranger trespassed the yard.

Meixiang: When we found him behind the hibiscus trellis,

　　　　　　He'd be punished in private or in court.

Maidservant, Meixiang: Now that he stays her,

　　　　　　He's in ecstasy with his wife.

Maidservant: Sister, a Master Lu dropped from the sky.

Meixiang: Not a Master Lu but a Master Donkey dropped from the sky.

Miss Cui: You silly maids! You are telling the naked truth. As my family has not accepted a son-in-law without office for seven generations, I'll send him to attend the imperial examinations. What do you think about it?

Maidservant: Wonderful! When he comes into office, you will become a distinguished lady.

[To the tune of Busuanzi]

(Enter Lu Sheng)

Lu Sheng: A long chat goes with a long night;

　　　　　　A broad love goes with a broad quilt.

　　　　　　A beauty graceful and coy.

　　　　　　Fills me with great joy.

(Sheng and Miss Cui greet each other)

Miss Cui: Master Lu,

　　　　　　(In the pattern of Collected Tang Poems) You enjoy your life ignoring fame,

Lu Sheng: As I enjoy Utopian life here best.

Miss Cui: With flower-brewed wine to entertain the guest.

Lu Sheng: I have a fairy beauty to my claim.

Miss Cui: Master Lu, since I married you here, we've become man and wife. By enjoying ourselves day and night to the best of our hearts' content, we have tasted all the pleasures of human life. However, as my family has not accepted a son-in-law without office for seven generations, what do you think of your official career?

Lu Sheng: To tell you the truth, I've read all the classics but haven't made much progress in these years. Now that we are living a happy life by heavenly bliss, I won't care about an official career.

Miss Cui: Alas, how can a scholar talk like this? May I ask how many examinations you have attended?

[To the tune of Zhunu'er]

Lu Sheng: I have forgotten how many exams I attended,

　　　　　But the examiners never mind what I write.

　　　　　All those who are at the top of the list

　　　　　Are from families of wealth and might.

All: Fame and name,

　Come at the right time,

　The prime minister will be to your claim.

Miss Cui: Families of wealth and might are not to blame. As you do not have many connections and you have not achieved fame, you have been delayed. Now that most of my relatives are in key positions, you have to pay respects to them when you arvive in Chang'an.

Lu Sheng: Yes, I see.

Miss Cui: Besides, it's by no means easy to contact these high officials. With the help of my elder brother, you can easily become the number-one scholar.

Lu Sheng: Will he do that for me?

Miss Cui: No problem.

赏评

　　《邯郸记》是中国明代戏剧家汤显祖"临川四梦"之一。《邯郸记》的剧情原型来自于唐代传奇《枕中记》，讲述了一个"黄粱美梦"的故事。

　　《邯郸记》的英译过程浩瀚，难度极大。从小到大涉及中国历史文化的各个层面，小到格律、押韵、修辞的独特性，大到时代背景的特殊性。译者在翻译过程中，采取了各种翻译技巧和理念，力求译文的"传神达意"。如，"生旦净末丑"属于典型的中国传统文化，如果采取音译的方法，则不能体现这些名称的角色内涵；若选择意译，则需要对背景知识加以解释，而戏剧表演的即时性和舞台性特点又不允许过长的解释，因此，译者选择了直接用人名代替角色名的翻译方法。

　　《赠试》中，汤显祖原曲字词精练，说唱结合，唱曲部分词句凝练，韵律悠扬，因此译者即便无法完全还原原文韵脚，但依旧尝试了其他形式的押韵，韵式从 abab 结构调整为 abba 或者 aabb。原文中存在的大量文化词汇需要通过文内增释的方式或者替换表达的方式来翻译。例如，文中崔小姐所述"我家七辈无白衣女婿"，这里的"白衣"是一种借代的表现手法。在古代，不同的衣着颜色有着不同意义。"白衣"，原意是白色之衣，代指穿白衣的人，即指无官无位的在野平民。白衣在古代为身份较低贱者所穿，如仆役、庶民等，所以便用它来借指庶民，也泛称没有做官的读书人。《西厢记》中的相国夫人便因张生未得功名，而以"俺三辈不招白衣女婿"的理由逼迫张生进京赴考。如直译"白衣"为 white cloth，则读者无法体会其中的文化内涵，因此，译者将"白衣女婿"译为：a son-in-law without office，既简洁又明了。又如，《朱奴儿》中出现的"翰林苑"，熟悉清宫剧的读者对此地一定不陌生，"翰林苑"是负责科举事宜的政府部门，"翰林"是历代科考人员的主试官，手握科考书生的生死大权，此外还负责修书撰史，起草诏书，为皇室成员侍读等，地位清贵。因此，"翰林苑"此处就代表了权力机关，又与科举挂钩，作者的真实意图也是用"翰林苑"婉转表达对翰林苑之人处事的愤愤不平。因此，译者就直截了当地译为 examiners。

《赠试》中还出现了大量唐诗的诗歌体律，译者也尽量做到了传神达意。例如，"不羡名公乐此身""风光别似武陵春""百花仙酿能留客""一面红妆恼煞人"。第一句来自无名氏的《杂曲歌词》："王孙别上绿珠轮，不羡名公乐此身"；第二句来自方干的诗："为是仙才登望处，风光便似武陵春"；第三句来自王昌龄的《题朱炼师山房》："叩齿焚香出尘世，斋坛鸣磬步虚人。百花仙酿能留客，一饭胡麻度几春"；第四句来自李白的诗歌："千杯绿酒何醉辞，一面红妆恼杀人。"因此，两人的对白都通过未曾写出的诗歌上下联隐隐表达，如若按照字面意思直译两人对话，则会令人不知所云，故而变通译为：

Miss Cui: You enjoy your life ignoring fame,

Lu Sheng: As I enjoy Utopian life here best.

Miss Cui: With flower-brewed wine to entertain the guest.

Lu Sheng: I have a fairy beauty to my claim.

这样的译法既保留了诗歌的韵律（abba），又能够连贯上下文，使读者不会跳脱出原文内容。（汪榕培，2003：113）

13.5 课后练习

雷 雨

曹禺

第一幕 选段

朴 （四凤端茶，放朴面前。）四凤，——（向冲）你先等一等。（向四凤）叫你跟太太煎的药呢？

四 煎好了。

朴 为什么不拿来？

四 （看繁漪，不说话）。

繁 （觉出四周有些恶相）她刚才跟我倒来了，我没有喝。

朴 为什么？（停，向四凤）药呢？

繁 （快说）倒了。我叫四凤倒了。

朴 （慢）倒了？哦？（更慢）倒了！——（向四凤）药还有么？

四 药罐里还有一点。

朴 （低而缓地）倒了来。

繁 （反抗地）我不愿意喝这种苦东西。

朴 （向四凤，高声）倒了来。

（四凤走到左面倒药）

冲 爸，妈不愿意，你何必这样强迫呢？

朴 你同你妈都不知道自己的病在那儿。（向繁漪低声）你喝了，就会完全好的。（见四凤犹豫，指药）送到太太那里去。

繁 （顺忍地）好，先放在这儿。

朴 （不高兴地）不。你最好现在喝了它吧。

繁 （忽然）四凤，你把它拿走。

朴 （忽然严厉地）喝了药，不要任性，当着这么大的孩子。

繁 （声颤）我不想喝。

朴 冲儿，你把药端到母亲面前去。

冲 （反抗地）爸！

朴 （怒视）去！

（冲只好把药端到繁漪面前）

朴 说，请母亲喝。

冲 （拿着药碗，手发颤，回头，高声）爸，您不要这样。

朴 （高声地）我要你说。

萍 （低头，至冲前，低声）听父亲的话吧，父亲的脾气你是知道的。

冲 （无法，含着泪，向着母亲）您喝吧，为我喝一点吧，要不然，父亲的气是不会消的。

繁 （恳求地）哦，留着我晚上喝不成么？

朴 （冷峻地）繁漪，当了母亲的人，处处应当替子女着想，就是自己不保重身体，也应当替孩子做个服从的榜样。

繁 （四面看一看，望望朴园又望望萍。拿起药，落下眼泪，忽而又放下）哦！不！我喝不下！

朴 萍儿，劝你母亲喝下去。

萍 爸！我——

朴 去，走到母亲面前！跪下，劝你的母亲。

（萍走至繁漪面前）

萍 （求恕地）哦，爸爸！

朴 （高声）跪下！（萍望着繁漪和冲；繁漪泪痕满面，冲全身发抖）叫你跪下！（萍正向下跪）

繁 （望着萍，不等萍跪下，急促地）我喝，我现在喝！（拿碗，喝了两口，气得眼泪又涌出来，她望一望朴园的峻厉的眼和苦恼着的萍，咽下愤恨，一气喝下！）哦……

（哭着，由右边饭厅跑下）

第 14 章　散文

散文文体与翻译

　　散文是文学文体中最随心所欲的文字,是无所不谈的文章。有的散文精粹精辟,有的谈笑风生,有的亲切感人,有的意趣无穷;有的散文三言两语,而能一语中的,立论警策,给人以哲理启迪;有的散文气象万千,如行云流水,使读者从不长的篇幅中观览古今。散文既能敏捷地反映社会生活,又能记录作者的所见、所闻、所感,抒写倏乎即逝的某种心态和情感,信手拈来,不拘成法。

　　散文可分为抒情散文、叙事散文和哲理散文三类,表现形式包括知识小品、社会生活杂感、文艺随感、旅行游记、读书偶感、私人日记和私人书简等。

　　散文具有真实性,富于激情,讲究意境、韵味、文采,表达自由活泼、舒卷自如等特点。英汉散文都十分讲究语言的音乐美,其音乐美主要通过声音节奏和意义节奏来实现。散文的音韵和节奏传达了情感,营造出情调和意境。散文语篇以书面语为主要表现形式,语域特征显著,文本表现形式灵动多变。

　　散文翻译必须充分考虑到语言的音乐美,优秀的散文翻译应该传达出原文语言的音乐美。

14.1 课前实践

14.1.1 抒情散文

The First Snow
Henry Wadsworth Longfellow

The first snow came. How beautiful it was, falling so silently all day long, all night long, on the mountains, on the meadows, on the roofs of the living, on the graves of the dead! All white save the river, that marked its course by a winding black line across the landscape; and the leafless trees, that against the leaden sky now revealed more fully the wonderful beauty and intricacies of their branches. What silence, too, came with the snow, and what seclusion! Every sound was muffled, every noise changed to something soft and musical. No more tramping hoofs, no more rattling wheels! Only the chiming of sleigh-bells, beating as swift and merrily as the hearts of children.

第一场雪
亨利·沃兹沃斯·朗费罗

第一场雪飘落，多么美啊！昼夜不停地下着，落在山岗，落在草场，落在世人的房顶，落在死人的墓地。遍地皆白，只有河流像一条黑色的曲线穿过大地；叶子落光的大树映衬在铅灰色的天幕下，越发显得奇伟壮观，还有那错落有序的树枝。下雪是多么寂寥，多么幽静！所有的声音都变得沉浊了，所有的噪音都变得轻柔而富有乐感。没有得得的马蹄声，没有辚辚的车轮声，只能听到雪橇那欢快的铃声如童心在跳动。

14.1.2 叙事散文

落花生
许地山

我们屋后有半亩隙地。母亲说，"让它荒芜着怪可惜，既然你们那么爱吃花生，就辟来做花生园罢"。我们几姊弟和几个丫头都很喜欢——买种的买种，动土的动土，灌园的灌园；过不了几个月，居然收获了！

Peanuts
Xu Dishan

Behind our house there lay half a *mu* of vacant land. Mother said, "it's a pity to let lie waste. Since you all like to eat peanuts so much, why not have them planted here." That exhilarated as children and our servant girls as well, and soon we started buying seeds, ploughing the land and watering the plants. We

妈妈说:"今晚我们可以做一个收获节,也请你们爹爹来尝尝我们的新花生,如何?"我们都答应了。母亲把花生做成好几样食品,还吩咐这节期要在园里的茅亭举行。

那晚上的天色不太好,可是爹爹也到来,实在很难得!爹爹说:"你们爱吃花生么?"

我们都争着答应:"爱!"

"谁能把花生的好处说出来?"

姊姊说:"花生的气味很美。"

哥哥说:"花生可以制油。"

我说:"无论何等人都可以用贱价买它来吃;都喜欢吃它。这就是它的好处。"

爹爹说:"花生的用处固然很多,但有一样是很可贵的。这小小的豆不像那好看的苹果、桃子、石榴,把它们的果实悬在枝上,鲜红嫩绿的颜色,令人一望而发生羡慕之心。它只把果子埋在地底,等到成熟,才容人把它挖出来。你们偶然看见一棵花生瑟缩地长在地上,不能立刻辨出它有没有果实,非得等到你接触它才能知道。"

我们都说:"是的。"母亲也点点头。爹爹接下去说:"所以你们要像花生,因为它是有用的,不是伟大、好看的东西。"

我说:"那么,人要做有用的人,不要做伟大、体面的人了。"

gathered in a good harvest just after a couple of months!

Mother said, "How about giving a party this evening to celebrate the harvest and invite your Daddy to have a taste of our newly-harvested peanuts?" We all agreed. Mother made quite a few varieties of goodies out of the peanuts, and told us that the party would be held in the thatched pavilion on the peanut plot.

It looked like rain that evening, yet, to our great joy, father came nevertheless. "Do you like peanuts?" asked Father.

"Yes, we do!"

We vied in giving the answer.

"Which of you could name the good things in peanuts?"

"Peanuts taste good," said my elder sister.

"Peanuts produce edible oil," said my elder brother.

"Peanuts are so cheap," said I, "that anyone can afford to eat them. Peanuts are everyone's favourite. That's why we call peanuts good."

"It's true that peanuts have many uses," said Father, "but they're most beloved in one respect. Unlike nice-looking apples, peaches and pomegranates, which hang their fruits on branches and win people's instant admiration with their brilliant colors, tiny little peanuts bury themselves underground and remain unearthed until they're ripe. When you come upon a peanut plant lying curled up to the ground, you can never immediately tell whether or not it bears any nuts until you touch them."

"That's true," we said in unison. Mother

爹爹说："这是我对于你们的希望。"

我们谈到夜阑才散，所有花生食品虽然没有了，然而父亲的话现在还印在我的心版上。

also nodded. "So you must take after peanuts," Father continued, "because they're useful though not great and nice-looking."

"Then you mean one should be useful rather than great and nice-looking," I said.

"That's what I expect of you," Father concluded.

We kept chatting until the party broke up late at night. Today, though nothing is left of the goodies made of peanuts, Father's words remain engraved in my mind.

14.1.3 哲理散文

Of Studies

Francis Bacon

论 读 书

弗朗西斯·培根

Studies serve for delight, for ornament, and for ability. Their chief use for delight, is in privateness and retiring; for ornament, is in discourse; and for ability, is in the judgment and disposition of business. For expert men can execute, and perhaps judge of particulars, one by one; but the general counsels, and the plots and marshalling of affairs come best from those that are learned.

To spend too much time in studies is sloth; to use them too much for ornament, is affection; to make judgment wholly by their rules, is the humor of a scholar. They perfect nature and are perfected by experience; for natural abilities are like natural plants, that need pruning by study; and studies themselves do give forth directions

读书足以怡情，足以傅彩，足以长才。其怡情也，最见于独处幽居之时；其傅彩也，最见于高谈阔论之中；其长才也，最见于处世判事之际。练达之士虽能分别处理细事或一一判别枝节，然纵观统筹，全局策划，则舍好学深思者莫属。

读书费时过多易惰，文采藻饰太盛则矫，全凭条文断事乃学究故态。读书补天然之不足，经验又补读书之不足，盖天生才干犹如自然花草，读书然后知如何修剪移接，而书中所示，如不以经验范之，则又大而无当。

有一技之长者鄙读书，无知

too much at large, except they be bounded in by experience.

Crafty men condemn studies, simple men admire them, and wise men use them; for they teach not their own use; but that is a wisdom without them, and above them, won by observation. Read not to contradict and confute; nor to believe and take for granted; nor to find talk and discourse; but to weigh and consider.

Some books are to be tasted, others to be swallowed, and some few to be chewed and digested; that is, some books are to be read only in parts; others to be read, but not curiously; and some few to be read wholly, and with diligence and attention. Some books also may be read by deputy, and extracts made of them by others; but that would be only in the less important arguments, and the meaner sort of books, else distilled books are like common distilled waters, flashy things.

Reading maketh a full man; conference a ready man; and writing an exact man. And therefore, if a man write little, he had need have a great memory; if he confer little, he had need have a present wit; and if he read little, he had need have much cunning, to seem to know that he doth not.

Histories make men wise; poets witty; the mathematics subtle; natural philosophy deep; moral grave; logic and rhetoric able to contend. *Abeunt studia in mores*. Nay, there is no stone or impediment in the wit, but may be wrought out by fit studies; like as diseases of the body may have appropriate exercises. Bowling is good for

者羡读书，唯明智之士用读书，然书并不以用处告人，用书之智不在书中，而在书外，全凭观察得之。读书时不可存心诘难读者，不可尽信书上所言，亦不可只为寻章摘句，而应推敲细思。

书有可浅尝者，有可吞食者，少数则须咀嚼消化。换言之，有只须读其部分者，有只须大体涉猎者，少数则须全读，读时须全神贯注，孜孜不倦。书亦可请人代读，取其所作摘要，但只限题材较次或价值不高者，否则书经提炼犹如水经蒸馏，淡而无味矣。

读书使人充实，讨论使人机智，笔记使人准确。因此不常做笔记者须记忆力特强，不常讨论者须天生聪颖，不常读书者须欺世有术，始能无知而显有知。

读史使人明智，读诗使人灵秀，数学使人周密，科学使人深刻，伦理学使人庄重，逻辑修辞之学使人善辩；凡有所学，皆成性格。人之才智但有滞碍，无不可读适当之书使之顺畅，一如身体百病，皆可借相宜之运动除之。滚球利睾肾，射箭利胸肺，慢步利肠胃，骑术利头脑，诸如此类。如智力不集中，可令读数学，盖演题须全神贯注，稍有分散即须重演；如不能辨异，可令读经院哲学，盖是辈皆吹毛求疵之人；如不善求同，不善以一物阐证另

the stone and reins; shooting for the lungs and breast; gentle walking for the stomach; riding for the head; and the like. So if a man's wit be wandering, let him study the mathematics; for in demonstrations, if his wit be called away never so little, he must begin again. If his wit be not apt to distinguish or find differences, let him study the Schoolmen; for they are *cymini sectores*. If he be not apt to beat over matters, and to call up one thing to prove and illustrate another, let him study the lawyers' cases. So every defect of the mind may have a special receipt.

一物，可令读律师之案卷。如此头脑中凡有缺陷，皆有特效可医。

14.2 文体特点

14.2.1 篇幅短小随意　形式不拘成法

　　散文在形式上篇幅短小，行文方便，语言精粹而优美，富有浓郁的文学色彩。散文的结构，是"散"与"不散"，形"散"而神"聚"的辩证统一。散文一般在行文上运笔如风，挥洒自如，对生活的反映具有极大的跳跃性。如秦牧的《土地》，作者时而立足现实，时而回首往事，时而极目万古，时而憧憬未来，思绪如脱缰之马，纵横驰骋，行文如万斛泉源，不择地而出，常行于所当行，常止于所不可止，文理自然，姿态横生。行文有时朴素，含蓄凝练，耐人寻味，鲜活质朴；有时华丽，炫目淳厚；有时单纯，返璞归真，纯真平淡。

　　散文在表达形式上的不拘成法是由其内容所决定的。散文的体裁，既有文笔犀利的杂文，又有婉约动人、余音袅袅的抒情散文和叙事散文；既有境界开阔、明净无尘的旅行游记，又有文采绚丽，如五光十色的玛瑙般的社会生活杂感。散文反映的生活领域宽广，内容丰富多彩，与之相适应，它表现内容的形式也必然不能囿于一种格式、一种风貌。

　　散文能够巧妙地运用各种语言形态，不仅力求选词用字的高度准确，而且注重语句布局的变幻多姿，在形式上取长补短，融会贯通，将内容与形式处理得和谐，进而形成精粹的思想、隽永的意境，使文章具有更多的艺术美感，生动而形象地感染人、教育人，启迪人的思想性。

14.2.2　语言千姿百态　情景交融如画

散文是不分行的诗。散文要有诗一样的文采、诗一样的构思、诗一样的手法，特别是要有诗一样的语言。散文的语言含义隽永，有的语音铿锵，文采风流，如《岳阳楼记》："衔远山，吞长江，浩浩汤汤，横无际涯；朝晖夕阴，气象万千。"真是情景如画，气势磅礴，极富绘画美和律动美。有的则是色彩明丽，刻画细腻，如明代散文家袁宏道的《满井游记》，描写京郊由冬入春的景象：水上的冰开始溶解，波光刚刚发出亮色，如鱼鳞一样的波纹荡漾水面，清澈见底；形容其明亮程度，则曰"晶晶然如镜之新开而冷光之乍出于匣也"；写四周山色，则曰"山峦为晴雪所洗，娟然如拭，鲜妍明媚，如倩女之靧面而髻鬟之始掠也。"刻画细腻，比喻贴切，寥寥数语，道尽了北国早春雪消冰解后的绮丽风光，达到了恰到好处、出神入化的地步。

散文语言之美体现在如下几点：

（1）直抒的情感美

散文有激动人心的情感美。如其他文学形式一样，散文也用形象思维来反映现实的生活。形象思维带有强烈的感情特点，是艺术形象的主体和核心，是人物形象和生活形象的映射，写人、写生活就必须写情。散文作家往往把他们对生活的热爱和礼赞、对丑恶的憎恨和诅咒或直接地、或曲折地、或明露地、或含蓄地倾诉给读者。行文中他们往往"缘情布景"，以一种感情为中心，把通过想象和联想汇集起来的材料贯穿起来，使感情得以抒发。即使是对山川日月、花鸟虫兽这些无情物的描绘，也往往都经过了作者感情的过滤。

（2）优雅的意境美

散文善用借景抒情、寓情于景、移情于景或直接抒情等多种写情手法。这些感情有时细腻，像涓涓小溪；有时粗犷，像奔腾江流；有时明快，像轻松愉快的小夜曲；有时含蓄，像晶莹透亮的露水珠。于是散文的情感也就有了细腻美、粗犷美、朦胧美、明丽美。这些情感和所写的景物、人物、画面、世态、风俗密切融合，作者把自己的感情寄寓到景物描写中，就使景物传神，神有所附，既写出了景物美，又表现了情感美。文中一切景语都成了情语。

散文的目的就是要使读者去感受这种意境美，去拨动他们心灵上共鸣的琴弦，和作者一起低吟浅唱、嬉笑怒骂，在优美的意境和健康的情感中获得陶醉和享受。

（3）深远的哲理美

散文的美还体现在它深刻的思想美。特别是那些寓情于事、寓理于景的名作，文中的一花一木、一皿一器，哪怕是一幅断笺、一片碎瓷，也无不揭示着邃密的哲理，体现着深刻的社会意义。散文和其他文学艺术形式一样，都是以形象感人，忌讳公式化、概念化，但不等于不要"理"；都是以情动人，反对干巴巴、空洞洞，但不等于排斥"理"。相反，正因为散文不能像小说那样完美地去创造典型的人物形象，不能像戏剧那样激烈地去展现矛盾冲突，不能像诗歌那样淋漓地去抒写感情，所以"理"的因素就更强烈、更突出。散文往往是根据主题的需要去写一些人物或景物，根据主题的需要去选用材料，去展开联想，去安排线索，去布置结构。

主题—哲理—思想，是散文创作的基础。"无理不成文"。散文里的形象是理性和直觉、思想和感情和谐地结合在一起而创作出来的形象。有了"理"，文章才有了灵魂，有了生命。散文的理不是简单的议论，散文的哲理往往借助于形象引发读者的深思。

（4）跳跃的音乐美

散文语言是作者思想情感的表达，作品的音韵节奏是语言美的重要因素。散文跳跃的音乐美是通过语言的流动过程中表现出的适度和谐的响度、快慢交替的节奏、抑扬顿挫的语调、灵活巧妙的停顿处理等方面体现出来，使人"听之则丝簧，味之则甘腴，佩之则芬芳"（《文心雕龙·总术》）。低婉回旋的韵律将散文语言的音乐美表现得尤为充分。音乐贵在声律之和谐，否则，就无法演唱。如高维敬写到江南的美的时候是这样开始的："说好了，我本应是那个掀起你红盖头的人啊！你究竟在哪里啊？我是那个最疼你又背离你的人啊！一千年了，你还负气恨我吗？还耿耿于怀不肯原谅我吗？我辜负了你如水的柔情，毁了你的年少春闺。竟让我用千年的时光来懊悔啊！可一千年的懊悔也换不回你青春的美丽啊！"文中每一句话的末尾相间使用了象声字"啊""吗"，语句重叠，句句押韵，形成一种跳脱的韵律之美，将作者的懊恼之情用音乐般的旋律舒缓地表达出来，顿时有了一种高山流水般的韵律之美。为了更为传神地刻画江南之美，作者接着写道："总幻觉着在某一个瞬间捕捉到你的声息，想象着你会在一个时刻来到我面前，轻灵美丽，笑语嫣然。我怎能不时刻等待，准备张开双臂拥你入怀。""只有江南的春雨年年如约而来，一样细细飘洒。雨丝温柔的滋润下，桃花也年年自在地盛开，那个佩剑少年却再没有出现。路上越来越热闹了，你却越来越寂寞。""轻灵美丽""张开双臂""热闹""寂寞"等字眼，使得作者对于江南的思念之情有了轻重缓急、抑扬顿挫之节奏美，急如波浪滔天，缓如潺潺流水，轻如柳絮飘转，重如石破天惊，真是变化多姿，妙不可言。由于作者调动了上述多种艺术手法，使其语言具有了音乐的音韵美，那种情感也如声遏行云，余韵绕梁，清浊委婉，舒缓自如，静听有声。

散文语言的音乐美还体现在一咏三叹的抒情上。音乐的节奏一般轻快而富于变化，在一个主旋律下，变化出多种音调，达到抒发情感的目的。散文与此有异曲同工之妙，这在很大程度上源于散文句式的错综和流动。

（5）绚丽的色彩美

散文语言具有绘画一般的"应物象形""随类赋彩"的表现力和造型力，能表现出一幅幅五彩缤纷、色彩绚丽、喧腾激越而又具体可感的艺术画面来。各种色彩相互映衬，增强了语言的绚丽美。

散文语言绚丽的色彩美可通过"实""虚"相宜的画面呈现。"实"是可以摸得着看得见的实物，是具体可感的。散文叙事的真实性，是散文产生独特魅力的重要因素。"虚"是指散文如绘画一样可以"裁出空白"，用"留白"的形式促使读者寻找作品的意义，就是对空白手法的美学概括。

散文语言绚丽的色彩美还可通过"静""动"相随的画面呈现出来。静态的色彩美是作者通过对事物平面的、静止的描写而呈现出来的耀人眼目的美；动态的色彩美是把客观事物立体的、活动的场面描写出来，呈现出喧腾激越的图画美。散文的色彩美因作者主观心理色彩的不同而呈现出不同的色调，流露出不同的情韵。语言的效果要能在读者的头脑中形成一幅鲜明的图面，呈现出纷繁各异的感情色彩。（艾湘涛，2009）

14.3 翻译要领

散文一般具有语言精练，以少胜多，思想缜密，刻画入微，隽永含蓄，深沉有味，朴实无华，清新自然等特点，最显著的特色是"体物写志，形散神聚"。其语言不仅具有表意功能，亦有美学功能。一篇优美的散文不但让读者浮想联翩，也会使人陷入沉思。无不给人以美的感受，其色、其声、其动、其静，令人尽情陶醉。因此，散文翻译，不仅要求语言地道，还要求内容畅达自然；不仅要求译文在形式上与原文对等，而且在思想艺术、审美情趣上也应相吻合。翻译时，译者通常通过微观的语言手段，如语音、词汇、句法、修辞等来实现语言转换，再现原文风格。

14.3.1 情融意境　神形逼现

散文之美美在语言，美在意境。意境是指抒情诗及其他文学创作中的一种艺术境界。这种艺术境界是由主观思想感情和客观景物环境交融而成的意蕴或形象，其特点是描述如画，意蕴丰富，能启发读者的联想和想象，有着超越具体形象的更广的艺术空间。散文看似形散而神不散，因而散文翻译绝不能随心所欲，不仅要兼顾语言与情境的有效传达，更要尽可能保持原作的风姿。散文翻译应充分考虑原文所体现的形式、内容和意境的完美统一，同时也应注意到译入语的语义结构和文化定势。译文应当和原文一样是美的文字，诗一般的语言。散文的意境总是通过形式、格调、局部细节等体现出来，情韵和意境相辅相成：散文中既不可能只有"情"，也不可能只有"意"——意境靠情韵烘托，情韵藉意境升华，并构成意境不可分割的一部分。因此，散文的翻译应用符合英汉语义结构的语言形式把文章的内涵和自己的感觉自然地表达出来，同时根据译入语文化的要求对原文进行调整。如：

原文 在南方每年到了秋天，总要想起陶然亭的芦花，钓鱼台的柳影，西山的虫唱，玉泉的夜月，潭柘寺的钟声。（郁达夫《故都的秋》）

译文 When I am in the South, the arrival of each autumn will put me in mind of Peiping's Tao Ran Ting, with its reed catkins, Diao Yu Tai with its shady willow trees, Western Hills with their chirping insects, Yu Quan Shan Mountain on a moonlight evening and Tan Zhe Si with its reverberating bell. （张培基译）

这段译文用了排比的修辞手法，用了四个 with 和一个 on 形成排比，极具平衡和音韵之美，巧妙地传达了原文的意境。原语和译语两种文字所叙述的是同一事件，而译文的感人力量主要来自于对原文的把握，首先要准确理解原文文字，深刻体会原文的意境，再来考虑如何表达的问题，才能取得好的艺术效果。

14.3.2　形散神聚　风格再现

风格即语言特点，是语言之美的体现。风格，即把合适的词放在适当的位置。人们往往用"形散神不散"来形容散文的特色。所谓"形散"是指散文句法灵活，形式多样；"神不散"则是中心思想明确，情感基调贯穿始终。散文文体的自由一方面给散文创作留下了充分发挥的空间，另一方面也使散文的风格难以把握，与其他文学体裁界限模糊。它既可以表达丰富的情感，也可以阐发深刻的思想。散文的风格不仅具体可感，而且有现实的内容，它透过句法结构自然而然地流露出来。对于散文作者而言，风格发之于内而形之于外；对于散文读者而言，风格寓之于句而感之于心。

对风格的准确把握是成功翻译散文的前提，而对风格的定位必须建立在对句法结构有效分析的基础上。散文句法结构的变动直接导致散文风格的飘忽不定。译者要想把握住原作的风格，必须要有对词句的微观分析和对篇章结构的宏观把握，既要见树木又要见森林。阅读一篇优秀的散文就像听着旋律优美的音乐，欣赏一幅清新自然的图画，音与画融为一体，使人产生身临其境的情感共鸣。可以说，散文的风格体现在抑扬顿挫的韵律之中，体现在情景交融的意境之中，也体现在触人心弦的情感之中。而这一切都只能通过遣词造句的灵活安排和句法结构的巧妙组合体现出来。如：

原文 人把它捕捉，将它制成标本，作为一种商品去出售，价钱越来越高。最后几乎把它捕捉得再也没有了。这一生物品种快要绝种了。（徐迟《枯叶蝴蝶》）

译文 Man captures it, makes a specimen of it and sells it in the market at increasingly high prices. What happens as a result is that there is hardly any of the butterfly to be found—the species is dying out. （刘士聪译）

原文作者以短促的句式来表达一种忧急如焚的心情，译者保持了这种特色。译者以 What happens as a result 来译"最后"，看似背离了原文句式短促的风格，实则既准确表达了前后的因果关系，又保持了原文朗朗上口的快节奏。

散文创作的生命力在于鲜明的风格，散文翻译的关键在于风格的再现。如果原文是为了体现激昂向上的情感，译文在形式上也应为节奏铿锵、明快的表达方式；如果原文表达一种悲怆、抑郁的意境，那么译文也就应采用节奏缓慢、音韵压抑的句式和词语。

14.3.3 节奏烘托　灵活变通

散文之美，美在节奏。要成功翻译散文作品的内容和情感，不可忽略节奏的再现。散文的节奏随文赋形，相对自由。英语语言节奏主要通过轻重音的对比交替而形成，汉语语言节奏主要通过平仄搭配而产生。英语的轻重与汉语的平仄并不形成对应关系，英语有轻重的地方用汉语翻译时不一定能译出平仄。因此，节奏的再现不是在对应成分之间进行的，而是依据节奏在原文句、段、章中的特殊表现经过变通再现出来的。

英语是拼音文字，借轻重音的搭配而形成抑扬顿挫，而汉语的节奏则呈跳跃型。所以翻译散文的节奏时，要注意两点：一是汉译英要注重双音节词的和谐，二是英译汉要注重轻重音的搭配。其次，节奏不仅是形式，也是内在结构，英语和汉语的句法结构不同，因而声响和节奏也不同，翻译时要透过字句之形，把握其中的情感和节奏。双音节词和轻重音的运用得当，对文本形成节奏美具有重要作用。译入语的节奏不能以原文节奏的构成要素为基础，而应以原文的风格和情感为基础。要使译入语的节奏也依附译文之形，首先得把握文本的风格，特别是情感类型。再以译入语的节奏来烘托之。节奏不是翻译的，而是再现的。翻译时必须采用灵活变通的翻译方法再现原作的神韵。

如果将一篇汉语散文比作一首中国传统乐曲，那么其英译文就应该是一首西洋乐曲，演奏的乐器不同，演奏方法自然也不同。对原文句法的机械复制充其量只能得原文之"形"，而不能得原文之"神"。译者必须深入感受、体会、领悟原文的旋律，再以恰当的翻译技巧再现其神韵，而这种再现同样应该自然流畅、毫无雕饰痕迹。如：

原文 曲曲折折的荷塘上面，弥望的是田田的叶子。叶子出水很高，像亭亭的舞女的裙。层层的叶子中间，零星地点缀着些白花……（朱自清《荷塘月色》）

译文 All over this winding stretch of water, what meets the eye is a silken field of leaves, reaching rather high above the surface, like the skirts of dancing girls in all their grace. Here and there, layers of leaves are dotted with white lotus blossoms…（朱纯深译）

作者利用叠词"曲曲折折""田田""层层"及双声词"零星"等营造了一种错落有致的抑扬之美，而译者利用英语中的头韵 winding、water、what 和 layers、leaves 等再现了原文悦耳动听的节奏感和静谧和谐的氛围。

14.4 译文赏评

14.4.1 哲理散文

原文

My 'fellow 'citizens of the 'world, / 'ask 'not / what Am'erica will 'do for 'you, / but what to'gether we can 'do for the 'freedom of man.

译文

　　全世界的同胞们，不要问美国能为你们做什么，而要问我们能共同为人类的自由做什么。

赏评

　　尽管英汉节奏的建构要素不尽相同，节奏和情感的类型却是相通的，完全可以在译文中予以再现。原文充满豪情，语气坚定，节奏也相应地铿锵、简洁。

　　原句中的 ask 和 not 各有一个重音，节奏铿锵，译文却无法以同样形式予以强调，只能按译入语的习惯，按常规的节奏译为"不要问"。

14.4.2 抒情散文（1）

原文

笑
冰心

　　严闭的心幕，慢慢地拉开了，涌出五年前的一个印象。——一条很长的古道。驴脚下的泥，兀自滑滑的。田沟里的水，潺潺地流着。近村的绿树，都笼在湿烟里。弓儿似的新月，挂在树梢。一边走着，似乎道旁有一个孩子，抱着一堆灿白的东西。驴儿过去了，无意中回头一看。——他抱着花儿，赤着脚儿，向我微微地笑。

译文

Smile
Bing Xin

A scene of five years ago slowly unveiled before my mind's eye. It was along ancient country road. The ground under my donkey's feet was slippery with mud. The water in the field ditches was murmuring. The green trees in the neighboring village were shrouded in a mist. The crescent new moon looked as if hanging on the tips of the trees. As I passed along, I somewhat sensed the presence of a child by the roadside carrying something snow white in his arms. After the donkey had gone by, I happened to look back and saw the child. Who was barefoot, looking at me smilingly with a bunch of flowers in his arms.

赏评

这幅"记忆"中的自然景致，有静有动，情景交融。原文中描写的景物有：古道、驴脚、泥；田沟、水流；绿树、湿烟；新月、树梢。从空间顺序来看，由下到上，从低处的古道一直描写到高空中的新月，可谓如诗如画；从句法上来看，使用了一系列精湛的短句，而且字数相当，如："驴脚下的泥……田沟里的水……近村的绿树……弓儿似的新月……"。在翻译时，为了再现原文意韵，译者注意了句式的变化，在同一语段里使用了一连串的主系表结构的句子，采用了形式整齐的句子结构，增强了译入语的句法优势，也加强了画面的动感，使译文充满了诗情画意。

14.4.3 抒情散文（2）

原文

荷塘月色
朱自清

这几天心里颇不宁静。今晚在院子里坐着乘凉，忽然想起日日走过的荷塘，在这满月的光里，总该另有一番样子吧。月亮渐渐地升高了，墙外马路上孩子们的欢笑，已经听不见了；妻在屋里拍着闰儿，迷迷糊糊地哼着眠歌。我悄悄地披了大衫，带上门出去。

沿着荷塘，是一条曲折的小煤屑路。这是一条幽僻的路；白天也少人走，夜晚更加寂寞。荷塘四面，长着许多树，蓊蓊郁郁的。路的一旁，是些杨柳，和一些不知道名字的树。没有月光的晚上，这些路上阴森森的，有些怕人。今晚却很好，虽然月光也还是淡淡的。

路上只我一个人，背着手踱着。这一片天地好像是我的；我也像超出了平常的自己,到了另一世界里。我爱热闹,也爱冷静;爱群居,也爱独处。像今晚上,一个人在这苍茫的月下,什么都可以想,什么都可以不想,便觉是个自由的人。白天里一定要做的事,一定要说的话,现在都可不理。这是独处的妙处,我且受用这无边的荷香月色好了。

曲曲折折的荷塘上面,弥望的是田田的叶子。叶子出水很高,像亭亭的舞女的裙。层层的叶子中间,零星地点缀着些白花,有袅娜地开着的,有羞涩地打着朵儿的;正如一粒粒的明珠,又如碧天里的星星,又如刚出浴的美人。微风过处,送来缕缕清香,仿佛远处高楼上渺茫的歌声似的。这时候叶子与花也有一丝的颤动,像闪电般,霎时传过荷塘的那边去了。叶子本是肩并肩密密地挨着,这便宛然有了一道凝碧的波痕。叶子底下是脉脉的流水,遮住了,不能见一些颜色;而叶子却更见风致了。

月光如流水一般,静静地泻在这一片叶子和花上。薄薄的青雾浮起在荷塘里。叶子和花仿佛在牛乳中洗过一样;又像笼着轻纱的梦。虽然是满月,天上却有一层淡淡的云,所以不能朗照;但我以为这恰是到了好处——酣眠固不可少,小睡也别有风味的。月光是隔了树照过来的,高处丛生的灌木,落下参差的斑驳的黑影,峭楞楞如鬼一般;弯弯的杨柳的稀疏的倩影,却又像是画在荷叶上。塘中的月色并不均匀;但光与影有着和谐的旋律,如梵婀玲上奏着的名曲。

荷塘的四面,远远近近,高高低低都是树,而杨柳最多。这些树将一片荷塘重重围住;只在小路一旁,漏着几段空隙,像是特为月光留下的。树色一例是阴阴的,乍看像一团烟雾;但杨柳的风姿,便在烟雾里也辨得出。树梢上隐隐约约的是一带远山,只有些大意罢了。树缝里也漏着一两点路灯光,没精打采的,是渴睡人的眼。这时候最热闹的,要数树上的蝉声与水里的蛙声;但热闹是它们的,我什么也没有。

忽然想起采莲的事情来了。采莲是江南的旧俗,似乎很早就有,而六朝时为盛;从诗歌里可以约略知道。采莲的是少年的女子,她们是荡着小船,唱着艳歌去的。采莲人不用说很多,还有看采莲的人。那是一个热闹的季节,也是一个风流的季节。梁元帝《采莲赋》里说得好:

> 于是妖童媛女,荡舟心许;鹢首徐回,兼传羽杯。櫂将移而藻挂,船欲动而萍开。尔其纤腰束素,迁延顾步。夏始春余,叶嫩花初,恐沾裳而浅笑,畏倾船而敛裾。

可见当时嬉游的光景了。这真是有趣的事,可惜我们现在早已无福消受了。

于是又记起《西洲曲》里的句子:

> 采莲南塘秋,莲花过人头;低头弄莲子,莲子清如水。

今晚若有采莲人，这儿的莲花也算得"过人头"了；只不见一些流水的影子，是不行的。这令我到底惦着江南了。——这样想着，猛一抬头，不觉已是自己的门前；轻轻地推门进去，什么声息也没有，妻已睡熟好久了。

1927年7月，北京清华园

译文

Moonlight over the Lotus Pond
Zhu Ziqing

I have felt quite upset recently. Tonight, when I was sitting in the yard enjoying the cool, it occurred to me that Lotus Pond, which I pass by every day, must assume quite a different look in such moonlight night. A full moon was rising high in the sky; the laughter of children playing outside had died away; in the room, my wife patting the son, Run'er, sleepily humming a cradle song. Shrugging on an overcoat, quietly, I made my way out, closing the door behind me.

Alongside the Lotus Pond runs a small cinder footpath. It is peaceful and secluded here, a place not frequented by pedestrians even in the daytime; now at night, it looks more solitary, in a lush, shady ambiance of trees all around the pond. On the side where the path is, there are willows, interlaced with some others whose names I do not know. The foliage, which, in a moonless night, would loom somewhat frighteningly dark, looks very nice tonight, although the moonlight is not more than a thin, grayish veil.

I am on my own, strolling, hands behind my back. This bit of the universe seems in my possession now; and I myself seem to have been uplifted from my ordinary self into another world. I like a serene and peaceful life, as much as a busy and active one; I like being in solitude, as much as in company. As it is tonight, basking in a misty moonshine all by myself, I feel I am a free man, free to think of anything, or of nothing. All that one is obliged to do, or to say, in the daytime, can be very well cast aside now. That is the beauty of being alone. For the moment, just let me indulge in this profusion of moonlight and lotus fragrance.

All over this winding stretch of water, what meets the eye is a silken field of leaves, reaching rather high above the surface, like the skirts of dancing girls in all their grace. Here and there, layers of leaves are dotted with white lotus blossoms, some in demure bloom, others in sky bud, like scattering pearls, or twinkling stars, our beauties just out of the bath. A breeze stirs, sending over breaths of fragrance, like faint singing drifting from a distant building. At this moment, a tiny thrill shoots through the leaves and flowers,

第14章 散文

like a streak of lightning, straight across the forest of lotuses. The leaves, which have been standing shoulder to shoulder, are caught trembling in an emerald heave of the pond. Underneath, the exquisite water is covered from view, and none can tell its color; yet the leaves on top project themselves all the more attractively.

The moon sheds her liquid light silently over the leaves and flowers, which, in the floating transparency of a bluish haze from the pond, look as if they had just been bathed in milk, or like a dream wrapped in a gauzy hood. Although it is full moon, shining through a film of clouds, the light is not at its brightest; it is, however, just right for me—a profound sleep is indispensable, yet a snatched doze also has a savor of its own. The moonlight is streaming down through the foliage, casting bushy shadows on the ground from high above, dark and checkered, like an army of ghosts; whereas the benign figures of the drooping willows, here and there, look like paintings on the lotus leaves. The moonlight is not spread evenly over the pond, but rather in a harmonious rhythm of light and shade, like a famous melody played on a violin.

Around the ponds, far and near, high and low, are trees. Most of them are willows. Only on the path side can two or three gaps be seen through the heavy fringe, as if specially reserved for the moon. The shadowy shapes of the leafage at first sight seem diffused into a mass of mist, against which, however, the charm of those willow trees is still discernible. Over the trees appear some distant mountains, but merely in sketchy silhouette. Through the branches are also a couple of lamps, as listless as sleepy eyes. The most lively creatures here, for the moment, must be the cicadas in the trees and the frogs in the pond. But the liveliness is theirs, I have nothing.

Suddenly, something like lotus-gathering crosses my mind. It used to be celebrated as a folk festival in the South, probably dating very far back in history, most popular in the period of Six Dynasties. We can pick up some outlines of this activity in the poetry. It was young girls who went gathering lotuses, in sampans and singing love songs. Needless to say, there were a great number of them doing the gathering, apart from those who were watching. It was a lively seasons, brimming with vitality, and romance. A brilliant description can be found in "Lotus Gathering" written by Yuan Emperor of the Liang Dynasty:

> *So those charming youngsters row their sampans, heart buoyant with tacit love, pass to each other cups of wine while their bird-shaped prows drift around. From time to time their oars are caught in dangling algae, and duckweed float apart the moment their boats are about to move on. Their slender figures, girdled with plain*

silk, tread watchfully on board. This is the time when spring is growing into summer, the leaves a tender green and the flowers blooming, —among which the girls are giggling when evading an outreaching stem, their skirts tucked in for fear that the sampan might tilt.

That is a glimpse of those merrymaking scenes. It must have been fascinating; but unfortunately we have long been denied such a delight.

Then I recall those lines in "Ballad of Xizhou Island":

Gathering the lotus, I am in the South Pond,/The lilies, in autumn, reach over my head;/Lowering my head I toy with the lotus seeds./Look, they are as fresh as the water underneath.

If there were somebody gathering lotus tonight, she could tell that the lilies here are high enough to reach over her head; but, one would certainly miss the sight of the water. So my memories drift back to the South after all.

Deep in my thoughts, I looked up, just to find myself at the door of my own house. Gently I pushed the door open and walked in. Not a sound inside, my wife had been asleep for quite a while.

Qinghua Campus, Beijing

July, 1927

赏评

散文《荷塘月色》是朱自清于1927年任清华大学教授时所写。当时作者正处在彷徨苦闷、矛盾挣扎之中。文中所描写的月色下的荷塘之景便是作者自己借以抒发复杂的心情。作者用重笔写景，虚实相生，动静结合，让月光下的荷塘以一幅精彩的画面呈现在读者面前。文章句式灵活，用词新颖，音韵优美，构架了极强的语言感染力，给人美不胜收之感。译文出自朱纯深先生之手，在表现原文艺术意境和思想性方面既做到了"信、达、切"，也达到了"化境"；读来朗朗上口，使人感觉如在读原汁原味的写景状物的英语散文一般。译文具有相当高的美学价值，语言准确、鲜明、生动、自然，在传达原文信息方面，可谓恰到好处，符合译语语言习惯，不露斧凿之痕，没有"不同语言习惯的差异而露出生硬牵强的痕迹"（钱锺书先生语）。下面从其美学艺术方面略加评析。

（1）叠音与双声叠韵词的翻译

《荷塘月色》这篇散文充分体现了以语言艺术形式来传达美学功能的独特性，叠音词的频繁出现是原文的文体特色之一，全文约莫二十多个叠音词，译者根据不同的上下文，做了灵活处理，力求产生相应的修辞效果。叠词本身可产生押韵的效果，在重复中开拓出新意，产生回环往复的艺术效果，并具有很强的描绘作用，准确、形象、逼真；当诉诸人的听觉、视觉、嗅觉等感官时，给人以如见其形、如辨其音、如闻其香，乃至身临其境之感；读起来音节舒展悠扬，抑扬顿挫，音韵美和音乐美油然而生。同时，它们又构成了这类文章的翻译难点，即如何把它们体现的审美转换到译语中去？朱译既考虑到了词语形式，又考虑到了表现效果。

例1 "迷迷糊糊地哼着眠歌"：sleepily humming a cradle song。此处的"迷迷糊糊"为叠词式成语，朱译用 sleepily 与之对应，体现了较好的音美。因为 sleepily 包含三个元音（即一个长音 [iː] 和两个短音 [ɪ]），相同或相近元音的重复就较好地照应了原词的重叠结构，而且与"迷迷"（读：mímí）谐音；sleepily 也比较贴切地实现了原词的意义传达，并对应了词性。

例2 "长着许多树，蓊蓊郁郁的"：in a lush, shady ambiance of trees。"蓊蓊郁郁"亦为叠词式成语，表意形象、准确。朱译用 lush 和 shady 两个词来表达原文树荫浓郁的意义。这两个英文词均有字母 -sh，前者在词尾，后者在词首，中间以逗号并列，发音相同为 [ʃ]，衔接紧密，有亲近和连续感。译者最大可能地让译文与原词实现结构形式和发音的对应。

例3 "虽然月光也还是淡淡的"：although the moonlight is not more than a thin, grayish veil。译者用了两个形容词加一个名词形成修饰关系来翻译"淡淡的"这个叠词，即"thin, grayish veil"，十分贴切地描绘出当晚的月色景象，也准确把握了作者的复杂心境，符合原文意境。两个形容词的使用也照应了原词的构架与节奏，并且均含有元音 [ɪ]，读起来轻缓绵延，音效节奏积极。

例4 "弥望的是田田的叶子……像亭亭的舞女的裙"：what meets the eye is a silken field of leaves... like the skirts of dancing girls in all their grace。跟例 3 相似，对本句中叠词"田田的""亭亭的"的翻译处理，朱译充分考虑了字数结构与节奏安排，用 a silken field of 及 in all their grace 来分别与原文对应。译者努力使翻译更接近忠实于原文，并把原文连绵往复的音美延续到译文中。

例5 "层层的叶子中间，零星地点缀着些白花，有袅娜地开着的……正如一粒粒的明珠，又如碧天里的星星"：Here and there, layers of leaves are dotted with white lotus blossoms, some in demure bloom... like scattering pearls, or twinkling stars。本例的原文在同一句中既使用了叠音词，又使用了双声叠韵词，"层层的""零星""袅娜"分别与 layers of、here and there、demure 对应。译者选用这几个英文词不仅能表意，而且巧妙地承袭了原文的音美——它们的尾音非常贴近 [ə]、[eə] 及 [ʊə]，押韵明显。为了达到延续原文绘声绘色的音美效果，译者还用了两个尾韵相同的形容词 scattering 和 twinkling 来翻译"一粒粒"和"星星"。这两词富有很强的动态美,通过视觉感官来实现升华荷花开放的月色意境之美。同时,以上诸词在译文中的分布也与原文的节奏对应。译文忠实于原文的意义和形式,并保留了相当的文采,还展示了原文的语言特色。

（2）韵律的翻译

韵律是散文的重要文体特色,汉语是一种带声调的语言,内涵丰富,具有很强的表音表意功能。英语是一种带重音的语言,注重表意与结构形式,所以对于汉译英来说,如何展现汉语文本的韵律是一个很大的挑战。鉴于汉英两种语言表现手段的差异,汉语叠词在英文中难以很好地体现出来。译者在译文中通过适当的选词用词来进行增补,发挥英文自身的表达优势,让译文最大程度、最宽泛地体现出原文叠词所彰显的音美、形美和意美。同时,译者的选词用词又是准确而精当的,忠实于原文的创作风格,产生了几近相同的感染力。

例1 "微风过处,送来缕缕清香,仿佛远处高楼上渺茫的歌声似的":A breeze stirs, sending over breaths of fragrance, like faint singing drifting from a distant building。本例原文十分典型,因为它还蕴含了重要的修辞手法——通感,为原文的语言特色锦上添花。作者把"缕缕清香"（嗅觉）转换成"渺茫的歌声"（听觉）,以此描写香气的时浓时淡、飘忽断续。微风轻拂,远处高楼传来的歌声也就似有似无,断断续续,给人渺茫之感。朱译成功地沟通了嗅、听这两类不同的感官功能。对原文的叠音词"缕缕"和双声叠韵词"仿佛""渺茫",朱译选择 breaths of、like 和 faint 三个词来表达,读起来与原文选词的重叠特点相去较远,但是,译者创造性地解决了这一问题,让韵律音美在译文中得到增补,这一技巧性的翻译处理着实巧妙。译者在译文中用四个 -ing 结尾的词——sending、singing、drifting、building 来表现叠音,对于"微风"和"清香",译者选择多个共有清辅音 [s] 的词——stirs、sending、breaths、fragrance、singing、distant 来体现意境和音效。此外,breeze 中的浊音 [z] 和 stirs 中的清音 [s] 同属摩擦音,发音很相近,音效明显,能弥补译文的个别缺憾。

例2 "像闪电般,霎时传过荷塘的那边去了":like a streak of lightning, straight across the forest of lotuses。本例中朱译承袭了原文使用大量叠词的语言特色,从全篇角度出发,尽可能多地运用语音上的重复或近似。朱译的 streak 和 straight 的词首有相同的 [str-] 读音,并且在译文中多词有摩擦音 [s],如 streak、straight、across、forest、lotuses,这也正是译者匠心独运的创造性的翻译。

例3 "树色一例是阴阴的,乍看像一团雾":The shadowy shapes of the leafage at first sight seem diffused into a mass of mist。原文使用了"阴阴的"叠音词,朱译把它译为 shadowy shapes。从翻译技巧上来分析,两英文词的词首有相同的 sha-,

发音一个为 [ʃæ]，一个为 [ʃeɪ]，极为相似，与原文叠词在语音上照应。虽然 shadowy 已经可以把"阴阴的"意义传达出来，译者还是创造性地进行了增补，让译文顿时生色许多。再考虑轻雾冉冉的意境，译者用语音之美来体现，并实现对原文叠词现象创造性的展示，音美顿现——first、sight、diffused、mass、mist、against 中共有的 [s]/[z] 音和 [t] 音即是相同语音的重复，弥补译文对原文叠音词、叠韵词翻译的不足之处。

例4 "可惜我们现在早已无福消受了"：but unfortunately we have long been denied such a delight。本例中的原文虽然没有叠词出现，但是译者在选词用词上却颇有技巧。译文里 denied、delight 二词，词首相同，即 de-，中间均有元音 [aɪ]，体现了音效美。同时，这种处理方式也能对全篇译文起到增补的效果。

朱纯深英译的《荷塘月色》，选用了最合适的词语来表现原文的语言特色——大量使用叠音词和双声叠韵词，并借助巧妙的翻译技巧、创造性的表达手法，再现了原文关于声音、意义、形式等方面的审美。朱译忠实于原文，不仅有意译，而且能重现原文文本的意境，把原文的文采风格体现得相当完美。

14.5 课后练习

（1）

It's time to plant the bulbs. But I put it off as long as possible because planting bulbs means making space in borders which are still flowering. Pulling out all the annuals which nature has allowed to erupt in overpowering purple, orange and pink, a final cry of joy. That would almost be murder, and so I wait until the first night frost anaesthetizes all the flowers with a cold, a creaky crust that causes them to wither; a very gentle death. Now I wander through my garden indecisively, trying to hold on to the last days of late summer.

The trees are plump with leafy splendor. The birch is softly rustling gold, which is now fluttering down like an unending stream of confetti. Soon November will be approaching with its autumn storms and leaden clouds hanging above your head like soaking wet rags. Just let it stay like this, I think, gazing at the huge mysterious shadows the trees conjure up on the shining green meadows, the cows languidly flicking their tails. Everything breathes an air of stillness, the silence rent by the exuberant color of asters, dahlias, sunflowers and roses.

（2）

　　江南的春天素称多雨，一落就是七八天。住在上海的人们，平时既感不到雨的需要，一旦下雨，天气是那么阴沉，谁也耐不住闷在狭小的家里；可是跑到外面，没有山，没有湖，也没有经雨的嫩绿的叶子，一切都不及晴天好；有时阔人的汽车从你身旁驰过，还得带一身泥污回来。

　　记得六七年前初来上海读书，校里的功课特别忙，往往自修到午夜；那年偏又多雨，淅淅沥沥，打窗飘瓦，常常扰乱我看书的情绪。我虽不像岂明老人那样额其斋曰："苦雨"，天天坐在里面嘘气，但也确有点"深恶而痛绝之"的念头。

　　可是这种事情只在上海才会有。少时留居家乡，当春雨像鹅毛般落着的时候，登楼眺望，远处的山色被一片烟雨笼住，村落恍惚，若有若无，雨中的原野新鲜而又幽静，使人不易忘怀！尤其可爱的是夜间。不知哪一年春天，我和两个同伴，摇着小船到十里外一个镇上看社戏，完场已是午夜，归途遇雨，船在河塘中缓缓前进，灯火暗到辨不出人面，船身擦着河岸新生的茅草，发出沙沙的声音。雨打乌篷，悠扬疾徐，如听音乐，如闻节拍，和着同伴们土著的歌谣,"河桥风雨夜推篷",真够使人神往。

这几年投荒到都市,每值淫雨,听着滞涩枯燥的调子,回念故乡景色,觉得连雨声也变大了。人事的变迁,更何待说呢!

第 15 章 诗歌

📖 诗歌文体与翻译

诗歌是一种高度集中地概括并反映社会生活的文学体裁。它通过凝练而极其形象的语言以及鲜明的节奏与和谐的音韵，充满音乐美地将诗人丰富的想象和情感充分地传达出来。

诗歌是一种独特的文学体裁，在分类、节奏、韵律、构思、词序、选词等方面都自成体系，以自己独特的形式展示着诗人对生活的理解。

诗歌在不同的时期、不同的环境背景下，有不同的存在形式。诗歌从叙写内容上可以大致分为抒情诗、叙事诗、哲理诗。从形式，即体式上来看，中诗有"风""骚"、赋、乐府与歌行、格律诗和律诗绝句、词、曲；英诗有四行体、六行体、八行体、十四行体、颂歌体、斯宾塞诗节、无韵诗、挽歌体等。

诗歌语言结构的组合方式是为内容服务的，有时利用巧妙的形式造成特殊的艺术效果，有助于读者理解诗意、加深印象。在语言上，诗歌文体的语言特别优美、精练，语句具有节奏性、音乐性，同时又大量运用比喻、象征等修辞手段，使之意境深远，耐人寻味。

诗歌的音韵和节奏传达了情感，营造出情调和意境。诗歌语篇，既有书面语体，也有口语体形式，语域特征显著。文本表现形式有时形象活泼，有时意义蕴含深刻，表达形式多样。

诗歌是思想感情、意境形象、音韵节奏和风格神韵等方面的统一体，翻译中要集意美、音美、形美于一体，提倡"以诗译诗"，充分考虑诗歌语言的音乐美，要做到传神得体，既要追求意义和情感上与原诗相当，又要贴合译语诗歌的文体特色。

15.1 课前实践

15.1.1 抒情诗

When You Are Old	当你老了
William Butler Yeats	威廉·巴特勒·叶芝

When you are old and gray and full of sleep,　　当你老了，白发苍苍，睡意朦胧，
And nodding by the fire, take down this book,　　在炉前打盹，请取下这本诗篇，
And slowly read, and dream of the soft look　　慢慢吟诵，梦见你当年的双眼
Your eyes had once, and of their shadows deep;　　那柔美的光芒与青幽的晕影；
How many loved your moments of glad grace,　　多少人真情假意，爱过你的美丽，
And loved your beauty with love false or true,　　爱过你欢乐而迷人的青春，
But one man loved the pilgrim Soul in you,　　唯独一人爱你朝圣者的心，
And loved the sorrows of your changing face;　　爱你日益凋谢的脸上的衰戚；
And bending down beside the glowing bars,　　当你佝偻着，在灼热的炉栅边，
Murmur, a little sadly, how Love fled,　　你将轻轻诉说，带着一丝伤感：
And paced upon the mountains overhead　　逝去的爱，如今已步上高山，
And hid his face amid a crowd of stars.　　在密密星群里埋葬它的赧颜。

15.1.2 叙事诗

诗经·魏风·硕鼠	Big Rats

硕鼠硕鼠，　　　　　Big rats, Oh! Big rats,
无食我黍！　　　　　Don't eat my millets.
三岁贯女，　　　　　I breed you for many years,
莫我肯顾。　　　　　But you don't care me a bit.
逝将去女，　　　　　I've decided to leave you,
适彼乐土。　　　　　I'll go to land without thieves.
乐土乐土，　　　　　Go to land, Oh! I will go,
爰得我所。　　　　　That place is my best home.
硕鼠硕鼠，　　　　　Big rats, Oh! Big rats,
无食我麦！　　　　　Don't eat my wheats.

三岁贯女，	I breed you for many years,
莫我肯德。	But you don't heed me a bit.
逝将去女，	I've decided to leave you,
适彼乐国。	I'll go country without thieves.
乐国乐国，	Go to country, Oh! I will go,
爰得我直。	That place is my right choice.
硕鼠硕鼠，	Big rats, Oh! Big rats,
无食我苗！	Don't eat my sprouts.
三岁贯女，	I breed you for many years,
莫我肯劳。	But you don't console me a bit.
逝将去女，	I've decided to leave you,
适彼乐郊。	I'll go to suburb without dirt.
乐郊乐郊，	Go to suburb, Oh! I will go,
谁之永号？	Who's been there to sing a song?

15.1.3　哲理诗

<table>
<tr><th>Gitanjali 82</th><th>吉檀迦利 82</th></tr>
<tr><th>Tagore</th><th>泰戈尔</th></tr>
</table>

Time is endless in thy hands, My lord. There is none to count thy minutes.

Days and nights pass and ages bloom and fade like flowers. Thou knowest how to wait.

Thy centuries follow each other perfecting a small wild flower.

We have no time to lose, and having no time we must scramble for our chances. We are too poor to be late.

And thus it is that time goes by while I give it to every querulous man who claims it, and thine alter is empty of all offerings to the last.

我的主上啊，你手中的光阴无穷无尽。无人能数算你的时分。

昼夜消隐，岁华开谢纷纷。你懂得等待的窍门。

你消磨一个又一个世纪，只为令一朵小小野花臻于完美。

我们没有时间可供荒废，没有时间的我们，只能手忙脚乱地争竞机会。我们实在困乏可怜，绝不敢误了行程。

我将时间给了所有那些愤愤不平的索取者，就这样耗去了光

> At the end of the day I hasten in fear lest thy gate be shut; but I find that yet there is time.
>
> 阴，而你的祭坛之上，始终不见分毫贡品。
>
> 日子的尽头，我在恐惧之中匆匆前行，生怕你已经关上大门；而我蓦然发现，时间尚未告罄。

15.2 文体特点

诗歌是语言的艺术。诗歌语言来自日常语言，遵循着日常生活语言的规范，但诗歌语言又有别于日常语言，常常偏离、突破日常语言规范，形成独特的"诗家语"。它的文体特点涉及语言的各个方面，如语音、语义、节奏和修辞等。

15.2.1 音韵优美　节奏鲜明

优美的音韵和鲜明的节奏感是诗歌文体的一个显著特点。诗歌往往通过轻重音节的有序排列，传达出一种有节奏的韵律，在加强语言的音韵美的同时，更加增强语言的表现力，把意义与音素直接联系起来，以最鲜明的手段来表现诗人的艺术审美。音韵往往带有诗人的个性化色彩，韵律的美不只是为了读起来有美感，更是为了体现一种意义，而且这种"意义"的表达与诗歌的韵法有着密切的联系。韵法是诗人用来表达一种意义的最鲜明的文体特点。它是诗歌中有规律的轻重抑扬变化连同韵式的变化，表现为行与行之间的押韵格式。

构成诗歌节奏的基础是韵律。诗歌以诗行中的音节和重读节奏为尺度（标准）来计算韵律。英诗的节奏主要由音节重读和非重读的有规律的重复构成，一个重读音节和一个或两个轻读音节搭配起来就组成一个音步。格律就是将诗划分成音步，并区分出是何种音步以及计算音步的数量。根据一首诗歌的音步数量，形成"单音步""双音步""三音步""四音步""五音步""六音步""七音步""八音步"。英语是以重音计时的语言，即重音节之间的时距大体相等。英文诗歌的韵律是依据音步包含音节的数量及重读音节的位置而加以区分的。传统音步有六种：即抑扬格（Lambus）、扬抑格（Trochee）、抑抑扬格（Anapaest）、扬抑抑格（Dactyl）及抑扬抑格（Amphibrach）。汉语是以音节计时的语言，汉字是单音节字，一个字一个音节。每一诗行音节越多（也就是汉字越多），吟诵所用时间越长。以每行字数来划分，汉诗可以分为"二言""三言""四言""五言""七言"和"九言"，其中以"五言"和"七言"最为普遍。一句诗中的音节一般是两个两个地组合在一起形成"顿"。"顿"，也叫"音组"或"音步"。四言二顿，每顿两个音节；五言三顿，每顿的音节是二二一或二一二；七言四顿，每顿的音节是二二二一或二二一二。顿的划分既要考虑音节的整齐，又要兼顾意义的完整。音节的组合不仅形成顿，还形成"逗"。逗就是诗句中最显著的那个顿。中国古体诗、近体诗建立诗句的基本规则，就是一句诗必须有一个逗，逗把诗句分成前后两半，其音节分配是：四言二二，五言二三，七言四三。

一首诗所用的音步大体上是一致的，但不是毫无变化的。正因为节奏的玄妙变化给诗歌带来了音乐性，使之优美动听，而且增加了诗的表达力。

15.2.2 形式多样　破格变异

从表现形式上看，诗歌的形式多种多样，如英诗中的两行诗节、英雄双韵体、三行诗节、四行诗节、歌谣体四行诗节、斯宾塞九行诗节、莎氏十四行诗、意大利十四行诗，等等。从体裁上看，诗歌又可具体分为许多类，主要有叙事诗、史诗、戏剧诗、故事诗、民谣、抒情诗、颂、哀歌、田园诗、爱情诗、说理诗、三行俳句诗、五行打油诗，等等。

不同的形式和体裁是对主题不同形式的演绎。诗人常常寻求某种形式上的变异来唤起读者的注意力。这种"变异"即表现为诗歌文体中常出现的形式的"陌生化"现象。形式的"陌生化"现象主要表现为诗人通过破格与变异来打破常规的语言模式，以一种新奇的手法来刺激读者对诗歌原有形式产生的审美疲劳。诗歌的"破格与变异"一方面是为了满足诗歌在韵律和节奏方面的需求，如为了适应节奏格律的需要，诗人灵活调整词序、主谓倒置、动宾倒置、将修饰词与被修饰词进行换位、使用一些特殊的缩略形式（如 tis = it is, o'er = over）等。诗人对语言行使的特权所带来的"个性化"结果，使诗歌具有独特的审美感受。另一方面，诗歌的"破格变异"现象表现为诗人对语言常规模式的有意偏离，是对语言的一种创造性使用。变异可以发生在诗歌语言的各个层面上，如语音、拼写、词汇、语法、诗式等。诗歌中的陌生化审美效果以及它所引起的审美感受不仅仅是为了造就一个新鲜的审美意象，而是为了创造一种蕴涵丰富的审美价值的特殊形式。当一首诗的独特文体以一种陌生化的形式进入人的审美视域的时候会使人惊奇，并带来强烈的审美感受。但在这令人惊异的陌生化形式背后是诗人所建构的一个新的、用来承载"意义"的空间，在这个空间里，各样的审美感受都会随着人们的"视域融合"而会聚为对"意义"的把握。从这个角度看，陌生化的形式不仅是对诗歌形式陈规的突破，更是对无限可能的意义的开拓，给读者以发现新的审美感受的可能性。

15.2.3 意象丰富　语域鲜明

诗人表情达意时往往诉诸意象。意象是"寄义于象，把情感化为可以感知的形象符号，为情感找到一个客观对应物，使情成体，便于把照玩味"（张保红，

2011: 92)。诗歌文体的语言若仅凭毫无经验的、抽象的情感表达往往是苍白的，难以动人的，而诉诸具象的、经验的情感表述则往往能让人感同身受，体会强烈而深刻。诗歌意象种类繁多，不同的意象种类，会引导读者从不同的视角与层面去感知与体味意象在诗中的特有的意蕴与丰富的审美内涵。诗歌意象既有心理学层面的，如视觉、听觉、触觉等；也有具体化层面的，如总称意象与特色意象，使得意象更具空间上的张力，更具清晰、明确性；还有存在形态层面的，如静态与动态，使得意象更具描写性和叙述性。

诗歌文体有自己独特的语域。诗歌是违反常规的话语，因而时常打破日常话语中必须遵守的规律。诗歌中大量使用古雅的辞藻。诗歌的语言讲究陌生化，英诗中常用古词、冷僻的词汇、外来语，另外还经常引用典故，尤其是古希腊罗马神话以及《圣经》中的故事。英诗中的语法和句法和一般文体不一样，注重对日常用语的扭曲和变形，有些语法也不合规范，有时缺省谓语，有时缺省主语，有时省略一些词。弥尔顿的诗歌语言最有特色，在他的代表作《失乐园》中不但大量运用古希腊罗马神话和《圣经》中的典故，句法的变化也极其多样。为了追求押韵或者音律的要求，有些词的读音在诗中也会发生变化。在用语和语域上，诗有所谓的"破格自由"，这与其他文体有着很大区别。

15.3 翻译要领

诗歌外在形式独特，音韵节奏突出，意境生成方式多样，蕴涵丰富。诗歌翻译是翻译艺术的顶峰，要集意美、音美、形美于一体，再现原作诗歌的审美艺术性，但同时又要具有灵活性和创造性，即对结构作相应的调整，从而尽可能完美地再现原作的音韵、意境和深沉内涵。

诗歌的主旨遁形于无迹，主题时时既在场又缺席，难以捕捉。诗歌翻译是从形式到内容对诗歌本身的全面再现。译者在翻译诗歌时，要表达出抽象的诗意，还要忠实于诗歌的具体形式、格律等。在诗歌翻译上的问题，更多集中在"神"而非"形"。译诗的"形"与原文的"形"在直观上便可以看出是否统一，因此对"神"的翻译便更重要，也更困难。

15.3.1 音美、形美 音义合一

诗歌的美，美在其音、其形。诗歌讲究音乐性，中英诗歌都对语言音韵、节奏有着自觉的追求。诗歌外在与内在的音乐性并不是刻意而为的，它们均有效地表征着诗歌的情感律动与意义传达，是"音义合一"与"音情合一"的完美体现。翻译中讲求"音美"就是要忠实传达原作的音韵、节奏、格律等方面所表现的美感，使译文"有节奏、押韵、顺口、好听"（张保红，2011：93）。

汉语的双声叠韵、四字成语，都是汉语独特音韵的表现形式。翻译时，为了追求在英语中达到相应的效果，应寻求目标语与原语相对应的音韵表达方式。汉语的抑扬顿挫源于汉语平上去入的四声特点，英语则是一词多音节，分轻重音。此外，中国古典诗歌在设定的字数、韵律、平仄的限制和框架下，运用双声叠韵等手段组合起来，谱出和谐的音韵之美；相较之下，英语诗歌的音韵则是通过诗歌格律、韵式来表现它的节奏美。和谐的音韵，有助于再现原文的意境，让译文的读者与原文的读者获得相同的声律美感。

诗歌以其独特的外在形式而有别于其他文学文体。诗歌文本语符各部分的排列方式，显示着诗歌作品的深沉美感；诗歌文本中语符的声音及字面意义，显示着诗歌作品的韵律美感；诗歌文本中语词语符的引发意义，显示着诗歌作品的诗性内涵；诗歌文本中的意象及其组合方式，显示着诗歌作品的主客体相互感触、融合而生发的美感信息，表征着作品的诗境美；诗歌文本中的内在本质结构的情感结构形式，显示着诗歌作品的民族审美情感与个体内在的情感境界；诗歌文本中某种习惯体系或公认的诗歌形式，显示着诗人继承与创新的形式因素。诗歌翻译中，形美一方面是要保持原诗的诗体形式。诗体形式有定型形式与非定型形式之分，前者对字数或音节数、平仄或音步、行数、韵式等均有较为严谨的要求，体现出鲜明的民族文化性。后者虽不受制于一定的诗体形式，但其呈现的外在形状却表征着诗情的流动与凝定。在这一意义上，传达形美也意味着传达原作所具有的文化特性与诗学功能。形美另一方面是指要保持诗歌分行的艺术形式。诗作中诗句是采用一行之内句子语义完整的煞尾句诗行，还是采用数行之内语义才可完结的待续句诗行，虽无一定之规，但不同的诗行形式演绎着不同的诗情流动路径，昭示着作者不同的表情意图。

15.3.2 境由象生　象境共存

"意境"的概念经由"意象"发展而来，是指文学作品情景交融、虚实相生、韵味无穷的特征。"境"是一种境界，是诗歌中所营造的立体艺术氛围的实际图画。意境来源于意象又高于意象，是可意会而不可言传的。意境之有无在于字里行间是否给读者带来真情与美感的体验。意境通常表现为情景交融，作者或着力写景，景中有情，或重在抒情，情中见景，结构上呈现虚实相生的特征，一面是身临其境如在眼前的实，另一面是只可意会不可言传的虚，从而带来韵味无穷的审美体验。作者常通过"写境""造境""留白"等手法创造言有尽而意无穷之感，给读者留下一定的想象空间。诗歌，尤其是中国古诗中的意境美不胜收，汉语的平平仄仄所达成的抑扬顿挫和英语的独特韵律和行文产生的效果是不同的。汉语是一种意合的语言，一个意群接着一个意群，犹如竹子一般，同时又是一种意境的语言，可以不着一字，尽得风流；而英语是形合的语言，犹如一棵大树，不管枝叶多么繁茂，主干始终清晰明朗，讲求客观的分析，注重逻辑。英语讲实，中文求虚；英语重意，中文造境。诗歌翻译，是两种艺术语言的激烈碰撞，能否如电光火石般绚丽，在于译者的功夫。诗歌翻译是在两种截然不同的语言体系和文化传统的背景下进行的，而每一种文化都具有自身独特的思维特点和表达方式，语言是最能反映文化的载体，包含深刻而独特的文化内涵，在很多语境中都很难找到意义能够完全对等的词汇，所以有时为了重现意境只能用解释的方式把作者隐含的意思表达出来。不同的语境、不同的文体，处理的方式不同，没有放之四海而皆准的法则，只能遇山开路，遇水搭桥，随机应变。

意象是诗歌中唯一永恒的东西，一首诗就是一个完整的意象。诗歌的意象永远是诗歌的生命法则，永远是诗人的试金石和荣耀。诗歌的意象指的是用语言勾勒出来的画面。一个修饰语、一个明喻或者暗喻都可以生成意象；意象可以由一个词或一个词组构成，也可以由一段表象为简单的描绘，实则向读者传达难以言表的感悟的描写构成。诗歌意象可以是单纯的情景的替代，也可以是隐喻的、象征的。意象是关于生活本身的书写，融化于诗歌的形式当中，言表诗人的胸臆与情怀。诗歌意象集中了诗歌的神韵和意境，承载着作者的思想情感，包含了丰富的民族文化内涵，是诗歌的整个中心所在。诗歌意象的翻译要注重遵循原文的意思，应尽量保证翻译的客观性，而不应该加入译者的主观想法。在对原文的意象进行翻译的过程中，可以利用新的意象来代替旧的意象，或者干脆删掉旧的意象，或者是利用原诗歌中没有明确表达的意象，要注意把握以下几点：

（1）保留

原诗歌中非比喻性的意象一般属于诗人对事物的真实感受，是对现实真切的反映。如果要对初始的意象进行删除或者是修改，就会在很大程度上丢失原文的意思，翻译的客观性将很难得到保证。因此对于非比喻性质的意象，在翻译的过程中最好遵循原文的意思，加以保留。

（2）替换

在译语体系中寻找原语意象的"替身"。诗歌的翻译应由表及里，管中窥豹，在从诗歌里的字句所表现出来的语义和观念的基础上，进一步通过诗人所采用的意象窥探其内心，因为意象是诗人心迹的表露，必须透过这些意象所展露出的蛛丝马迹进行思考和联想，洞察其内含的意蕴，然后在另一个语言体系里搜索，寻找相应的能够代其所言的"替身"，这个"替身"绝不等同于在辞典里所找到的翻译对应词。

（3）模糊化

对原诗意象进行改变或作模糊化处理。在诗歌翻译中，对意象的理解是翻译成功的关键，既要翻译出意象，又不能为了意象而牺牲意境。意象是为了营造渲染意境服务的，直译不是对意象翻译的唯一方法，必须注意对意象的直译要能够为译诗的读者所理解，倘若直译意象不能被理解或者容易造成歧义，则译者可以对意象进行模糊化处理，以期达到与原文相同的审美效果。

（4）变通

由于生活习惯和文化背景的差异，如果所翻译的意象无法引起不同文化背景下读者的共鸣，那么可以添加一些意象或者是形容性的词，使得原诗歌中的意思能够更好地体现出来，以求实现和原文同样的功能。另外，在中文古诗词中有很多名词，如果不知道这些名词的隐含意义而直接翻译的话，读者往往也不解其意。在这种情况下可以变通一下，将这种意象省略或者是不进行直接翻译。

（5）加注

有些比较隐晦的比喻诗，诗人在比喻的时候本体并没有显现出来，需要读者在赏析的过程中自己去思考本体到底是什么。在翻译这类诗的过程中，一定要一丝不差地遵循原文的意思，在深刻理解原文的基础上再对其进行翻译，但又不能将作者的意思在翻译过程中直接说出来，否则就破坏了作者特意制造的朦胧美。因此在必要的情况下可采取注释的方式将作者的隐喻体现出来。

15.3.3 风格对等 神韵再现

诗歌的文体风格是诗歌的外在表现形式，诗歌的翻译必须兼顾形似与神似，要展现原诗的美学效果及作者的创作风格和理念，忠实于诗歌的灵魂。要灵活运用翻译技巧，使译文形神兼备，最大限度地再现原作的文体风格特色。形式的等值是诗歌翻译中整体等值非常重要的一部分，诗歌形式是文体风格的重要表现形式之一，因此，在诗歌翻译中注重文体风格的等值就不能忽视诗歌形式。从诗歌的审美意义来看，诗的形式是至关重要的。可以说没有诗歌的形式也就没有诗歌的美。文体等值即译文能够最大限度地传递原诗语言形式方面的审美特征及诗人的文体风格，使译语读者的感受等同或接近于原语读者的感受。

诗歌语言的一个显著特征便是它的偏离性，这种对于规律的偏离可表现在：词汇偏离、语音偏离、语法偏离、语相偏离、语义偏离等几个层面。翻译时应尽可能忠实地传达出诗歌的文体风格，即偏离之处，随文体风格的差异而调整尺度，保证译文与原文文体风格相适应。在保持原作的风格（如民族风格、时代风格、语体风格和作者的语言风格）的同时，还要了解不同民族的文化背景，不只是寻找确切的对等说法，还应寻找相同的感情色彩，相同的分寸和轻重，有时要力求忠实于原作，恪守原诗格律，有时要侧重于曲传神韵，不论是新鲜或古雅、通俗或书卷气、平铺直叙或形象化等，都应通过文体风格来阐释一个民族的精神。翻译不仅是语言问题，还是一种社会行为，译者必须了解原诗的意义，也就是要了解目的语国家的社会情况，使读者能感受原作所处的社会背景及其风格。译者要使译文具有同样的活力，就应该掌握诗人的感情脉络，使译文在风格上毫无二致。原文慷慨激昂、气韵跌宕，译文也应气势雄浑、荡气回肠；原文郁抑悲怅、萧瑟凄楚，译文也应感情凝重、幽冷苍凉。

15.4 译文赏评

15.4.1 意象派诗歌

原文

The Red Wheelbarrow

William Carlos Williams

so much depends

upon

a red wheel

barrow

glazed with rain

water

beside the white

chickens

译文1

红色手推车

威廉·卡洛斯·威廉斯

这么多的事物都依赖于

那一辆红色轮子的手推车

它湿漉漉的沾满雨水

站在一群白色的小鸡旁边

译文 2

红色手推车
威廉·卡洛斯·威廉斯

一群
白色的鸡雏旁

一辆
红色的手推车

雨水中
晶莹闪亮

承载着
如许分量

赏评

威廉斯的《红色手推车》描写了一幅色彩鲜明的日常生活画面,描述的是一个躲雨时见到的场景。威廉斯选择红、白对比色以及雨水冲洗后的锃亮,写出了人类与大自然共创理想生活的一面。威廉斯用红色装饰手推车的轮子,隐喻人类积极的劳动,劳动造就了人类积极向上的欢快精神,用"小鸡"和"雨水"来表达他对自然的崇敬。这首诗仿佛是一幅西洋油画,色彩鲜明,线条突出,立体感强,折射出大自然的光亮,整体画面宁静完美,富有和谐感,它向世人展示了20世纪美国人民的时代精神和民族情结。这首诗运用语相偏离的方法,使诗歌以非传统的形式出现。

(1)字体印刷对常规的偏离

此类的偏离包括对斜体、黑体、大写、非大写等的人为操纵。这首诗中很显然,整首诗没有一个标点符号,而且每一行开头字母也都没有大写。不同的语言之间有共通性,标点符号是汉语和英语所共同具备的文字标识系统,所以对于译文来说,省略标点是很容易做到的,但是非大写这一点是汉语译文难以表现的。汉语和英语属于两种不同语系,汉语文字没有大小写之分,这就属于汉英两种语言之间的不可译因素,对于译者来说,即英语中的大小写在汉语中的等值成分为零,是无法通过其他的途径来实现的,译者只能放弃。从这一点来说,诗歌翻译的可译性是有限度的,译诗一般不可能完全再现原诗的风姿。所以,在这个层面的语相偏离,两种译文的效果是同样的,都没有、也无法等值地再现原作的特征。

(2) 诗形偏离

诗形偏离指的是文学作品尤其是诗歌的整体形状偏离常规，与众不同，以此来凸显特定的作品主题。一般来说，特殊的形式一定蕴含着作者特定的意图，即作者想通过形式表达诗歌的意义，因此形式的偏离也是引起读者注目的一种方式。要赏析译文在这方面是否等值地再现了原作特点，必须首先对原诗进行分析。原诗最引人注目的特征之一是诗歌文字的排列形式，奇数行第一、三、五、七行都是三个单词，偶数行第二、四、六、八行都只有一个单词，因此整首诗有头重脚轻之感。这在形式风格上偏离了常规，与一般诗歌的外部形式迥然不同。诗人对诗歌的外部形式的处理意在昭示读者：诗歌的排列形状类似一辆载满了重物的手推车，看起来头重脚轻，读者眼前仿佛是一辆负重的手推车的画面。所以诗形的偏离是本诗的一大亮点，暗含本诗的主题，因此译者必须如实地实现译文在这个层面的等值。译文 1 的翻译完全抛弃了原诗的诗形结构，而译文 2 则采用了第一、三行两个字，第二、四行六个字；第五、七行三个字，第六、八行四个字，将全诗分为两个部分，虽然在外在诗形上没有完全与原诗对等，但是基本传达了原诗独特的诗形特点。

(3) 语法单位嵌入诗歌单位

句子是一个由词构成的意义完整的单位，一个句子可以再切分为几个更小的语义单位。实际上原诗的几个意义单位是 so much depends upon、a red wheel barrow、glazed with rain water、beside the white chickens。但是诗人却把这几个相对完整的意义单位进行再切分，成为：so much depends/upon、a red wheel/barrow、glazed with rain/water、beside the white/chickens。对词的切分也同时造成了意义的切分，使一个原本完整的意义单位分割开来：depends/upon、wheel/barrow、rain/water、white/chickens。但正是通过这种违反常规的切分，使诗歌获得一种一气呵成的感觉。因为每一行诗在意义上的切分都会吸引读者情不自禁地往下读，被吸引着一气读下去一探究竟。这就是诗行止于不当止处，使读者欲止难止。译诗也必须实现这种效果，寻求意义切分的等值形式，对诗行进行恰当地切分。译文 2 对原文的再现真正达到了较为传神的程度，译文的读者和原文的读者对这首诗的感觉会大体一致，这样就做到了最大限度的风格等值。

分析两种译文，译文 1 没有传达出原诗诗形偏离和意义切分的特色。译文 1 的整体排列形态与原诗相去甚远，没有使用等值的形式来翻译。译文 2 的形式看起来更有负重之感，更接近原诗，也更能传达出诗人通过诗歌形式表现的内在含义及外在的美学效果，因此是以最贴切的对等形式翻译的译文。

15.4.2 山水诗

原文

江 雪

柳宗元

千山鸟飞绝,万径人踪灭。

孤舟蓑笠翁,独钓寒江雪。

译文1

River in the Snow

No bird appears in hills,

no trace of human on all trails.

In a solitary boat, straw hat and cape,

an old man fishes alone—cold river in the snow.

译文2

River Snow

A hundred mountains and no bird,

a thousand paths without a footprint.

In a boat a straw-coaked old guy,

is fishing on river in snow.

译文3

Fishing in Snow

Birds in mountains fly and hide in places unknown,

there are no human footmarks on any road I note.

A straw coak'd man afloat, behold!

Is fishing snow on river cold.

译文4

Fishing in Snow

From hill to hill no bird in flight,

From path to path no man in sight.

A straw-cloak'd man in a boat, lo!

Fishing on river clad in snow.

第15章 诗歌

赏评

　　唐代诗人柳宗元的《江雪》一诗前两句"千山鸟飞绝，万径人踪灭。"中的"千山"和"万径"两个意象相互照应衬托，塑造了广阔无边、万籁俱寂的背景：远处峰峦叠嶂却无飞鸟，万径纵横交错却不见人踪。译文1采用了直译法，使用并列结构，诗句的原意能够一目了然地表达出来，但由于没有把"千"和"万"这两个数词所要表达的"山"和"径"之多的意思翻译出来，因而缺乏一种气势，未达"言有尽而意无穷"之效。译文2采用数字译数字的"对应式换码"，用 a hundred 和 a thousand 来指代群山和小径的数量，显得呆板，因为诗句中的"千"和"万"并非实指，而是用来体现山峦巷道规模之大。这种以实译虚的翻译方式反映出译者没有了解中文古诗用词的特点，并在某种程度上扼杀了读者的想象空间，无法正确表达出原诗句的意境。译文3在句式结构的布置上显得很随意，既无对称也无对比，没有将山、径之量多体现出来，因此也无法还原原诗句的意境。译文4语言简练，能体现出汉语诗歌本身的特点；句式中采用"淡化式换码"的方法，把"千山"和"万径"分别译为 from hill to hill 和 from path to path，一来准确传达了原诗句的信息，巧妙地避免了数字实对实的翻译；二来营造出山峦起伏、万巷交错的磅礴气势，使得原诗开阔的意境得以再现，彰显了译者的高明手法；工整自然的对仗以及和谐的尾韵锦上添花，为诗句平添了韵律美，读者诵读之际一股苍茫寂寥之感油然而生。较之前三个译本，译文4更好地保留了原诗的意境。

　　"孤舟蓑笠翁，独钓寒江雪。"虽然只由一个副词"独"、一个动词"钓"和"孤舟""蓑笠""（老）翁""寒江""雪"这几个名词组成，但表达出来的意境绝不是这些个体意象的简单堆砌，而是意象相互交融所产生的孤傲不群、超然物外的意蕴。译文1结构松散，语言拖沓，无法展现原诗语言高度凝练的特点，影响了诗的意蕴。译文2的形式整体紧凑，表达方式却平淡无奇，没有传达出老翁在寒江之上独自垂钓的孤寂幽僻之感。译文3采用了增词法，译者通过增加动词 behold（注视）将老翁专注垂钓的画面惟妙惟肖地描绘了出来，整体上使诗句更加生动。然而与译文2类似，"独"字的缺译，使清高孤傲的诗境无法再现，美中不足。译文4出自翻译名家许渊冲之手，前一句中的 lo 对应原诗中的"独"。lo 之妙处在于它并非一个完整的词，品诗者完全可以任意理解为 lonely、alone、lonesome 等；lo 位于 boat 和 snow 之间，与这两词分别压行内韵和尾韵，将"孤舟"和"雪"两个意象个体紧密联系在一起，进而使人领略到诗中凄冷孤寂的意境；此外，lo 还是一个能表达惊讶或者唤起注意的感叹词，意为"看哪，瞧啊"，通过呼唤，将品诗者的注意力转移到垂钓翁身上，也是译者的匠心独运。clad 有"覆盖；穿衣"义，在原诗句中并无对等词，译者别出心裁地添加，生动地给江河穿上了冰雪大衣，同时也反映出冰天雪地的寒冷，传神地再现了原诗中白雪皑皑的气氛。由此，原诗的意境

也跃然纸上。（娄梦佳等，2015：154-155）

 课后练习

（1）

London

William Blake

I wander through each charter'd street,
Near where the charter'd Thames does flow,
And mark in every face I meet
Marks of weakness, mark of woe.

In every cry of every Man,
In every Infant's cry of fear,
In every voice, in every ban,
The mind-forged manacles I hear.

How the Chimney-sweeper's cry
Every blackening Church appalls;
And the hapless Soldier's sigh
Runs in blood down Palace walls.

But most through midnight streets I hear
How the youthful Harlot's curse
Blasts the new-born Infant's tear,
And blights with plagues the Marriage hearse.

（2）

乡　愁

余光中

小时候
乡愁是一枚小小的邮票
我在这头
母亲在那头

长大后
乡愁是一张窄窄的船票
我在这头
新娘在那头

后来啊
乡愁是一方矮矮的坟墓
我在外头
母亲在里头

而现在
乡愁是一湾浅浅的海峡
我在这头
大陆在那头

参考文献

艾湘涛. 2009. 散文语言艺术美初探. 湖南社会科学（2）：148-150.

曹黄金，柴跃廷，刘义. 2011. 动态系统影响优化分析. 清华大学学报（自然科学版）（3）：304-308.

曹明伦. 2007. 谈翻译中的语言变体和语域分析. 中国翻译（5）：87-88.

曹雪芹. 1978. A dream of red mansions. 杨宪益，戴乃迭，译. 北京：外文出版社.

曹雪芹，高鹗. 1987. 红楼梦. 长沙：岳麓书社.

陈国华. 1997. 论莎剧重译（下）. 外语教学与研究（3）：48-54.

陈静. 2003. 哈代悲剧小说的美学价值. 宜宾学院学报（2）：38.

陈科龙. 2012.《汉宫秋》中英剧比较. 戏剧文学（9）：69-72.

程雨民. 1989. 英语语体学. 上海：上海外语教育出版社.

戴湘涛，张勤. 2013. 实用文体汉英翻译教程. 北京：世界图书出版公司.

董晓波. 2013. 实用经贸文体翻译. 北京：对外经济贸易大学出版社.

方梦之. 2002. 译学辞典. 上海：上海外语教育出版社.

弗朗西斯·司各特·菲茨杰拉德. 1925/2015. 了不起的盖茨比. 吴建国，译. 上海：上海文艺出版社.

高壮丽. 2016. 戏剧翻译中语言动作性的解读——以《李尔王》四个汉译本为例. 哈尔滨学院学报（5）：108.

郭著章，李庆生. 2003. 英汉互译实用教程（第三版）. 武汉：武汉大学出版社.

何纤夫. 2014. 莎士比亚戏剧的文体教学. 文学教育（9）：50-52.

何自然，冉永平. 2006. 语用学概论（修订本）. 长沙：湖南教育出版社.

侯维瑞. 2008. 文学文体学. 上海：上海外语教育出版社.

忽思乐，曹阳. 2012. 对德国德累斯顿理工大学职业学院职业与技术教师教育课程设置结构的分析. 语文学刊（6）：113-115.

胡宝慧. 2015.《HUBCO 项目土建投标书》英汉翻译实践报告. 西北师范大学硕士学位论文：i-ii.

黄芳.2008.论表演性对戏剧翻译的启示——从书斋把玩到优人搬弄的转变.四川外语学报(6):105-108.

贾丽梅.2009.英语语域标志及在翻译中的应用.山西农业大学学报(1):15.

焦菊隐.1979.戏剧论文集.上海:上海文艺出版社.

卡勒德·胡赛尼.2003/2006.追风筝的人.李继宏,译.上海:上海人民出版社.

李基亚,冯伟年.2004.论戏剧翻译的原则和途径.西北大学学报(7):161-165.

李玲,李志岭.2010.从《红色手推车》看诗歌文体风格的等值翻译.吉林省教育学院学报(2):72-74.

李梅.2012.《中国名园》英译策略探讨.中国翻译(1):83-86.

李明.2006.翻译批评与赏析.武汉:武汉大学出版社.

李文革.2013.应用文体翻译实践教程.北京:国防工业出版社.

李运兴.2000.语篇翻译引论.北京:中国对外翻译出版公司.

刘宓庆.2012.文体与翻译.北京:中国对外翻译出版公司.

刘肖言,关子安.2002.试论戏剧翻译的标准.齐齐哈尔大学学报(11):5-7.

刘知洪.2012.《荷塘月色》语言特色译文赏析.西昌学院学报·社会科学版(3):44-47.

刘重德.1994.论风格的可译性.北京:中国对外翻译出版公司.

刘著妍.2012.多元化译论对实用文体翻译文本的解读.天津大学学报(社会科学版)(4):342-345.

龙仕文,郝丽娜,王志林.2011.散文翻译中的情境再现探析——以《英译中国现代散文选》为例.重庆交通大学学报(社会科学版)(2):129-132.

娄梦佳,宫丽.2015.浅谈中国古诗英译过程中对意境的把握——以柳宗元《江雪》为例.现代语文(2):154-155.

罗书肆.1983.介绍泰特勒的翻译理论.外国翻译理论评介文集.北京:中国对外翻译出版公司.

冉永平,侯海冰.2009.人际冲突下隐含修正用意的语用分析.外语教学与研究(6):430-480.

任晓霏,张吟,等.2014.戏剧翻译研究的语料库文体学途径——以戏剧翻译中的指示系统为案例.外语教学理论与实践(2):86.

芮雪梅.2012.口语体文学《麦田里的守望者》翻译研究.安徽工业大学学报(社会科学版)(6):90.

邵璐.2012.西方翻译文体学研究(2006—2011).中国翻译(5):10-14.

邵璐. 2013. 莫言《生死疲劳》英译中隐义明示法的运用：翻译文体学视角. 外语教学（2）：100-104.

申丹. 1995. 文学文体学与小说翻译. 北京：北京大学出版社.

申丹. 1998. 叙述学与小说文体学研究. 北京：北京大学出版社.

申丹. 2002. 论文学文体学在翻译学科建设中的重要性. 中国翻译（1）：11-15.

申丹. 2008. 西方文体学的新发展. 上海：上海外语教育出版社.

沈国荣. 2011. 一则汉英摘要翻译的话语分析理论研究. 河南工业大学学报（社会科学版）（2）：ii；13.

孙大雨. 1997. 古诗文英译集. 上海：上海外语教育出版社.

泰戈尔. 1916/2010. 飞鸟集. 郑振铎，译. 北京：外语教学与研究出版社.

谭载喜. 1999. 新编奈达论翻译. 北京：中国对外翻译出版公司.

汤显祖. 1598/2003. 牡丹亭. 汪榕培，译. 北京：外语教学与研究出版社.

汤显祖. 1601/2003. 邯郸记. 汪榕培，译. 北京：外语教学与研究出版社.

托马斯·哈代. 1891/1984. 德伯家的苔丝. 张若谷，译. 北京：人民文学出版社.

托马斯·曼. 1901/2009. 布登勃洛克一家. 傅惟慈，译. 上海：译林出版社.

王方路. 2016. 文化自觉关照下的典籍翻译——以《诗经》为例. 北京：光明日报出版社.

王致远，赵唯安，刘玲娟，等. 2017. 新生小鼠心肌肌钙蛋白 I 相互作用蛋白的鉴定与功能预测. 解放军医学杂志 42（9）：769-774.

王佐良，丁往道. 1987. 英语文体学引论. 北京：外语教学与研究出版社.

威廉·萨默赛特·毛姆. 1919/2009. 月亮和六便士. 傅惟慈，译. 上海：译文出版社.

文殊. 1989. 诗词英译选. 北京：外语教学与研究出版社.

吴鹏，秦家慧. 2014. 构建商务英语学科教学知识的研究框架. 外语界（2）：18-24.

谢谦. 2005. 文学文体学与诗体戏剧中"语言变异"的翻译——以《哈姆雷特》为例. 广东外语外贸大学学报（7）：19-52.

谢延秀. 2006. 实用文体与文学文体之分野及融合. 理论导刊（4）：75-77.

熊婷婷. 2006. 论巴斯奈特的戏剧翻译观. 西华师范大学学报（哲学社会科学版）（5）：6.

许渊冲. 1988. 唐诗三百首新译. 北京：中国对外翻译出版公司.

许渊冲. 1992. 中诗英韵探胜从《诗经》到《西厢记》. 北京：北京大学出版社.

许渊冲. 2003. 文学与翻译. 北京：北京大学出版社.

杨晓荣. 2005. 英语专业八级考试辅导丛书——快速通关（汉译英分册）. 北京：中国宇航出版社.

余东，刘士聪. 2014. 论散文翻译中的节奏. 中国翻译（2）：92-96.

俞东明. 1996. 戏剧文体与戏剧文体学. 浙江大学学报（人文社会科学版）（1）：101.

袁子阳. 2009. 抗辐射加固"龙芯"处理器的空间辐射环境适应性研究及航天计算机设计评估. 中国科学院空间科学与英语研究中心硕士学位论文：i-iii.

曾冬萍，蒋利玲，曾从盛，等. 2013. 生态化学计量学特征及其应用研究进展. 生态学（18）：5484-5490.

张保红. 2011. 文学翻译. 北京：外语教学与研究出版社.

张光明，陈葵阳，李雪红，等. 2009. 英语实用文体翻译. 合肥：中国科学技术出版社.

章华. 2009. 每天读一点英文. 陕西：陕西师范大学出版社.

张培基. 1999. 英译中国现代散文选. 上海：上海外语教育出版社.

张培基. 2007. 英译中国现代散文选（二）. 上海：上海外语教育出版社.

张庭琛等. 1991. 一百丛书. 北京：中国对外翻译出版公司.

张威. 2014. 戏剧翻译的理论与实践——英若诚戏剧翻译评析. 广东外语外贸大学学报（2）：68-71.

郑穹. 2013. 翻译中的文体对应——以罗经国英译《陋室铭》为例. 海外英语（23）：188-191.

郑亚兰. 2012.《硅胶项目报告》英译实践报告. 广东外语外贸大学硕士论文：ii.

周筠. 2012. 面向生物医学仿真的表面重建和四面体化技术研究. 中南大学博士论文：i-iv.

周中明. 1982. 论《红楼梦》语言的绘画美. 红楼梦学刊（2）：65-98.

朱姝，张春柏. 2013. 对戏剧翻译中动态表演性原则的反思. 东北师范大学学报（哲学社会科学版）（1）：109-112.

Bassnett, S. (1990). *Poetry and translation*. Shanghai: Shanghai Foreign Language and Education Press.

Bronte, C. (2012). *Jane eyre*. London: Canterbury Classics.

Crystal, D. (1999). *The penguin dictionary of language*. London: Penguin Books.

Fowler, R. (1977). *Linguistics and the novel*. London: Methuen Publishing.

Halliday, M. A. K. (1978). *Language as social semiotic: The social interpretation of language and meaning*. London: Edward Arnold.

Hawkes, D. & Minford, J. (2003). *The story of the stone*. Shanghai: Shanghai Foreign Language Education Press.

Leech, G. N. & Short, M. H. (1981). *Style in fiction*. London: Longman.

Newmark, P. (1988). *A textbook of translation*. Shanghai: Shanghai Foreign Language Education Press.

Nida, E. A. (1982). *The theory and practice of translation*. Leiden: E. J. Brill.

Nord, C. (2001). *Translating as a purposeful activity: Functionalist approaches explained*. Shanghai: Shanghai Foreign Language Education Press.

Trudgill, P. (1983). *Sociolinguistics: An introduction to language society*. Harmondsworth: Penguin Books.